Microsoft® EXCEL 5 For Windows™

Step by Step

MicrosoftPress

PUBLISHED BY
Microsoft Press
A Division of Microsoft Corporation
One Microsoft Way
Redmond, Washington 98052-6399

Library of Congress Cataloging-in-Publication Data pending.

ISBN: 1-55615-587-5

Printed and bound in the United States of America.

10 11 12 13 MLML 9 8 7 6

Distributed to the book trade in Canada by Macmillan of Canada, a division of Canada Publishing Corporation.

Distributed to the book trade outside the United States and Canada by Penguin Books Ltd.

Penguin Books Ltd., Harmondsworth, Middlesex, England
Penguin Books Australia Ltd., Ringwood, Victoria, Australia
Penguin Books N.Z. Ltd., 182-190 Wairau Road, Auckland 10, New Zealand

British Cataloging-in-Publication Data pending.

PostScript is a registered trademark of Adobe Systems, Inc. HP and LaserJet are registered trademarks of Hewlett-Packard Company. 1-2-3 and Lotus are registered trademarks of Lotus Development Corporation. Microsoft, MS-DOS, and Visual Basic are registered trademarks and Autosum and Windows are trademarks of Microsoft Corporation. Arial is a registered trademark of The Monotype Corporation PLC. Paintbrush is a trademark of ZSoft Corporation.

For Catapult, Inc.
Managing Editor: Donald Elman
Author: Samantha J.W. Robertson
Associate Editor: Ann T. Rosenthal
Production/Layout Editor: Jeanne K. Hunt

For Microsoft Press
Acquisitions Editors: Lucinda Rowley and Marjorie Schlaikjer
Project Editor: Casey D. Doyle

Catapult, Inc. is a national software training company dedicated to providing the highest quality application software training. Years of PC and Macintosh instruction for major corporations and government institutions provide the models used in building Catapult's exclusive Performance-Based Training program. Based on the principles of adult learning, Performance-Based Training materials ensure that training participants leave the classroom with the confidence and ability to apply skills acquired during the training day. Both visual design and textual content are planned to motivate the adult learner to accomplish specific course objectives. This approach presents the required information about concepts and commands, allows for practice of newly learned skills, and provides additional follow-up to ensure skills retention. Catapult's adherence to Performance-Based Training is the basis for the approach Catapult brings to the Microsoft Press *Step by Step* series.

Catapult's development team builds into every *Step by Step* tutorial the knowledge gained from training hundreds of thousands of students. After gathering classroom feedback from individual entrepreneurs, session evaluations from employees of Fortune 500 companies, and input from decision makers at state and government agencies nationwide, Catapult analyzes the data to determine which skills can provide increased productivity. This information is applied to each *Step by Step* model. Then, working directly with software developers at Microsoft, Catapult's development team creates effective lessons and exercises that enhance skills to solve specific needs by utilizing the full power of your Microsoft applications and operating systems.

The Product Development group at Catapult is pleased to share their training experience with a wider audience through the *Step by Step* series. *Microsoft Excel 5 for Windows Step by Step* is the ninth in this series to be produced by Catapult Press. This book and others in the collection will help you to develop the confidence necessary to achieve increased productivity with your Microsoft products.

Catapult Software Training Centers provide instructor-led Performance-Based Training nationwide in their open-enrollment classrooms or as dedicated classes at customer sites. Catapult's corporate headquarters are in Bellevue, Washington.

WE'VE CHOSEN THIS SPECIAL LAY-FLAT BINDING

to make it easier for you to work through the step-by-step lessons while you're at your computer.

With little effort, you can make this book lie flat when you open it to any page. Simply press down on the inside (where the paper meets the binding) of any left-hand page, and the book will stay open to that page. You can open the book this way every time. The lay-flat binding will not weaken or crack over time.

It's tough, flexible, sturdy—and designed to last.

Contents

Lesson 3   **Formatting Your Data   45**

Part 1   Review & Practice   65

Part 2   Charting and Printing Your Data

Lesson 4   **Charting Your Data   71**

Part 3 Managing Your Data

Part 4   Analyzing and Sharing Your Data

Appendix

About This Book

Microsoft Excel version 5 for Windows is a powerful spreadsheet application that you can use for charting, managing, and analyzing your data. *Microsoft Excel 5 for Windows Step by Step* shows you how to use Microsoft Excel to simplify your work and increase your productivity. You can use *Microsoft Excel 5 for Windows Step by Step* in a classroom setting, or you can use it as a tutorial to learn Microsoft Excel at your own pace and at your own convenience.

You also get hands-on practice using the files on the accompanying disk. Instructions for copying the practice files to your computer's hard disk are in "Getting Ready," the next section in this book.

Finding the Best Starting Point for You

This book is designed for new users learning Microsoft Excel for the first time, and for experienced users who want to learn and use the new features in Microsoft Excel version 5 for Windows. Either way, *Microsoft Excel 5 for Windows Step by Step* will help you get the most out of Microsoft Excel.

This book is divided into five major parts, each containing several related lessons. At the end of each part, you will find a Review & Practice section that gives you the opportunity to practice the skills you learned in that part. Each Review & Practice section allows you to test your knowledge and prepare for your own work.

Use the following table to determine your best path through the book.

If you are	Follow these steps
New to a computer or graphical environment, such as Microsoft Windows	Read "Getting Ready," the next section in this book, and follow the instructions to install the practice files. Carefully read the sections on "If You Are New to Microsoft Windows" and "If You Are New to Using a Mouse." Next, work through Lessons 1 through 3 for a basic introduction to Microsoft Excel. Work through Lessons 4 through 15 in any order.
Familiar with the Microsoft Windows graphical computer environment, but new to using Microsoft Excel	Follow the instructions for installing the practice files in the "Getting Ready" section in this book. Next, work through Lessons 1 through 3 for a basic introduction to Microsoft Excel. Work through Lessons 4 through 15 in any order.

If you are	Follow these steps
Familiar with Lotus 1-2-3, but new to Microsoft Excel	Follow the instructions for installing the practice files in the "Getting Ready" section in this book. Next, work through Lessons 1 through 3 for a basic introduction to Microsoft Excel. Work through Lessons 4 through 15 in any order. Watch for the margin notes that explain differences or similarities between Lotus 1-2-3 and Microsoft Excel.
Experienced with Microsoft Excel	Follow the instructions for installing the practice files in the "Getting Ready" section in this book. Next, read through "New Features in Microsoft Excel 5," following "Getting Ready" for an introduction to the new features in version 5. Complete the lessons that best fit your needs.

Using This Book As a Classroom Aid

If you're an instructor, you can use *Microsoft Excel 5 for Windows Step by Step* for teaching computer users. You might want to select certain lessons that meet your students' particular needs and incorporate your own demonstrations into the lessons.

For information about an instructor kit for this book, call 1-800-MSPRESS.

If you plan to teach the entire contents of this book, you should probably set aside up to three days of classroom time to allow for discussion, questions, and any customized practice you might create. Lessons 1 through 3 cover Microsoft Excel basics like entering data, writing formulas, and formatting data. Lessons 4 through 6 discuss charting and printing your data. Lessons 7 through 10 cover managing your data by working with workbooks, lists, and reports. Lessons 11 through 13 cover analyzing your data with simple analysis tools and worksheet models, and sharing your data with other users and applications. Lessons 14 and 15 discuss customizing Microsoft Excel with toolbars and windows, and using macros to automate repetitive tasks.

Conventions Used in This Book

Before you start any of the lessons, it's important that you understand the terms and notational conventions used in this book.

Procedural Conventions

- Hands-on exercises that you are to follow are given in numbered lists of steps (1, 2, and so on). A triangular bullet (▶) indicates an exercise with only one step.

- The word *choose* is used for carrying out a command from a menu or a dialog box.

- The word *select* is used for highlighting directories, filenames, text boxes, and menu bars and options, and for selecting options in a dialog box.

Notational Conventions

- Characters or commands that you type appear in **bold lowercase** type.

- Important terms (where first defined) and titles of books appear in *italic* type.

- Names of files, paths, or directories appear in ALL CAPITALS, except when they are to be directly typed in.

Keyboard Conventions

- Names of keys that you press are in small capital letters, for example, TAB and SHIFT.

- A plus sign (+) between two key names means that you must press those keys at the same time. For example, "Press ALT+TAB" means that you hold down the ALT key while you press TAB.

- A comma (,) between two or more key names means that you must press each of the keys consecutively, not together. For example, "Press ALT, T, X" means that you press and release each key in sequence. "Press ALT+W, L" means that you first press ALT and W together, and then release them and press L.

- You can choose menu commands with the keyboard. Press the ALT key to activate the menu bar, and then sequentially press the keys that correspond to the highlighted or underlined letter of the menu name and of the command name. For some commands, you can also press a key combination listed in the menu.

Mouse Conventions

- *Click* means to point to an object and then press and release the mouse button. For example, "Click the AutoSum button." The word "click" is used for selecting command buttons, option buttons, and check boxes.

- *Drag* means hold down the mouse button while you move the mouse. For example, "Drag the contents of cell B5 to C10."

- *Double-click* means to rapidly press and release the mouse button twice. For example, "Double-click the Microsoft Excel icon to start Microsoft Excel."

- *Click the right mouse button* means to point to an object and then press and release the right mouse button. For example, "Select cell A1 and click the right mouse button." Clicking the right mouse button opens a shortcut menu that provides easy access to commands associated with the current action.

Other Features of This Book

- Text in the left margin provides tips, additional useful information, or keyboard alternatives.

- The "One Step Further" exercise at the end of each lesson introduces new options or techniques that build on the commands and skills you used in the lesson.

- Each lesson has a summary list of the skills you have learned in each lesson and gives a brief review of how to accomplish particular tasks.

- The optional "Review & Practice" activity at the end of each part provides an opportunity to use the major skills presented in the lessons completed so far. These activities present problems that reinforce what you have learned and encourage you to recognize new ways that you can use Microsoft Excel.

Print

- You can carry out many commands by clicking a button at the top of the Microsoft Excel window. If a procedure instructs you to click a button, a picture of the button appears in the left margin, as the Print button does here.

- In the Appendix, "Matching the Exercises," you can review the options used in this book to get the results you see in the illustrations. Refer to this section of the book when your screen does not match the illustrations or when you get unexpected results as you work through the exercises.

Cross-References to Microsoft Excel Documentation

References to the *Microsoft Excel User's Guide* at the end of each lesson direct you to specific chapters for additional information. Notes and other references also direct you to your Microsoft Excel documentation. Use these materials to take full advantage of the features in Microsoft Excel.

Online Help

The Help system in Microsoft Excel provides a complete online reference to Microsoft Excel. You'll learn more about the Help system in "Getting Ready," the next section in this book.

Microsoft Excel User's Guide

This manual includes information about setting up and starting Microsoft Excel, using the Help system, and working with the application. It also provides explanations of the application's features.

Microsoft Excel Visual Basic User's Guide

This manual provides detailed information about creating and editing macros using the Visual Basic language. Lesson 15 of this Step by Step book introduces you to macros to automate repetitive tasks.

Getting Ready

This section of the book prepares you for your first steps into the Microsoft Excel environment. You will review some useful Microsoft Windows techniques as well as terms and concepts important in your understanding of how to use Microsoft Excel.

You will learn how to:

- Install the step-by-step practice files on your computer's hard disk.
- Start Microsoft Windows.
- Start Microsoft Excel.
- Use important features of the windows, menus, and dialog boxes in the Microsoft Windows graphical operating system.
- Use the online Help system in Microsoft Excel.

Installing the Step by Step Practice Files

At the back of this book, you'll find a disk labeled "Microsoft Excel for Windows Step by Step Practice Files." A special program on the Practice Files disk copies these files onto your computer hard drive into a directory named PRACTICE.

Copy the practice files onto the hard drive

1 Turn on your computer.

2 Insert the Practice Files disk into drive A or B of your computer.

3 If Windows is already running, open the Program Manager and choose Run from the File menu. If you have not started Windows yet, skip to step 5.

4 In the Command Line box, type **a:\install** (or **b:\install**), choose OK, and then skip to step 6.

Do not type a space between the drive letter and the slash.

5 At the MS-DOS command prompt (usually C:\>), type **a:\install** (or **b:\install**) and press ENTER.

Do not type a space between the drive letter and the slash.

6 Follow the instructions on the screen to complete the installation process.

The Step by Step setup program copies the practice files from the floppy disk onto the hard disk in a subdirectory called PRACTICE of the Microsoft Excel for Windows home directory (called EXCEL, or whatever it happens to be named on your system).

You'll need to remember the name of the drive and directory where the practice files are stored so you can open a file for each lesson.

Lesson Background

The practice files are used in the lessons to simulate what you might encounter using Microsoft Excel in a typical business setting. Imagine that you work for a company called West Coast Sales. Throughout these lessons, you use Microsoft Excel to assist you in your daily tasks at West Coast Sales.

Starting Microsoft Windows and Microsoft Excel

This book assumes that you have Microsoft Windows and Microsoft Excel installed on your system. After you install the practice files, you can start Microsoft Windows, if it is not already running, and Microsoft Excel.

Use the following procedures to start Microsoft Windows and Microsoft Excel. Your screen might be different from the following illustrations, depending on your particular setup and the applications installed on your computer. For more information about Microsoft Windows, see the *Microsoft Windows User's Guide*.

Start Microsoft Windows from the MS-DOS command prompt

1   At the command prompt, type **win**

2   Press ENTER.

    After the initial startup, the Program Manager window looks like the following illustration. You can start all of your applications, including Microsoft Excel, from Program Manager.

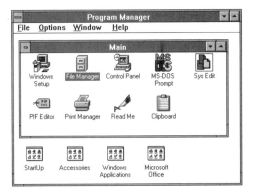

When Microsoft Windows is active, everything on your screen (called the *desktop*) is displayed in *windows*. You can adjust each window to the size you want, and you can move windows anywhere on the desktop. You can have multiple windows open at the same time to compare and share information easily.

Within the Program Manager window are symbols called *icons* that represent applications and documents. The icons are organized in program groups, usually related to applications. The normal installation of Microsoft Excel creates a new group or uses an existing group, and then creates an icon within that group for the Microsoft Excel program. Double-clicking the group icon that contains Microsoft Excel 5.0 opens the program group window that holds the icon for Microsoft Excel.

As you become more familiar with Windows, you will find that you can customize the startup screen to your personal working style.

Start Microsoft Excel

Microsoft
Excel

1 Double-click the group icon containing Microsoft Excel 5.0.

This opens the program group.

2 Double-click the Microsoft Excel program icon.

3 Click the Maximize button on the Microsoft Excel application window.

If You Are New to Microsoft Windows

For new Microsoft Windows users, this section provides a general overview of what you can accomplish within this graphical environment. Windows is designed to be easy to use while still providing sophisticated functions. It helps you handle all of the daily work that you carry out with your computer. Microsoft Windows provides a common interface shared by many different application programs—both in the way they share data and in the way you control their operation.

Once you become familiar with the basic elements of Microsoft Windows, you can apply these skills to learn and use Microsoft Excel, as well as many other types of applications including word processing and graphics.

Using Microsoft Windows

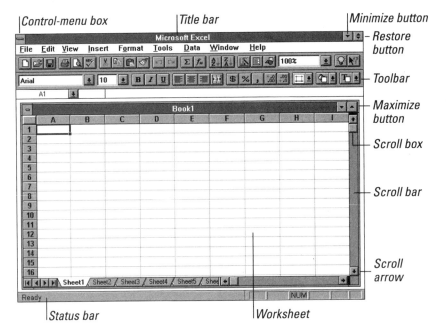

Control-menu box · Title bar · Minimize button · Restore button · Toolbar · Maximize button · Scroll box · Scroll bar · Scroll arrow · Status bar · Worksheet

You can scroll, move, size, and close a window by using the mouse.

To	Do this
Scroll through a window	Click the scroll bars or drag the scroll box.
Change the size of a window	Drag any of the window edges or corners.
Enlarge a window to fill the screen	Double-click the title bar or click the Maximize button.
Shrink a window to an icon	Click the Minimize button.
Restore a window to its previous size	Click the Restore button.
Move a window	Drag the title bar.
Close a window	Double-click the Control-menu box.

Using Windows in Microsoft Excel

Like any Windows-based application, Microsoft Excel has a main program window that displays the application name, "Microsoft Excel," in the title bar. This window can be maximized to fill the entire screen, restored to fill part of the screen, or minimized to an icon at the bottom of the screen.

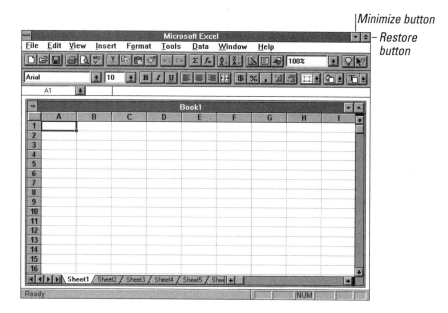

Minimize button

Restore button

Using Menus

In Microsoft Excel, menus and commands work according to Microsoft Windows conventions. Menu names appear in the *menu bar* across the top of the screen. A list of commands appears when you click a menu. To choose a command, you click the menu name to open the menu and then click the desired command.

The following illustration shows the Edit menu opened from the Microsoft Excel menu bar.

Some options have a *shortcut key* combination listed to the right of the command name. Once you are familiar with the menus and commands, these shortcut keys can save you time.

All commands have keyboard equivalents. If you are not using a mouse, you make selections by pressing ALT and the underlined character of the menu. To select a command from a menu, you can simply type the underlined character when the menu is displayed.

When a command name appears dimmed, it doesn't apply to your current situation and is unavailable. For example, the Paste command on the Edit menu appears dimmed if you have not first used either the Copy or Cut command.

When a command name displays a check mark to its left, the command is already in effect.

When a command name is followed by an arrow, another level of choices will appear when you choose the command. For example, when you choose the Clear command from the Edit menu, a list of further choices appears. You can clear All, Formats, Contents, or Notes.

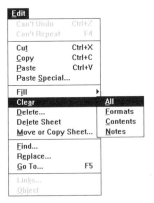

To close a menu without choosing a command, click the menu name again, or press ESC.

Using Dialog Boxes

When you choose a command that is followed by an ellipsis (. . .), Windows-based applications display a *dialog box* so that you can provide more information. Depending on the dialog box, you type the information or select from a group of options.

After you enter information or make selections in the dialog box, you can click the OK button with the mouse or press the ENTER key to carry out the command. You can also choose the Cancel button or press ESC to close a dialog box without carrying out an action.

For example, the Page Setup dialog box appears when you choose the Page Setup command from the File menu. In the dialog box, you specify the options you want. The Page Setup dialog box looks like the following illustration.

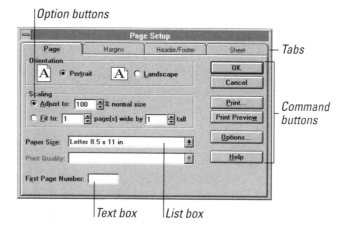

Every dialog box has one or more of the following types of items (called *controls*) to help you supply the information necessary to carry out the command.

Text box   You type information in a text box. For example, in the Page Setup dialog box, you can type a number in the First Page Number text box to start your page numbers with a specific number.

List box   Available choices appear in a list. If the list is longer than the box, you can use the scroll bar or the down-arrow button to see the rest of the list.

Option buttons   You can select only one option at a time from a group of option buttons. A selected option button has a black dot in its center.

Check boxes   You can select multiple check boxes at a time from a group of check boxes. A selected check box has an X in its center.

Command buttons   You choose a command button to carry out an operation or to display more options. If a command button is dimmed, it is unavailable. An ellipsis following the name of a command button means that more options are available. In the

Page Setup dialog box, you can choose the OK button to apply the options, you can choose the Print or Options button to open another dialog box with more options, or you can choose the Cancel button to cancel.

Tabs   You choose a tab to view another section of the dialog box. In the Page Setup dialog box, you can view different options by clicking the Margins, Header, Footer, or Sheet tabs.

Selecting Dialog Box Options

To move around in a dialog box, you can simply click the item you want. You can also hold down ALT and press the key for the underlined letter at the same time. Or, you can press TAB to move between items.

Use the procedures in this table to select options in a dialog box with the mouse.

To	Do this
Select an option button	Click the option button.
Clear an option button	Select another option button.
Select or clear a check box	Click the check box.
Select an item in a list	Click the item.
Move to a text box	Click the text box.
Select text in a text box	Double-click a word or drag through the characters.
Scroll through a list	Use the scroll bars.
Select a tab	Click the tab.

Using Toolbars

Located below the menu bar are the *toolbars*. When you first install and start Microsoft Excel, both the Standard toolbar and the Formatting toolbar are displayed. These bars contain buttons that are shortcuts for choosing commands and for working with Microsoft Excel. For example, clicking the Open button on the toolbar is the same as choosing the Open command from the File menu.

You can select different toolbars, depending on what tools you need. To change to a different toolbar, use the Toolbars command on the View menu, and then select the toolbar you want from the list.

Although initially you might feel more comfortable using the keyboard for making menu selections, it is generally much faster to use the mouse to click a button on the toolbars. The instructions in this book emphasize using the toolbars as the most efficient method for most of the basic Microsoft Excel operations.

If You Are New to Using a Mouse

Menu bars, toolbars, and many other features of Microsoft Excel and other Windows-based applications were designed for working with a mouse. Although you can use the keyboard for most actions in Microsoft Excel, many of these actions are easier to do with the mouse.

Mouse Pointers

The mouse controls a symbol on the screen called the *pointer*. You move the pointer by sliding the mouse over a flat surface in the direction you want the pointer to move. If you run out of room to move the mouse, you can lift it up and put it down again. The pointer moves only when the mouse is touching a flat surface.

Moving the mouse pointer across the screen does not affect the document; the pointer simply indicates a location on the screen. When you press the mouse button, an action occurs at the location of the pointer.

When the mouse pointer passes over different parts of the Microsoft Excel window, it changes shape, indicating what you can do with it at that point. Most of your work in this book will use the following mouse pointers.

This pointer	Appears when you point to
⌖	The menu bar and toolbars to choose a command or a button, the title bar to move a window, or the scroll bars to scroll through a document.
I	Text in a text box or cell. When you click the mouse in a text box, a blinking vertical bar called the *insertion point* appears.
⊕	A cell on the worksheet.
+	The fill handle on a selected cell or range.
↔ ↕	A column heading boundary or row heading boundary to change column width or row height.
↕ ↔	A split box on the scroll bar to split a window vertically or horizontally.
�	A button on a worksheet or a term in a Help topic that you can click to go to another topic.

Using the Mouse

The following describes the four basic mouse actions that you use throughout the lessons in this book.

Pointing   Moving the mouse to place the pointer on an item is called *pointing*.

Clicking   Pointing to an item on your screen and then quickly pressing and releasing the mouse button once is called *clicking*. You select items on the screen and move around in a document by clicking.

Double-clicking   Pointing to an item and then quickly pressing and releasing the mouse button twice is called *double-clicking*. This is a convenient shortcut for many tasks in Microsoft Excel.

Dragging   Holding down the mouse button as you move the pointer is called *dragging*. You can use this technique to select data in the rows and columns in a worksheet.

Try the mouse

Take a moment to test drive the mouse. Simply slide the mouse so that the pointer moves around the Microsoft Excel screen.

1   Slide the mouse until the pointer is over the menus and tools at the top of the screen. The pointer is now a left-pointing arrow.

2   Slide the pointer around the document window.

    The document window is the area in which you work with the text on a worksheet. The pointer now looks like a large plus sign.

3   With the pointer over any cell in the worksheet, click the mouse button; then slide the pointer over the formula bar, above the worksheet.

    The pointer now looks like an I-beam.

4   With the pointer over any cell in the worksheet, click the right mouse button.

    A shortcut menu appears, listing commands that you can perform for the selected cell.

Note Microsoft Excel version 5 has several shortcut menus that you can use when you click with your right mouse button over different areas of the screen. You see one menu when you click a cell, another when you click over the toolbars, and another when you click over the title bar of your document window. You'll use these shortcut menus throughout this book to access commands quickly.

---

5 Click another cell outside of the shortcut menu.

The shortcut menu closes.

Using Help

Microsoft Excel includes Help, a complete online reference. You can access Help information in several ways.

To get Help information	Do this
By topic or activity	From the Help menu, choose Contents.
While working in a window or dialog box	Press F1 or choose the Help button in the dialog box.
About a specific command, tool, or other element on the screen	Click the Help tool, and then click the command, tool, or other screen element.
By keyword	Double-click the Help tool. In the Search dialog box, type a keyword and then select a Help topic.

Display the list of Help topics

▶ From the Help menu, choose Contents.

The Microsoft Excel Help Contents window looks like the following illustration.

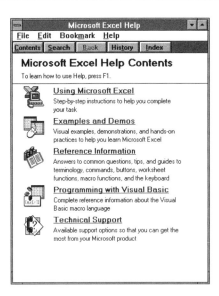

You can size, move, and scroll through a Help window. You can switch between the Help window and Microsoft Excel, or you can choose the Help On Top command to keep the Help window on top of other windows so that you can refer to Help while you work.

Getting Help on Help

To learn how you can make best use of all the information in Help, you can read through instructions for using Help.

Learn to use Help

1   Press F1.

The Contents For How To Use Help list appears.

2   Locate the phrase "scroll bar" which has a dotted underline, and click it.

A definition of the term appears in a popup box.

Note   Clicking an underlined term "jumps" you to a related topic. Clicking a term with a dotted underline displays a popup definition in a topic window.

---

3   Click the phrase again.

The definition popup box closes.

4   Locate the phrase "Help Basics" which has a solid underline, and click it.

A new screen appears with information about Help.

5 Click the term "jumps" which has a dotted underline.

Another popup definition appears.

6 Click the term again.

The definition closes.

Getting Help on a Specific Topic

The Help system allows you to find information on a topic in several ways. First, the Contents list allows you to choose from among a list of functionally organized topics and subtopics. Second, the Search option allows you to quickly locate Help topics by using a key word. If you know the command or term you want help on, you can go directly to the topic. You can also use the Index or the Help button on the Standard toolbar to find Help.

In the next exercises, you look for information using the Contents list and the Search option.

Use the Contents list

1 In the Help window, click the Contents button.

The Contents list appears.

2 Scroll downward in the list, and click any topic that is underlined in green.

A new screen appears with information about the topic.

Search for a specific topic

1 Click the Search button.

2 In the Search dialog box, type **print**

The printer options and printing topics appear in the list.

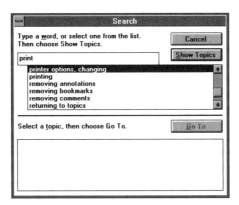

3 In the list of topics, scroll downward if necessary and select "printing," and then choose the Show Topics button.

4 Select a topic from the list at the bottom of the dialog box, and then choose the Go To button.

The Help window displays the selected topic.

5 In the Help window, from the File menu, choose Exit.

The Help window closes.

Quitting Microsoft Excel

If you would like to quit Excel and return to the Program Manager window, do the following:

Quit Microsoft Excel

▶ From the File menu, choose Exit.

If you see the Save dialog box, click No.

Note   You can also double-click the Control-menu box in the upper left corner of the application window to leave Microsoft Excel.

Quitting Microsoft Windows

If you would like to quit Windows, here is a simple way to exit the program.

Quit Microsoft Windows

1 From the File menu, choose Exit Windows.

2 When you see a box with the message "This will end your Windows session," press ENTER.

New Features in Microsoft Excel 5

The following table lists the major new features in Microsoft Excel for Windows version 5 that are covered in this book. The table shows the lesson in which you can learn about each feature. For more information about new features, see the *Microsoft Excel User's Guide*.

To learn how to	See
Automatically fill a custom series into a range of cells.	Lesson 1
Edit text directly in the cell.	Lesson 1
Use the Name box to create names and go to named ranges.	Lesson 2
Create formulas easily with the Function Wizard.	Lesson 2
Create grand totals automatically with AutoSum.	Lesson 2
Copy formatting quickly with the Format Painter button.	Lesson 3
Add data to a chart by dragging it from the worksheet.	Lesson 4
Draw arrows, text boxes, and other graphic objects directly on your worksheet or chart.	Lesson 5
Create standardized charts with automatic formatting or your own custom autoformats.	Lesson 5
Move chart items, such as titles and legends, to any position on the chart.	Lesson 5
Add trendlines to a data series in a chart.	Lesson 5
Use built-in headers or footers.	Lesson 6
Find files easily with the Find File command, even if you don't know their names.	Lesson 7
Filter your data automatically, to show only the data you need to see.	Lesson 8
Sort your data easily, using the column labels in your list.	Lesson 8
Add subtotals and grand totals automatically.	Lesson 9
Create summary reports easily with the PivotTable Wizard.	Lesson 10
Create and edit scenarios with the Scenario Manager.	Lesson 11

To learn how to	See
Activate and edit objects from other applications without leaving Microsoft Excel.	Lesson 13
Create and customize toolbars.	Lesson 14
Use the Full Screen and Zoom commands to see more of your document at once.	Lesson 14

1 Getting Started with Microsoft Excel

Entering Data

With Microsoft Excel, it's easy to enter information into a worksheet and change, delete, or add to the information. You don't need to worry about entering your data perfectly or completely the first time. You can always edit your data or fill in the rest of a series later. And, with version 5, you no longer have to create workbooks with contents pages and bound or unbound sheets. Every file in Microsoft Excel 5 is a workbook with several worksheets that you can switch between easily and enter information in quickly. You can arrange the sheets in a workbook and name them so that you can locate the information you need quickly. In this lesson, you'll learn how to work with worksheets and workbooks; open, save, and close a file; and enter and edit data in a worksheet.

You will learn how to:

■ Enter and edit data in a worksheet.

■ Work with workbooks.

Estimated lesson time: 40 minutes

Entering Data in Worksheets

Opening and Saving a File

If you haven't started Microsoft Excel or installed the practice files yet, work through "Getting Ready," earlier in this book. Then return to this lesson.

Whenever you start Microsoft Excel, a blank workbook opens, ready for you to work in. This workbook consists of several worksheets in which you can enter and edit information. When you start working in Microsoft Excel, you can either begin working on the blank workbook that Microsoft Excel creates, or you can open an existing file to work on instead.

In the next exercise, you open an existing file in your PRACTICE directory called 01LESSN.XLS. You use this file throughout this lesson to learn about entering data in a sheet.

Open an existing workbook

1 Click the Open button on the toolbar.

The Open dialog box appears.

Open

The Open command is like /File Retrieve, /File List, /File Directory, and /File Import in 1-2-3.

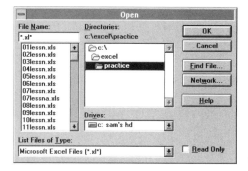

2   In the Directories list, be sure that the PRACTICE directory is selected.

3   In the File Name list, select the file 01LESSN.XLS and then choose OK.

The file 01LESSN.XLS, a budget sheet for West Coast Sales, opens. Your screen should look like the following.

If your screen does not match the illustrations in this lesson, see the Appendix, "Matching the Exercises."

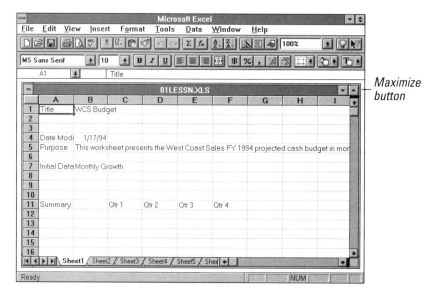

Maximize button

4   Click the Maximize button on the workbook window, if it is not already maximized.

You'll be using this budget file in several of the lessons in this book. You start each lesson by opening a file from the PRACTICE directory. You then save the file with a new name before making any changes to it to preserve the file to use again later. In the next exercise, you save the 01LESSN.XLS file that you just opened as LESSN01.XLS.

Save the workbook with a new name

*The Save As
command asks for a
filename, the same
as /File Save in 1-2-3.*

1 From the File menu, choose Save As.

The Save As dialog box appears. Be sure the correct directory and drive are selected.

*After you name a
worksheet, the Save
command (or the
equivalent Save
button) is like
/File Save Replace in
1-2-3.*

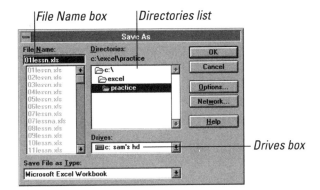

File Name box   *Directories list*

Drives box

2 In the File Name box, type **lessn01**, and then choose OK.

The extension XLS is added to the name automatically. The dialog box closes and your workbook is saved with the new name.

Moving Around in a Worksheet

A worksheet consists of *columns* and *rows*. Columns run vertically and are identified by letters; rows run horizontally and are identified by numbers. The intersection of a column and a row is called a *cell*. Cells are named by their positions in the rows and columns. This combination of the column letter and row number for a cell is called a cell *reference*. The intersection of the first column with the first row is a cell called A1. The cell one column to the right is called B1. The cell one row down from A1 is A2, and so on.

Note If your columns are identified by numbers instead of letters, it is because your reference style option is set to R1C1 style instead of A1 style. For this book, all references are in A1 style. To change to the A1 reference style, use the Options command on the Tools menu, and select the General tab. In the Reference Style box, click A1, and then choose OK.

---

*The active cell in
Microsoft Excel is
like the current cell
in 1-2-3.*

When you select a cell with the mouse button or with the cursor keys, you make that cell the *active cell*. When you make a cell active, you can type new data into it or edit the data it contains. The active cell has a border around it. You can always determine the reference for the cell you are in by looking in the name box on the formula bar.

The menu bar, formula bar, and status bar are like the control panel in 1-2-3.

In the following illustration, cell A1 is the active cell. Notice the border around the cell and the reference in the name box, which indicate the cell is active.

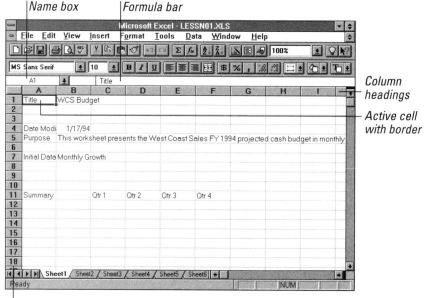

To change the active cell with your mouse, simply click a new cell. To change the active cell with your keyboard, use the arrow keys. The following table lists the keys you can use.

You can also use the scroll bars, scroll boxes, or scroll arrows to move to other areas in your worksheet. When you scroll through your worksheet, however, the cell that was active before you began scrolling remains the active cell.

To move	Press
Left one cell	LEFT ARROW
Right one cell	RIGHT ARROW
Up one cell	UP ARROW
Down one cell	DOWN ARROW
Up one screen	PAGE UP
Down one screen	PAGE DOWN
To the first cell in a row that contains data	CTRL+LEFT ARROW
To the last cell in a row that contains data	CTRL+RIGHT ARROW
To the start of the worksheet	CTRL+HOME
To the cell at the intersection of the last row and column that contains data	CTRL+END

In the next exercise, you use the keyboard commands to move around in your worksheet and select specific cells.

Select cells in a worksheet

1 Press the RIGHT ARROW key.

The active cell changes to cell B1, one cell to the right of A1.

2 Press CTRL+RIGHT ARROW.

The active cell changes to the last cell in the row, cell IV1.

3 Press CTRL+END.

The active cell changes to the cell at the intersection of the last row and column that contains data.

4 Press PAGE UP.

The active cell changes to the cell one screen up from the previous active cell.

5 Press CTRL+HOME.

The active cell changes to the first cell in the sheet, cell A1.

Selecting Multiple Cells

You can select several cells at once by holding down either the SHIFT or CTRL key while you click the mouse. To select several adjacent cells, you select the first cell in the set, hold down SHIFT, and then select the last cell in the set. Or, you can select the first cell and drag to the last cell. Either way, every cell between the first and last cell is selected. When you select more than one adjacent cell, you are selecting a *range* of cells. To select several non-adjacent cells, you simply click the first cell, hold down CTRL, and click the next cell that you want.

Note You can also select a range of cells on several sheets at once. You will learn more about working with sheets in your workbooks later in this lesson.

In the next exercise, you'll practice selecting multiple cells using the SHIFT and CTRL keys.

Select multiple cells in a worksheet

1 Click cell A1.

2 Hold down SHIFT and click cell B5.

All of the cells between cell A1 and cell B5 are selected.

3 Press CTRL+HOME.

Pressing CTRL+HOME makes cell A1 active again.

4   Hold down CTRL and click cell B5.

By holding down CTRL and clicking cell B5, you select only cells A1 and B5, and not all of the others between them.

5   Click cell A1.

Cell A1 becomes the active cell again.

6   Drag from cell A1 to cell B5.

All of the cells between A1 and B5 are selected.

7   Click cell A1.

Entering and Editing Data

Text in Microsoft Excel is like labels in 1-2-3.

You can enter text, numbers, and formulas into any cell on a worksheet. You simply select a cell and then type. You'll start your projected budget worksheet for West Coast Sales (WCS) by entering text in column A to label the rows of your budget sheet. You will label the rows with descriptions, such as Created by, Budget Model Area, and so on. When you label your worksheets, you and others are able to understand your worksheet's purpose, logic, and assumptions, making your worksheets easier to use.

Whatever you type appears in both the active cell and the formula bar. You can enter your data in the active cell by clicking the enter box (the box with a check on it) in the formula bar or by pressing ENTER. You can cancel the entry by clicking the cancel box in the formula bar or by pressing ESC. If you make a mistake while you're typing in a cell, you can use the BACKSPACE key or the arrow keys to move the *insertion point*, the blinking vertical line that indicates where you can enter text.

Enter the heading information

As you type the row titles, long entries will appear to spill into other columns, or be truncated if something is in the next column, even though they are contained in column B. You'll learn to correct this by changing column widths in Lesson 3, "Formatting Your Data."

If the active cell does not change when you press ENTER, choose Options from the Tools menu and select Move Selection After Enter on the Edit tab. See the Appendix, "Matching the Exercises," for more information.

1   Select cell A3, and then type **Created by**

2   Press ENTER.

3   Select cell B3.

4   Type your name, and then press ENTER.

5   Select cell A18.

6   Type **Budget Model Area**

7   Press ENTER.

Your worksheet should look like the following.

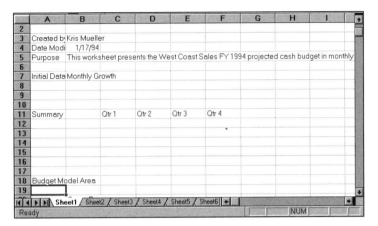

You can save time entering data in a range of cells if you select all of the cells in the range first. As you enter data in each cell and press ENTER, the next cell in the range becomes the active cell in a top-to-bottom, left-to-right order. Or, you can use TAB to move from left-to-right and then top-to-bottom in your range.

Note   Ranges are usually referred to by listing the first cell reference in the range, followed by a colon, and then the last cell reference in a range. For example, the range of cells from cell B8 to cell C9 would be referred to as B8:C9.

Start by selecting the range B8:C9, where you will enter the initial data for your budget sheet. The first cell you select remains the active cell. If you make a typing mistake and want to move backward through the selection, hold down the SHIFT key and press TAB or ENTER.

Select a cell range and enter the initial data

1   Drag from cell B8 to cell C9.

2   Type **Sales Growth** TAB **1.50** TAB **COGS Increase** TAB **0.90** TAB.

When you reach the last cell in the range and press TAB, the first selected cell becomes the active cell again. You can also press ENTER to move from the last cell to the first cell in your range. Your document should look like the following.

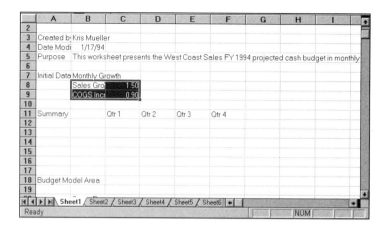

Editing Data in a Cell

You can edit data in two places on a sheet. You can select the cell and edit the data in the formula bar, or you can edit the data right in the cell. You simply double-click the cell and then move the insertion point to wherever you need it in the cell. You can then either type the new information or delete the information that's incorrect. Editing directly in the cell is useful when you're editing text in a cell, and it's even more useful when you're working with formulas, as you will see in Lesson 2.

In the next exercise, you edit the title of the worksheet.

Edit data in a cell

1   Double-click cell B1.

Cell B1 contains the title of the worksheet.

2   In cell B1, click just before the word "Budget," and type **Cash** followed by a **space**.

3   Click just after the word "Budget," type a colon followed by a space, and then type **1994 Fiscal Year**

4   Press ENTER.

Your new title appears in cell B1. Your worksheet should look like the following.

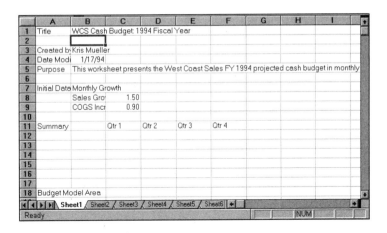

Entering a Series of Data into Cells

As you saw in the last exercise, you can select a range of cells and enter data into each of them. You can also enter a series of data, either numbers or text, into several cells. To do this, you type the first two numbers or text entries in the series and then use AutoFill to enter the rest of the series. For example, you can type "1" into the first cell, and "2" in the second cell, and then use AutoFill to quickly fill in 3, 4, 5, and 6.

If you are entering a set series, such as the months of the year, or the days of the week, you can type the first item in the series, and then fill in the rest of the series without typing anything else. For example, if you want to enter the months of the year into a row, you simply type "Jan," and then use AutoFill to fill in the rest.

Dragging the fill handle to enter a series is like using /Data Fill in 1-2-3.

You can either use the AutoFill command on the Edit menu, or you can drag the fill handle on the cell border to fill your series in quickly. In the next exercise, you add month labels to your budget sheet using AutoFill.

Use AutoFill to enter a series of numbers

1 Select cells C19:D19.

2 Type **1** ENTER **2**

3 With both cells still selected, move your pointer over the black box (the AutoFill handle) in the bottom right corner of cell D19 until the pointer changes to a solid plus sign. Your pointer should look like the following.

4 Drag the AutoFill handle to cell L19.

You can enter month or day names either in full (January) or short (Jan) form. When you fill the series into the other cells, the rest of the series will either be in full (February) or short (Feb) form as well.

Use AutoFill to enter a series of months

1 Select cell C19.

2 Type **Jun** and press ENTER.

3 Click cell C19 again, and then drag the AutoFill handle to cell N19.

The rest of the series is entered into the cells.

4 Press CTRL+HOME.

The active cell changes to cell A1.

Removing Data from Cells

If you need to remove data from a cell, you can easily delete the information and replace it with new information by typing new information into the cell. You can also remove data from a cell by either selecting the cell and pressing DELETE, or by using the Clear command on the Edit menu. Usually, however, selecting a cell and typing the new information over the old data is the quickest method.

In the next exercise, you enter new information by typing over the old data.

Clear a cell and enter new information

The Clear command is like /Range Erase in 1-2-3, except that you can specify which cell attributes you want to clear.

1 Select cell B4.

This cell reflects the date on which the budget sheet was last modified.

2 Type the current date in the form *mm/dd/yy*, and then press ENTER.

The date is removed from the cell and the new date is entered. Your sheet should look similar to the following.

In Lesson 2, "Writing Formulas," you learn how to create a formula that automatically displays the current date.

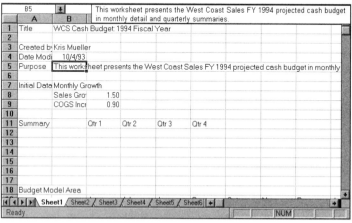

Undoing Changes

You can always correct mistakes while you are typing by pressing the BACKSPACE key and retyping the correct letters or numbers. But what if you select a cell and clear it or type over the contents of a cell by mistake? You can recover from such mistakes by using the Undo command on the Edit menu, or the Undo button on the toolbar. If you decide that you want to keep the change after all, you can use the Redo command on the Edit menu.

In the next exercise, you delete the contents of a cell and then restore them.

Undo previous actions

1   Select cell B4.

2   Press DEL.

The date is removed from the cell.

3   From the Edit menu, choose Undo Clear.

The data is restored. The name of the Undo command changes to reflect the specific action that you need to Undo. If you had typed new text, the Undo command would have been the Undo Entry command instead of the Undo Clear command.

4   From the Edit menu, choose Redo (u) Clear, or press CTRL+Z.

The Undo command changes to Redo since you've just used Undo. CTRL+Z is the shortcut key for both Undo and Redo. The date you typed in the last exercise is cleared from cell B4.

Note   In some instances, the Undo command is not available. If you have just saved your workbook, for example, and you open the Edit menu, you will see Can't Undo in the place of the Undo command.

Working with Workbooks

In Microsoft Excel 5, files are called *workbooks*. Workbooks can contain multiple worksheets, chart sheets, and Visual Basic modules. You'll learn more about charts and chart sheets in Lessons 4 and 5, "Charting Your Data" and "Modifying Your Charts." You'll learn more about Visual Basic modules in Lesson 15, "Automating Repetitive Tasks." For now, you'll work mostly with worksheets. With the workbooks in Microsoft Excel 5, you can switch between sheets easily, enter data in more than one sheet at a time, and name the sheets separately to make them easy to distinguish. You don't need to use a contents page to switch between sheets or view the sheet names within a workbook, or save sheets separately. Instead, all of the sheets are accessible at all times, and you save the entire workbook at once.

Moving Around in a Workbook

You can move between sheets in a workbook by clicking the tabs at the bottom of the sheets. You can use the arrows at the lower-left corner of the screen to move to the first sheet, one sheet backward, one sheet forward, or to the last sheet in a workbook. You can also use keyboard shortcuts to move between sheets. If you press CTRL+PAGE DOWN, you'll move to the next sheet. If you press CTRL+PAGE UP, you'll move to the previous sheet. The following illustration shows the tabs and arrows you can use to move around in a workbook.

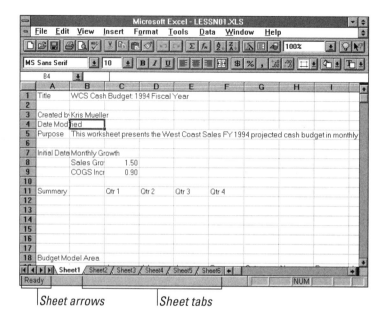

Sheet arrows   *Sheet tabs*

You can also select several sheets at a time in the same way that you select several cells at a time. You select several adjacent sheets by holding down SHIFT and selecting the tabs on the sheets that you want, or you select several non-adjacent sheets by holding down CTRL and selecting the sheet tabs.

When you select several sheets in a workbook, you can enter the same data on each sheet all at once. You simply select the sheets that you want the data to appear on, and then type the data on one of the sheets. The data appears in the same cell on each selected sheet.

In the next exercise, you move to different sheets in the workbook and enter data in them.

Move to other sheets and enter data

1   Click the tab for Sheet4.

Sheet4 becomes the active sheet.

2 Click the tab for Sheet5.

Sheet5, the next sheet in the workbook, becomes the active sheet.

3 Hold down SHIFT and click the tab for Sheet3.

Sheets 3 through 5 are selected, but Sheet5 remains the active sheet.

4 On Sheet5, select cell B3.

5 Type **Kris Mueller** and press ENTER.

6 Click the tab for Sheet4.

Sheet4 becomes the active sheet. Your workbook should look like the following.

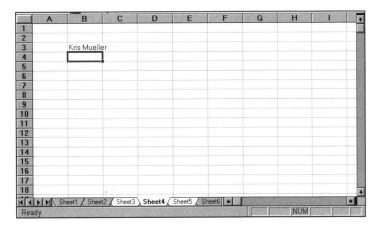

Notice that the name appears on Sheet4, even though you typed it only on Sheet5. When you select several sheets and then type on one, the data is entered in each selected sheet in the same place. Notice also that Sheet3 and Sheet5 are still selected, even though Sheet4 is now the active sheet.

7 Click the Sheet2 tab.

Clicking this tab clears the other sheet selections. Sheet2 becomes the active sheet.

Inserting, Deleting, and Renaming Sheets

When you open a new workbook, you have 16 blank sheets named Sheet1, Sheet2, and so on. You can leave these sheets in place, if you like, or you can customize your workbook by adding, removing, or renaming the sheets. You can have from 1 to 255 sheets in a workbook. You use the Worksheet command on the Insert menu to insert a new worksheet, and the Delete Sheet command on the Edit menu to remove a sheet. You can also rename sheets to describe their purpose or contents.

In the next exercise, you'll remove a sheet and insert a new one. Then, you'll rename a sheet to make its purpose clearer.

Remove, add, and rename sheets within a workbook

1 Be sure that Sheet2 is the active sheet, and then from the Edit menu, choose Delete Sheet.

A dialog box opens, informing you that the sheet will be deleted permanently.

2 Choose OK.

The dialog box closes and the sheet is deleted. Notice that Sheet2 is gone, and Sheet3 now follows Sheet1.

3 From the Insert menu, choose Worksheet.

A new sheet is inserted before Sheet3.

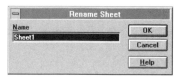

Last Tab Scroll

4 Click the Last Tab Scroll button.

The sheet tabs scroll so that you can see Sheet16.

Note There are two right arrows and two left arrows for scrolling through the sheets in your workbook. The arrows with the bar (Last Tab Scroll and First Tab Scroll buttons) move to the beginning or end of the sheet tabs. The arrows without the bar move forward or backward in your workbook one sheet at a time.

First Tab Scroll

5 Click the First Tab Scroll button.

The sheet tabs scroll so that you can see Sheet1.

6 Double-click the Sheet1 tab.

The Rename Sheet dialog box opens.

7 In the Name box, type **1994 Budget** and then press ENTER.

Sheet1 is renamed to 1994 Budget. Your worksheet should look like the following.

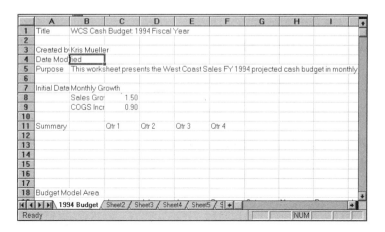

One Step Further

In this lesson, you learned that you can automatically enter a series of data into a series of cells. Microsoft Excel recognizes several standard series, such as 1, 2, 3; Qtr1, Qtr2, Qtr3; and the series of months that you used earlier. You can also define custom series. With the Options command on the Tools menu, you can create a custom list that you can fill into cells in your worksheets.

In the next exercise, you create a customized series.

Create a custom list of data

1 From the Tools menu, choose Options.

The Options dialog box opens.

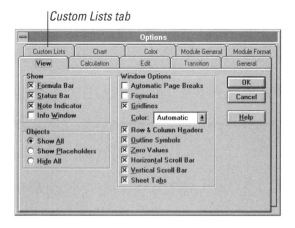

Custom Lists tab

2   Click the Custom Lists tab.

3   In the Custom Lists list, select NEW LIST.

4   In the List Entries box, type **Gross Revenue** ENTER **Cost of Goods Sold** ENTER **Gross Profit** ENTER **Expenses** ENTER **Operating Income**

5   Click the Add button.

Your new custom list is added to the Custom Lists in the dialog box.

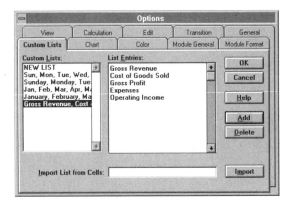

6   Choose OK.

7   Move to Sheet4 and select cell B12.

8   In cell B12, type **Gross Revenue** ENTER.

9   Select cell B12, and then drag the fill handle downward four rows to cell B16.

The series labels are automatically filled in.

If You Want to Continue to the Next Lesson

1   From the File menu, choose Save.

2   From the File menu, choose Close.

If You Want to Quit Microsoft Excel for Now

▶   From the File menu, choose Exit.

If you see the Save dialog box, click Yes.

Lesson Summary

To	Do this	Button
Open a workbook	Click the Open button on the toolbar. Select the drive, directory, and filename, and then choose OK.	
Save a workbook with a new name	From the File menu, choose Save As. In the File Name box, type the filename, and choose OK.	
Enter data	Select a cell and type the data.	
Edit data	Double-click in the cell that contains the data. Place the insertion point where you want to edit and either type over the data or use the backspace key to delete data.	
Fill data into a series of cells	Type in the data for the first two cells in the series, and then drag the AutoFill handle to fill in the rest of the series.	
Clear a cell	Select the cell, and then press DEL. *or* From the Edit menu, choose Clear, and then choose OK.	
Undo a change	From the Edit menu, choose Undo, if it is available.	
Repeat a change	From the Edit menu, choose Redo or Repeat, if it is available.	
Insert a worksheet into a workbook	From the Insert menu, choose Worksheet.	
Delete a worksheet from a workbook	Select the sheet tab, and from the Edit menu, choose Delete Sheet.	
Rename a sheet	Double-click the sheet tab. Type the new name in the Name box and choose OK.	
Close a workbook	From the File menu, choose Close. *or* Double-click the Control-menu box on the worksheet window.	

For more information on	See in the *Microsoft Excel User's Guide*
Opening, saving, and closing a workbook	Chapter 6, "Managing Workbook Files"
Entering data	Chapter 9, "Entering Data"
Editing data	Chapter 11, "Editing a Worksheet"
Filling a series of data into cells	Chapter 9, "Entering Data"
Clearing cells	Chapter 11, "Editing a Worksheet"
Undoing changes	Chapter 11, "Editing a Worksheet"
Inserting, deleting, and renaming sheets	Chapter 7, "Working in Workbooks"

Preview of the Next Lesson

In the next lesson, you'll learn how to copy, paste, and move information into other cells on a worksheet. You'll learn how to use simple formulas to perform mathematical and other kinds of operations, and how to use cell references in formulas to point to the cells you need. You'll also learn more about ranges and naming them so that you can quickly find and use the information you need.

Writing Formulas

You can perform calculations with your data using *formulas*, which are made up of *data operators* and often *functions*. Microsoft Excel comes with hundreds of functions that you can use in formulas, including automatic functions, like *AutoSum*, that totals data in rows or columns. The *Function Wizard* makes it easy to create formulas.

In this lesson, you'll learn how to total data in rows and columns, create simple formulas, and name ranges to make formulas and references easy to understand. You'll learn how to copy, paste, and move data with ease, and why the difference between relative and absolute references is important when you copy or move data.

You will learn how to:

- Total rows and columns automatically.
- Create simple formulas.
- Create formulas with the Function Wizard.
- Name ranges.
- Copy and paste data between cells.
- Move data between cells.
- Create formulas with relative and absolute references.

Estimated lesson time: 50 minutes

If your screen does not match the illustrations in this lesson, see the Appendix, "Matching the Exercises."

Start the lesson

1 From your PRACTICE directory, open 02LESSN.XLS.

2 Save the workbook as LESSN02.XLS.

3 Click the Maximize button on the workbook window, if it is not already maximized.

Totaling Rows and Columns Automatically

One of the tasks that you will probably do frequently in Microsoft Excel is total rows and columns. You could create a new formula every time you needed to total a row or column, but Microsoft Excel provides an easier way. The AutoSum button on the Standard toolbar automatically creates a formula to total the rows and columns for you.

You can use AutoSum in three ways—to locate and total the rows or columns in the range nearest to the current cell, to total any range that you select, or to add grand totals to a range containing other totals. To automatically total the nearest range, you click the AutoSum button and then press ENTER, or double-click the AutoSum button. To total a specific range, you select the range and then click the AutoSum button. When you use the AutoSum button, the Sum formula is created and entered. When you click the AutoSum button once, the formula is created, and then you have the option of accepting it (by pressing ENTER), or modifying it.

Whichever method you use, be sure that there is a blank row and column around your data for the cells you want to total. In the next exercises, you total the cost of goods sold data for June, and then total the summary data on your budget sheet using the AutoSum button.

Total the cost of goods sold

1 Be sure that the 1994 Budget sheet is the active sheet.

2 Select cell C29.

You will use AutoSum to enter a total for the range C25:C28.

3 Click the AutoSum button on the Standard toolbar once.

AutoSum

The range C25:C28 on the worksheet is surrounded by a moving line, and a sum formula, =SUM(C25:C28), appears in the formula bar. When you click the AutoSum button once, you can decide whether the selected range is the range that you want totaled. Your worksheet should look like the following.

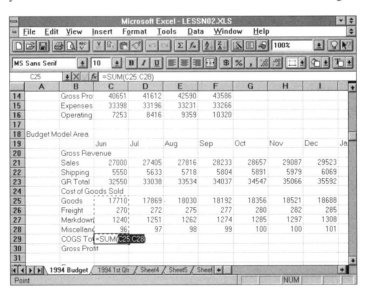

4 Press ENTER.

The result is entered into cell C29.

Total the other summary ranges

1 Select the range C12:G16.

This range contains the summary data and the totals column.

2 Click the AutoSum button.

The totals for the rows appear in cells G12:G16.

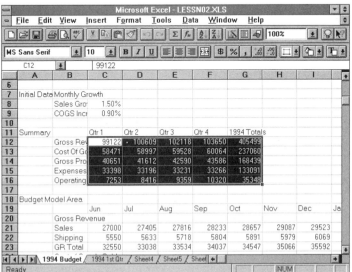

Creating Simple Formulas

When you need to perform a calculation in Excel, you use a formula. You can create formulas to perform calculations as simple as adding the values in two cells, or as complex as finding how much a particular value deviates from other values in a set. To tell Microsoft Excel that you're entering a formula in a cell, you must begin the entry with an arithmetic operator such as an equal sign (=). You can also type +, −, or @ to begin a formula; Microsoft Excel converts these to an equal sign. A simple formula, such as adding, subtracting, multiplying, or dividing cells, requires two parts: an operator to begin the formula, and at least one cell reference.

When you create formulas that perform calculations or use formulas that generate information from your data, you need to tell Microsoft Excel where to find the data. You can either type a cell reference or a range name, or you can point to the cells while you are creating the formula. The cells you point to are surrounded by a dotted line called the *moving border* so that you can see which cells are selected while you work with the formula.

In the next exercise, you create a formula in cell C30 to find the gross profit for June. You'll use the pointing method to create the formula.

Find the gross profit

1   Select cell C30.

2   Type =, and click cell C23.

3   Type –, and click cell C29.

4   Press ENTER.

The formula is entered, and the gross profit amount appears in the cell.

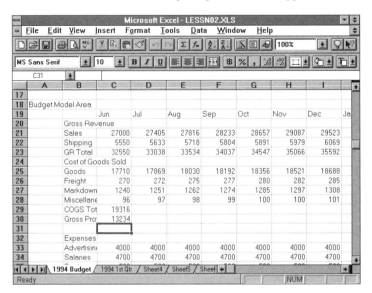

Writing Formulas Using the Function Wizard

A number in Microsoft Excel is like a value in 1-2-3.

A simple formula can consist of arithmetic operators and cell references. More complex formulas can also include numbers and functions. Microsoft Excel has hundreds of *worksheet functions* to help you perform specialized calculations easily. A worksheet function is a special built-in formula that performs an operation on the values you provide. For example, the formula "=AVERAGE(C22:C26)" uses a function to average the values in the cell range C22:C26. It gives you the same result as the formula "=(C22+C23+C24+C25+C26)/5", which adds the values and divides them by the number of values. Functions can be used alone or nested within other functions. You can enter functions by typing them in the cell with the other information needed for the formula. You can either type a formula with a function, or use the Function Wizard to enter a function automatically.

A function is like an @function in 1-2-3.

Certain functions are complete on their own; you do not need to include any cell references or other information for them to work. For example, the TODAY function enters the current system date into a cell. The NOW function is another function that does not require any additional information. In the next exercise, you'll use the TODAY function to display the current date.

Display the current date

1   Select cell B4 and press DELETE.

2   In cell B4, type **=today()**

You can type function names in either uppercase or lowercase type. When you press ENTER, they are converted automatically to uppercase.

3   Press ENTER.

The formula is entered, and the current system date appears in the cell.

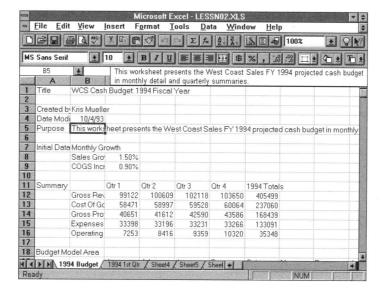

Most formulas that you create will require more than just a function name. You might need to include either cell references or values or both to complete the formula. These additional elements in a formula are called *arguments*. For example, in the summary formulas you entered with the AutoSum button, the formula was broken down into the function (=SUM) that determines what the formula does, and the argument (C25:C28) that determines which cells are used.

You can also use values in certain formulas, such as some financial functions that determine loan payments or future values of investments. Arguments usually appear within parentheses, such as in the sum formula =SUM(C25:C28). In fact, whenever you use a function, you must have parentheses, even if you don't need any arguments, such as when you entered the TODAY function, =TODAY(). Some functions, such as many statistical or financial functions, require more than one argument. In these cases, individual arguments are separated by commas.

For more information about specific functions, search in online Help for the function name.

When you work with a function that requires arguments, it can become difficult to keep track of the information that you need. Microsoft Excel now has a Function Wizard that prompts you for any arguments that are required to complete a formula. In the next exercise, you'll use the Function Wizard to create a formula that averages the sales for the entire year.

Average the sales for the entire year

Function Wizard

1   Select cell C50, and then click the Function Wizard button on the Standard toolbar.

The Function Wizard opens.

2   In the Function Category list, select Statistical.

A list of statistical functions appears in the Function Name box.

3   In the Function Name box, select AVERAGE, and then choose the Next button.

The next step in the Function Wizard appears.

4   Click the title bar of the Function Wizard dialog box, and drag the dialog box downward to the bottom of your screen.

You need to move the dialog box out of the way so that you can select the range you want to average on your budget sheet.

5   Click in the Number1 box.

6   Scroll upward in your budget sheet, until you can see row 21.

7 Drag to select cells C21:N21 in the budget sheet.

Notice that as you drag to select the cells, the value in the Value box in the Function Wizard dialog box changes to reflect your selection. The references C21:N21 appear in the Number1 box.

Value box

8 Choose the Finish button, and scroll downward in the budget sheet until you can see cell C50.

The average of the year's sales, 29343, appears in cell C50.

Naming Ranges

Any rectangular group of cells on a worksheet is called a *range*. As you saw in the AutoSum section of this lesson, you can refer to a range by listing the cell reference for the first cell in the range, followed by a colon, and then the last cell in the range. Often, you use ranges to refer to a group of similar data that falls within a rectangular area on the worksheet, like the sales data for a particular project, or the year's data for the freight category in the budget. When you need to refer to a range in a formula (as you will learn a little later in this lesson), you can either list the range by its cell references, or you can name the range and then use the name in the formula. Naming ranges can save you time and effort, since a name is easier to remember than the beginning and ending cell references for a range.

Creating Names

The Create Names command is like /Range Name Labels in 1-2-3, except that Create Names acts on multiple cells.

Creating names for a range is easy. You can either select the range and then use the name box on the formula bar to define a name, or you can create names automatically based on row or column headings. You can also use the Name command on the Insert menu to define names.

Range names can be as long as you need them to be, provided that you don't use any spaces, commas, or periods. Usually, a range name consists of one word, or a few words separated by underscore characters between words. For example, both the names "Freight" and "Printer_Sales" are acceptable range names. "Printer Sales" or "Printer.Sales" are not. In general, you should use names that you can easily remember and type.

You can create several names within a range all at once by selecting them and then using the Name command and the Create command on the Insert menu. To use the

Create command, you must have either row or column headings as part of the selection. The row and column headings then become the range names for the selection.

In the next exercise, you define a range with a name you type, and then create names for a larger range using the Create command.

Create range names

1   Select the range C20:C46.

You will define a name for this range.

Name

2   Click in the name box on the formula bar, and then type **June93_Budget**

3   Press ENTER.

The name June93_Budget is defined for the range C20:C46.

4   Select the range B19:N46.

This range contains the headings and all of the data in your budget.

5   From the Insert menu, choose Name, and then choose Create.

The Create Names dialog box opens. Notice that the options to use the headings in the top row and left column are already selected.

6   Choose OK.

The names are created. Each row becomes a range named with the row title, and each column becomes a range named with the column title.

Tip   A keyboard shortcut for creating range names is CTRL+SHIFT+F3.

Editing Names

The Name Define command is like /Range Name Create and /Range Name Delete in 1-2-3.

With the Name command, you can edit the range name or change the specific cells included in a named range after you create it. In the next exercise, you expand the range to include additional cells and then edit the range name.

Expand a range and edit a name

1   From the Insert menu, choose Name, and then choose Define.

The Define Name dialog box opens. Notice all of your new names listed in the Names In Workbook list.

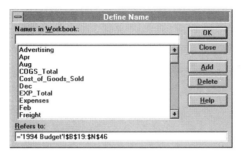

2   Scroll downward in the list, if necessary, and select the name June93_Budget.

This is the first range that you created.

3   In the Refers To box, select 20, and type **19**

This expands the range to include cell C19.

4   In the Names In Workbook text box, select the text "e93" in the June93_Budget name and press DEL.

Your dialog box should look like the following.

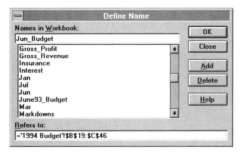

5   Click the Add button.

Clicking the Add button adds your modified name, Jun_Budget, to the list of ranges. Notice that June93_Budget is still on the list.

6   Select the range June93_Budget, and choose the Delete button in the dialog box.

The range is deleted from the list.

7   Choose Close.

The dialog box closes.

Going to Ranges

You can move around in your worksheet more quickly now that you have named your ranges. Instead of scrolling or moving to another area on the worksheet to select a range, you can use the name box on the formula bar to move to and select a range in one step. You select the range from the list in the name box.

In the next exercise, you use the name box to move around in your worksheet.

Select ranges using the name box

1   Click the down arrow next to the name box.

A list of ranges opens for you to choose from.

2   Scroll downward and select the Jun_Budget range.

Cells C19:C46 are selected.

3   Click the name box arrow again, and then scroll downward and select Sales.

Sales is a range name that was created automatically when you used the Create command. The Sales range, cells C21:N21, is selected.

Note   You can also use the name box on the formula bar to move to a specific cell. Instead of typing a name into the box, type a cell reference, such as N56, to select that cell.

Using Names in Formulas

You can use range names in place of cell references in formulas. Instead of listing the reference for the range C19:C46, you can use the name "Jun" that you created earlier in this lesson. Names can make your formulas much easier to understand if you ever need to backtrack and figure out exactly what a formula is for.

In the next exercise, you use the Function Wizard to find the maximum sales value, and then you type a formula to find the minimum sales value in your budget data.

Find the maximum and minimum sales values

Function Wizard

1   Select cell C51 and click the Function Wizard button on the Standard toolbar.

The Function Wizard opens.

2 In the Function Category box, be sure that Statistical is selected, and then in the Function Name box, scroll downward and select MAX.

This function finds the maximum value in a selected range.

3 Click the Next button.

The next step in the Function Wizard appears.

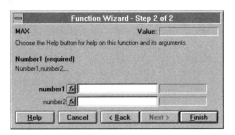

4 Click in the Number1 box.

5 Click the down arrow next to the name box on the formula bar.

The list of range names in the sheet opens.

6 Scroll downward in the list and select Sales.

The range name "Sales" appears in the Number1 box.

7 Click the Finish button.

The formula is completed and the value appears in cell C51.

8 Select cell C52.

9 Type **=min(Sales)**

This finds the minimum value in the range "Sales."

10 Press ENTER.

Your worksheet should look like the following.

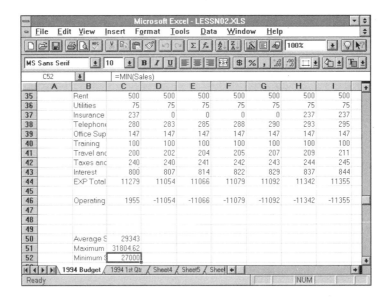

Rearranging Cell Contents

When you enter data in your cells, including text, numbers, and formulas, you are not locked in to the arrangement. You can always rearrange the data if you need to, although you should use some caution if you are working with formulas. You can copy and paste data between cells; insert and delete cells, rows, and columns; and even move data between cells.

Copying and Pasting Data Between Cells

If you need to copy information to another place on the worksheet, you can either use the Copy and Paste buttons on the toolbar, use the Copy and Paste commands on the Edit menu, or use the mouse to drag the data to a new location. To copy data with the mouse, you select the cell to be copied, hold down CTRL, and then drag the data into the new cell. This copying method is much quicker if you are copying onto the same sheet. If you need to copy to another sheet, however, you use the menu commands.

Pressing CTRL and dragging selected cells by their borders is like using /Copy in 1-2-3.

In the next exercises, you use the mouse to copy data on the budget sheet, and you use the Edit menu commands to copy data onto another sheet.

Copy data using the menu and the mouse

1   Select cells M19:N46.

2   Position the pointer over any part of the range border, and then hold down CTRL.

When you hold down CTRL with your pointer positioned over the range border, your pointer displays a small plus sign near its tip. This plus sign indicates that you are ready to copy the contents of the range. Your pointer should look like the following.

3   Drag the gray border surrounding the range to the new range O19:P46, and then release the mouse button and CTRL.

The information is pasted into the new cell range.

Tip   You can also copy data from one cell or range into an adjoining cell or range with another method. If your data is not a series that can be filled automatically into cells (such as the months of the year, days of the week, or consecutive numbers), you can copy the data by dragging the fill handle. Simply select the cell or range, drag the fill handle to the adjoining cell or range, and release. The data or series of data is copied into the cells.

---

4   From the Edit menu, choose Undo Drag And Drop.

The information is removed from the cells.

Copying Formulas

You can copy (or fill) formulas into a range of cells just as you can fill data into a range. To fill a formula into a range, you select the cell that contains the formula and then drag the fill handle over or down as far as you need. The formula is automatically copied into the new cells. In the next exercise, you fill your Cost of Goods Sold formula across the row.

Fill a formula into a range

1   Select cell C29.

2   Drag the fill handle to cell N29 and release.

The Cost of Goods Sold sum formula is filled into cells D29:N29. Your worksheet should look like the following.

	F	**G**	**H**	**I**	**J**	**K**	**L**	**M**	**N**
19	Sep	Oct	Nov	Dec	Jan	Feb	Mar	Apr	May
20									
21	28233	28657	29087	29523	29966	30415	30872	31335	31805
22	5804	5891	5979	6069	6160	6252	6346	6441	6538
23	34037	34547	35066	35592	36125	36667	37217	37776	38342
24									
25	18192	18356	18521	18688	18856	19026	19197	19370	19544
26	277	280	282	285	287	290	293	295	298
27	1274	1285	1297	1308	1320	1332	1344	1356	1368
28	99	100	100	101	102	103	104	105	106
29	19842	20021	20201	20383	20566	20751	20938	21127	21317
30									
31									
32									
33	4000	4000	4000	4000	4000	4000	4000	4000	4000
34	4700	4700	4700	4700	4700	4700	4700	4700	4700
35	500	500	500	500	500	500	500	500	500
36	75	75	75	75	75	75	75	75	75

Cell reference: COGS_Total   =SUM(C25:C28)

Sheet tabs: 1994 Budget / 1994 1st Qtr / Sheet4 / Sheet5 / Shee

Copying and Pasting Specific Aspects of a Cell

You can copy both cell entries and formats, just as you do in 1-2-3.

When you copy and paste, you can paste every aspect of the cell as you did in the last exercise, or you can paste only certain aspects of the data in the cell. For example, if the cell contains a formula, you can paste only the value, or only the result, of the formula to the new cell. You can also paste only the formatting of a cell, as you will learn in Lesson 3, "Formatting Your Data."

To copy and paste specific aspects of a cell selectively, you use the Copy command or button as usual, but you use the Paste Special command on the Edit menu instead of the Paste command. The Paste Special command allows you to choose which aspects of the cell you want to paste. For example, if a particular cell contains a formula, but you want to copy only the value that results from the formula, you can copy the cell and then use the Paste Special command to paste only the value, instead of the formula, into the new cell.

In the next exercise, you copy the totals information from the budget area and paste only the values into a summary area.

Copy only the values of the first quarter budget data to another sheet

1   Select B19:E30.

2   Click the Copy button on the toolbar.

3   Switch to the 1994 1st Qtr sheet and select cell B9.

Copy

4   From the Edit menu, choose Paste Special.

The Paste Special dialog box opens.

5   Under Paste, select the Values option button and then choose OK.

The dialog box closes and only the values are pasted into the new cell range.

Moving Data Between Cells

Just as you can copy data by dragging with the mouse or by using menu commands, you can also move data by either method. When you use the Cut and Paste commands on the Edit menu, you can cut data from one cell and paste it into another. With the mouse, you simply select a cell and drag the cell by its border to a new location. When you move data, you do not need to hold down CTRL or any other keys while you drag.

Dragging selected cells by their border is like using /Move in 1-2-3.

In the next exercise, you move a cell in the budget sheet to another location.

Move a cell

1   Switch back to the 1994 Budget sheet and select the range B30:C30.

2   Position the mouse pointer over part of the range border, hold down the mouse button, and drag the range border to B31:C31.

Be sure that you do not select the lower-right corner, which will automatically fill the data from cells B30:C30 into cells B31:C31, rather than moving the data.

3   Release the mouse button.

The data is dropped into place in the new location. Your worksheet should look like the following.

		Microsoft Excel - LESSN02.XLS							

File Edit View Insert Format Tools Data Window Help

B31			Gross Profit						
	A	B	C	D	E	F	G	H	I
19			Jun	Jul	Aug	Sep	Oct	Nov	Dec	Ja
20		Gross Revenue							
21		Sales	27000	27405	27816	28233	28657	29087	29523
22		Shipping	5550	5633	5718	5804	5891	5979	6069
23		GR Total	32550	33038	33534	34037	34547	35066	35592
24		Cost of Goods Sold							
25		Goods	17710	17869	18030	18192	18356	18521	18688
26		Freight	270	272	275	277	280	282	285
27		Markdown	1240	1251	1262	1274	1285	1297	1308
28		Miscellane	96	97	98	99	100	100	101
29		COGS Tot	19316	19490	19665	19842	20021	20201	20383
30									
31		Gross Pro	13234						
32		Expenses							
33		Advertisin	4000	4000	4000	4000	4000	4000	4000
34		Salaries	4700	4700	4700	4700	4700	4700	4700
35		Rent	500	500	500	500	500	500	500
36		Utilities	75	75	75	75	75	75	75

1994 Budget / 1994 1st Qtr / Sheet4 / Sheet5 / Sheet

Ready   NUM

Inserting and Deleting Cells, Rows, and Columns

The Columns and Rows commands are like /Worksheet Insert Column and /Worksheet Insert Row in 1-2-3.

You can copy cells to rearrange the data in your worksheet, but what if you just need more room in one particular area? You can insert or delete cells, rows, or columns easily, if you need to. When you delete a cell, you are not just clearing the contents. You are removing the entire cell from the sheet, and other cells must move into the deleted cell's place, either from the right or bottom of the deleted cell. To insert a cell, row, or column, you can use the Cells, Rows, or Columns commands on the Insert menu. To delete a cell, row, or column, you can use the Delete command on the Edit menu.

When you insert or delete a row or column, you must select the entire row or column, not just part of it. To select an entire row or column, click the header button at the left of a row or the top of a column.

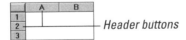 *Header buttons*

When you insert a cell, column, or row, you need to select the cell, column, or row immediately to the right or below where you want the new cell, column, or row to appear. When you use the menu commands to insert a cell, you can decide which cells will move to make space for the new cell. When you delete a cell, you can decide which cells will move to take the place of the deleted cells.

You can also insert or delete entire columns or rows, and move them around, just as you can insert, delete, and move cells. In the next exercise, you insert a new column in your budget and move your columns around so that you have a blank column between your area labels, such as Budget Area, and your data.

Insert and rearrange columns

1 Click the column header for column A.

You move to cell A1 so that you can see the data in column A move when you drag it in step 4.

2 From the Insert menu, choose Columns.

A new column is inserted.

3 Click the column header for column B.

4 Position the pointer on the right side of the range border and drag to the new column.

The data from column B moves to column A. You now have a blank column between your labels and your data. Your worksheet should look like the following.

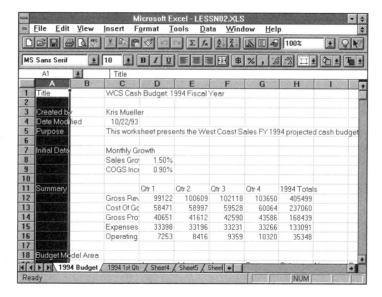

Creating Formulas with Relative and Absolute References

When you copied the formula for totaling the Cost of Goods Sold from cell C29 to D29:N29, the cell references used in the formulas were automatically adjusted to reflect the column that the formula was in. References that change automatically when you move them are called *relative references*. When you copy a formula containing relative references, the references are adjusted to reflect the new location of the formula. However, you can also use formulas with *absolute references,* references that always refer to the same cell, regardless of where the formula is copied.

A relative reference describes the location of a cell in terms of its distance, in rows and columns, from another cell. Relative references are analogous to giving directions, such as "Cross the street and go to the fifth house on the left." In the following worksheet, the formula in cell D23 totals the values in cells D21:D22. The formula in cell E23 totals the values in cells E21:E22. Likewise, the formulas in F23 and G23 total the values in cells F21:F22 and G21:G22, respectively.

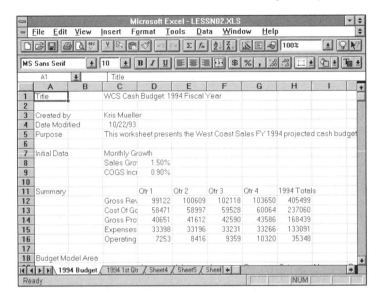

An absolute cell reference describes a specific cell address. Absolute references are analogous to giving directions, such as "Deliver the newspaper to 405 114th Avenue S.E., Bellevue, WA 98004." In the preceding illustration, the formulas in cells E21:O21 calculate the sales increase between months based on a fixed percentage. However, each of these formulas refers to cell $D$8, the cell that contains the sales growth rate (1.50%). The dollar signs ($) indicate an absolute reference to cell $D$8. No matter where the sales growth formula is copied, it always refers to cell $D$8.

Usually, when you use a cell reference in a formula, the reference is relative. For example, in the following illustration, the formula in cell C2 uses a relative reference to cell B4, two rows down and one column to the left of cell C2.

	A	B	C	D
1				
2			formula	
3				
4		data		
5				

If you copy the formula one cell to the right, as in the following illustration, the formula will continue to look for data in the cell two rows down and one column to the left of its new location. But your data remains in the same spot, which is now two rows down and two columns to the left of the formula. Now the formula is in cell D2, and it refers to cell C4, two rows down and one column to the left, while the data remains in cell B4.

	A	B	C	D
1				
2				formula
3				
4		data		
5				

You can change a relative reference to an absolute reference so that even if you move or copy the formula, it will always point to the same cell. To change a relative reference to an absolute reference, you select the reference in the formula and press F4. Or, you can type a dollar sign ($) before both the column and row indicators in the cell reference($D$8).

In the next exercise, you copy a formula made up of relative references and see what happens. Then you change the reference to an absolute reference and see how it changes again.

Copy a formula and change it to an absolute reference

1   Select cell O23.

This cell contains a formula with relative references.

2   Copy cell O23 to cell P23.

The formula moves to the new cell. Notice that you now get a result of 0 instead of the original value. This is because the relative reference now points to cells with nothing in them. Your worksheet should look like the following.

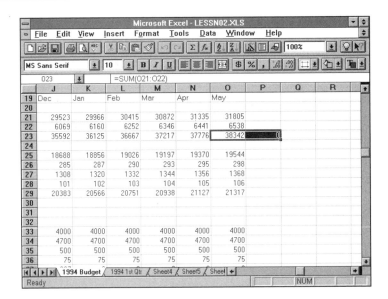

3 From the Edit menu, choose Undo Paste or Undo Drag And Drop.

4 Select cell O23.

5 In the formula bar, select "O21:O22."

6 Press F4, and then press ENTER.

This changes the references to absolute references.

Note You can press F4 several times to cycle among the different types of references. You can change both the row and column references to absolute references (such as $A$1), only the row reference to an absolute reference (such as A$1), only the column reference to an absolute reference (such as $A1), or both to relative references (such as A1).

---

7 Copy cell O23 to cell P23.

The formula is copied to the new cell, but retains its value since you changed the relative references to absolute references.

One Step Further

Microsoft Excel 5 comes with many functions that can help with mathematical, financial, statistical, and other formulas. You already saw a few of the functions you'll probably use most often, SUM, AVERAGE, MAX, MIN and TODAY. Some others that you'll probably use often are the NOW, COUNT, and COUNTA functions. The NOW function is very similar to the TODAY function, except that it enters both the current date and time. COUNT and COUNTA count how many cells have numbers in them and how many cells have any entries in them, respectively. For example, if you have a range with the following data: one, 2, 3, 4, 5; and you use the COUNT function to find out how many numbers are in the range, the result will be four. If you use the COUNTA function with the same range, the result would be five.

In the next exercise, you use the NOW and COUNTA functions to look at the information in your worksheets.

1 Switch to the 1994 1st Qtr sheet, and select cell B4.

2 Type **=now()** and press ENTER.

The current date and time appear in the cell.

Function Wizard

3 Select cell C23 and click the Function Wizard button.

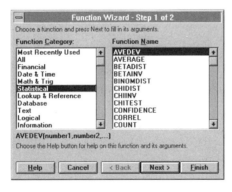

4 In the Function Category list, select Statistical, if it is not already selected.

5 In the Function Name list, scroll downward and select COUNTA, and then click the Next button.

6 Drag in the spreadsheet to select the range C11:C19.

7 Click the Finish button.

The result of the function, 8, appears in the cell. Your worksheet should look like the following.

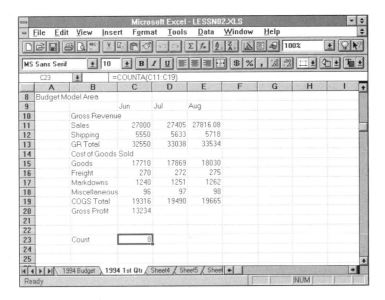

If You Want to Continue to the Next Lesson

1   From the File menu, choose Save.

2   From the File menu, choose Close.

If You Want to Quit Microsoft Excel for Now

▶   From the File menu, choose Exit.

   If you see the Save dialog box, click Yes.

Lesson Summary

To	Do this	Button
Total a range	Select the range and click the AutoSum button on the Standard toolbar.	Σ
Define a name for a range	Select the range and click in the name box on the formula bar. Type the name and press ENTER.	
Create several names within a range	Select the range. From the Insert menu, choose Name, and then choose Create.	

To	Do this	Button
Edit a name	From the Insert menu, choose Name, and then choose Define. Select the name in the list and edit the name or the definition. Choose OK.	
Go to a range	Click the arrow next to the name box on the formula bar and select the name. *or* Type the name in the name box.	
Write a formula with the Function Wizard	Select a cell and click the Function Wizard button on the Standard toolbar. Select the function category, and then the function name. Click the Next button. Enter the arguments needed, and click the Finish button.	*f*ₓ
Type a formula	Select a cell and type an equal sign followed by the formula. Press ENTER.	
Copy and paste data	Select the cell or range and from the Edit menu choose Copy, or check the Copy button. Select the new cell and, from the Edit menu, choose Paste or click the Paste button. *or* Select the cell with the data in it, hold down CTRL, and drag the cell border to the new range. Release the mouse button.	
Move data	Select the cell or range and drag it to the new location.	
Insert a cell, row, or column	Select the cell, row, or column to the right or below where you want the insertion. From the Insert menu, choose Cells, Rows, or Columns.	
Delete a cell, row, or column	Select the cell, row, or column and, from the Edit menu, choose Delete. In the Delete dialog box, choose the option you want, and then choose OK.	
Change a relative reference to an absolute reference	Select the reference in the formula or cell and press F4.	

For more information on	See in the *Microsoft Excel User's Guide*
Totaling and naming ranges	Chapter 10, "Creating Formulas and Links"
Writing formulas	Chapter 10, "Creating Formulas and Links"
Copying, pasting, and moving data	Chapter 11, "Editing a Worksheet"
Inserting and deleting cells, rows, and columns	Chapter 11, "Editing a Worksheet"
Using relative and absolute references	Chapter 10, "Creating Formulas and Links"

Preview of the Next Lesson

In the next lesson, you'll learn how to format your data and make it easier to understand. You'll learn how to use AutoFormat to format your data, and how to copy formats to other cells. You'll also learn how to control formatting elements individually with the buttons on the toolbar.

Formatting Your Data

When you are working on a sheet to be used in a presentation or a report, it's important to make the information clear and easy to understand. You can format your data so that the information communicates and is more meaningful. By formatting your data, you can also integrate your sheet with the rest of the presentation or report. With AutoFormat, Format Painter, and the formatting buttons on the toolbar, you can easily create clearer and better-looking sheets. In this lesson, you'll learn how to use AutoFormat to improve the look of your sheets. You'll learn how to quickly copy your formatting to other areas of your sheets, or onto other sheets in your workbook. Finally, you'll learn how to use the buttons on the Formatting toolbar to adjust formatting elements individually.

You will learn how to:

- Format your data with AutoFormat and Format Painter.
- Format data with the buttons on the Formatting toolbar.
- Copy formats to other cells.

Estimated lesson time: 35 minutes

If your screen does not match the illustrations in this lesson, see the Appendix, "Matching the Exercises."

Start the lesson

1 From your PRACTICE directory, open 03LESSN.XLS.

2 Save the workbook as LESSN03.XLS.

3 Click the Maximize button on the workbook window, if it is not already maximized.

Formatting Data Automatically

When you prepare data to show to someone else, either in a presentation or by itself, you want your data to look professional and be easy to understand. You can create a professional and consistent look for your data by using the AutoFormat command on the Format menu. AutoFormat lets you choose between standard table formats that include borders, shading, font colors, and other formatting options. With AutoFormat, you can easily apply the same format to multiple sheets.

To apply a format automatically, you select a range and then choose the AutoFormat command on the Format menu. You can then select one of seventeen different table formats, including formats for financial data, accounting data, lists, and even colorful or three-dimensional formats. You can also use the Options button to select the exact elements of the formats that you want to use. With the Options button, you can apply predefined number, border, font, pattern, alignment, and width or height formats to your table by turning these options on or off. By default, all of these options are turned on and applied when you choose AutoFormat.

In the next exercises, you select ranges and then apply different table formats to them with AutoFormat.

Note   When you format a range automatically, your data might not look exactly the way that you want. Later in this lesson, you'll learn additional formatting techniques to achieve the look you want.

Format data with AutoFormat

1   Select the range C11:H16.

2   From the Format menu, choose AutoFormat.

The AutoFormat dialog box opens.

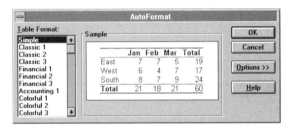

3   In the Table Format list, scroll downward and select List 2, and then choose OK.

Your data is formatted in the List 2 style. Your worksheet should look like the following.

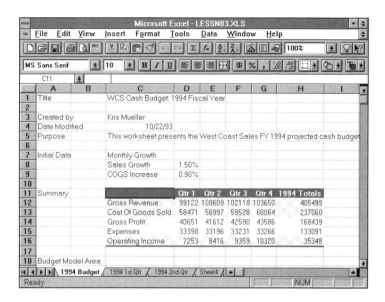

Format another range of data and turn off an option

1   Select the range C19:O46.

2   From the Format menu, choose AutoFormat.

The AutoFormat dialog box opens.

3   In the Table Format list, select Classic 3, and choose the Options button.

The AutoFormat dialog box expands to display the formatting options.

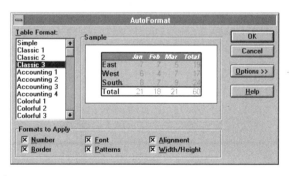

4 In the Formats To Apply box, click the Number and Width/Height check boxes.

This turns off these AutoFormats and ensures that the number formats, column widths, and row heights in each cell remain as they are in the worksheet. Applying an AutoFormat option changes the number format, column width, and row height for the selected area unless you choose not to apply these formats.

5 Choose OK.

The AutoFormat dialog box closes and the changes take effect. Your worksheet should look like the following.

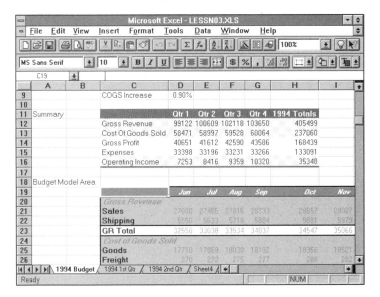

In the next exercise, you format the Summary Area to look the same as the Budget Model Area.

Repeat AutoFormatting

1 Select the range C11:H16.

2 From the Edit menu, choose Repeat AutoFormat.

The Classic 3 format is applied to the summary range.

Copying Formats to Other Cells

When you want to copy the formatting used in one section of your worksheet to another, you can use the Format Painter button. The Format Painter button lets you copy formats quickly. You simply select a cell with the format that you like, click the Format Painter tool, and then select the cell or range to which you want to apply the formatting.

When you click the Format Painter button once, you can only paste the formats once. If you need to copy formatting from one area of the worksheet to several nonadjacent areas, you can double-click the Format Painter button. When you are finished with the formats, you simply click the Format Painter button again to turn it off.

In the next exercise, you use the Format Painter button to copy the formatting from the Summary Area to the Initial Data area.

Copy a format with the Format Painter button

1 Select the range C11:D13.

2 Click the Format Painter button on the toolbar.

The pointer changes to look like a paintbrush with a plus sign.

Format Painter

3 With the new pointer, select C7.

The formatting is copied to the range C7:D9. If you had selected only one row, you would have copied only one row of formatting. By selecting three rows, you'll copy the formats in each of the three rows to the three rows in the destination range. Your worksheet should look like the following.

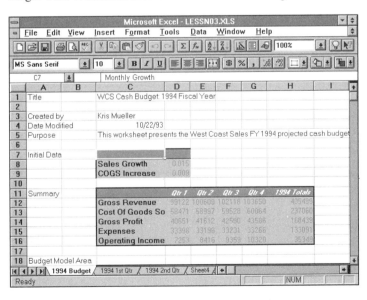

Formatting Data with the Formatting Toolbar

You might not want all of the standard settings in a table format, or perhaps you might want to emphasize a section of the sheet by applying different formats from the rest of your sheet. You can format specific cells, rows, columns, or ranges easily with the buttons on the Formatting toolbar.

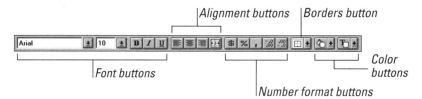

Changing Number Formats

You can format the numbers in a cell by using the Currency Style, Percent Style, and Comma Style buttons on the toolbar. Each of these styles has a default number of decimal points that you can change with the Increase Decimal and Decrease Decimal buttons.

In the next exercise, you change the number formats for your budget data to currency style, and the Monthly Growth figures to percent style. You also adjust the number of decimal places for the budget data.

Change number formats

1 Select cells D20:O45.

2 Click the Currency Style button on the Formatting toolbar.

This adds a dollar sign, a decimal point, and two decimal places to your numbers.

Currency Style

Note When you change to the currency format, some of the cells might display a row of number signs (#) rather than the actual values. Do not worry about losing any data; the number signs merely indicate that the columns are not wide enough to display the entire numbers. Later in this lesson, you change the size of the columns to make your data visible.

Decrease Decimal

3 Click the Decrease Decimal button on the toolbar twice.

This removes the decimal places from your numbers.

4 Select D21 and click the Format Painter button.

5 With the Format Painter pointer, select cells D12:H16.

Format Painter

Percent Style

6 Select cells D8:D9 and click the Percent Style button on the toolbar.

The cells are formatted as percentages. Your worksheet should look like the following.

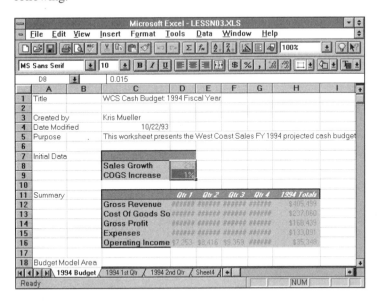

These commands are similar to the /Range Format options in 1-2-3.

You can also change number formats with the shortcut menu. Select the cells you want to change, click the right mouse button, and then choose Format Cells. With the Format Cells command, you have more choices of number formats than you do with the buttons on the toolbar. In the next exercise, you use the Format Cells command to change the format of cell C4, which contains the date the sheet was modified.

Change to date format

1 Select cell C4.

2 Click the right mouse button to open the shortcut menu.

3 From the shortcut menu, choose Format Cells.

The Format Cells dialog box opens.

4 In the dialog box, click the Number tab, if it is not already selected.

The Number tab opens, displaying the formatting options for numbers.

Number tab

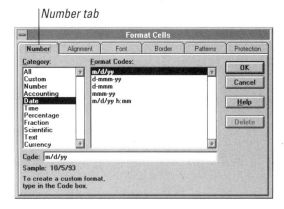

5   In the Category list, select Date.

As you can see, there are many number formats to choose from.

6   In the Format Codes list, select d-mmm-yy.

This code changes your date to display the day followed by the month and then the year. For example, July 5, 1994 would display as 5-Jul-94.

7   Choose OK.

Your date changes to display in the d-mmm-yy format. Your worksheet should look like the following.

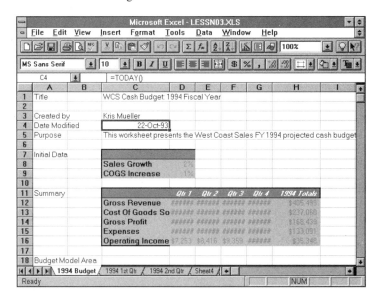

Changing Fonts

To make a formatting change for the entire worksheet, you start by selecting the worksheet and then make the change.

Not only can you change the number style of your data, you can also change other aspects of your text's appearance. You can quickly change fonts and font sizes with the Font and Font Size boxes on the Formatting toolbar, or you can use the Format Cells command. You can also use the Bold, Italic, or Underline buttons on the toolbar.

In the next exercises, you change the font, font size, and attributes used in your budget sheet.

Change fonts and sizes

1 In the top-left corner of the worksheet grid, click the Select All button. Or, press CTRL+SHIFT+SPACEBAR.

Select All button

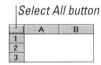

The entire worksheet is selected.

Font

2 Click the down arrow next to the Font box on the Formatting toolbar.

A list of fonts appears. The fonts available will vary depending on what fonts you have installed.

3 Select MS Serif.

Your text and numbers change to MS Serif.

Font Size

4 Click the down arrow next to the Font Size box on the Formatting toolbar.

A list of font sizes appears.

5 Select 12.

The font size changes to 12 points.

6 Click the down arrow next to the Font Size box again, and select 10 from the list.

The font size changes to 10 points. Your worksheet should look like the following.

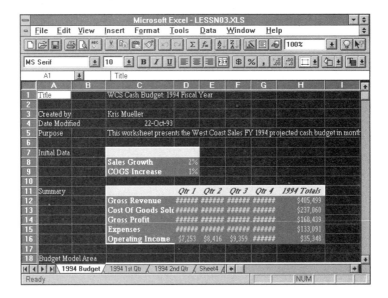

Note   You can also change your font, font size, and other attributes by choosing Format Cells from the shortcut menu. Select the cells you want to change, click the right mouse button, choose Format Cells, and click the Font tab in the Format Cells dialog box. Pick a font name, size, and other attributes and choose OK.

Change font attributes

1   Click cell C1, hold down CTRL, and then click cell C3.

Both cells are selected.

Bold

2   Click the Bold button on the Formatting toolbar.

3   Select cell C1.

C1 becomes the active cell and cell C3 is no longer selected.

Font Color

4   Click the down arrow next to the Font Color button on the Formatting toolbar.

A grid of color choices appears, similar to the following.

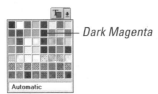

— *Dark Magenta*

5   Select Dark Magenta.

The title text is shaded Dark Magenta.

6 Click the column header for column A.

The entire column is selected.

Italic

7 Click the Italic button on the Formatting toolbar.

The fonts in column A are changed to italics.

Bold

8 Click the Bold button on the Formatting toolbar.

The fonts in column A are changed to bold.

9 Press CTRL+HOME.

Cell A1 becomes the active cell. Your worksheet should look like the following.

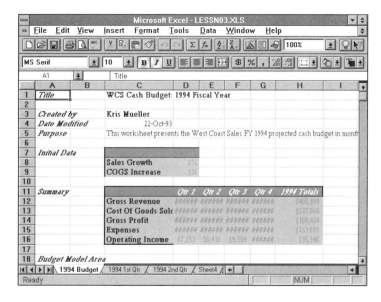

Changing Row Heights and Column Widths

Occasionally, your data will not fit within the standard column width. This is often the case when you are working with long labels, with large font sizes, or with data formatted as currency. You can easily change the column width or row height without using any menu commands or special keys. All you need is the mouse. By double-clicking the right border between column headers or the top border between row headers, the column or row is sized to fit the width of the longest entry in the column or the height of the largest font in the row.

The Column Width command is like /Worksheet Global Column-Width and /Worksheet Column Set-Width in 1-2-3.

In the next exercise, you use the mouse to adjust column widths to fit the data within each column.

Change column width to best fit

1 Select columns D through O.

2   Move the pointer over the border between any two selected column headers.

The pointer changes to a two-headed arrow.

3   Double-click the border between the column headers.

The column widths change to fit the widest data in each column. Your worksheet should look like the following.

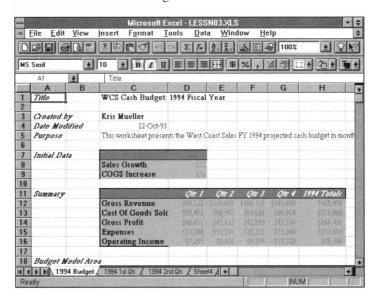

Note   You can also change column widths and row heights to any size you like by dragging the column or row header border to the desired width.

Changing Cell Alignments

The Alignment options are comparable to the /Range Label and /Worksheet Global Label Prefix in 1-2-3.

When you open a new sheet and begin entering data, your text is automatically left-aligned and your numbers are automatically right-aligned. However, you might decide that you want labels to be right-aligned or data to be centered in the cells. Perhaps you have a title that you want to center across the top of the worksheet. You can easily align text to the right, left, or center, or center text across columns using the buttons on the Formatting toolbar. You simply select the cell or range that you want to change, and then click the Align Left, Center, or Align Right buttons on the Formatting toolbar.

The default text and number alignment is the same as in 1-2-3, but you can change number alignment as well as text alignment in Microsoft Excel.

If you want to align a title across several columns, you select the cells that you want the text to be centered in and click the Center Across Columns button on the Formatting toolbar.

In the next exercise, you change the alignment of your label data, and then center the title across the top of the data.

Change cell alignments

1   Click the column header button for column A.

The entire column is selected.

Align Right

2   Click the Align Right button on the Formatting toolbar.

The entire column is right-aligned.

3   Double-click the column header border between column A and column B.

The column width is adjusted to fit the text in the cells.

Align Left

4   Select cell C4, and then click the Align Left button on the Formatting toolbar.

5   Select cells C1:L1.

This range includes the title of the sheet.

Center Across Columns

If you want to use the same alignment prefixes as in 1-2-3, choose Options from the Tools menu and select the Transition tab. Select the Transition Navigation Keys check box, and then choose OK.

6   Click the Center Across Columns button on the Formatting toolbar.

The title is centered across the selected columns. Your worksheet should look like the following.

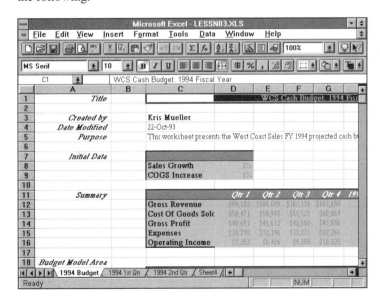

Adding Borders and Color

You can emphasize particular areas of the sheet or specific cells by using borders and color. Borders add lines above, below, or to either side of a cell. You can add a single line, or multiple lines, along one side of a cell or around it. You can shade a cell in one of many patterns or colors. Adding borders or color is as simple as selecting a cell, clicking the Borders or Color buttons on the toolbar, and selecting a style or color. You can also change the color of your text with the Font Color button on the toolbar. In the next exercises, you add borders to the Monthly Growth area on your spreadsheet and shade the cells with a light gray color to emphasize them. You then add a double border, or accountants' underline, to the Operating Income row.

Add borders and color

Borders

1   Select D8:D9.

2   Click the down arrow next to the Borders button on the Formatting toolbar.

A box with the different border options opens.

3   Select the third border in the third row.

A thin border appears around the range.

Color

4   Click the down arrow next to the Color button on the Formatting toolbar.

A box with the different color options opens.

5   Select the dark gray color.

The cells are shaded with dark gray. Your worksheet should look like the following.

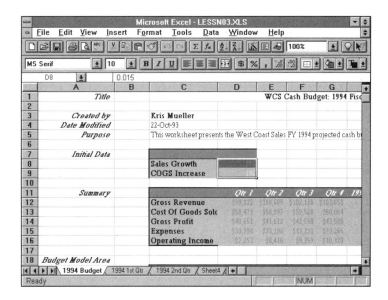

Add a double border to the bottom of the Operating Income row

1 Select D43:O43.

Borders

2 Click the down arrow next to the Borders button on the toolbar.

The different border options appear.

3 Select the first border in the second row.

A double border appears at the bottom of each cell. The underlining should look similar to the following.

Double-border underlining

One Step Further

As you saw throughout this lesson, there's more than one way to access the formatting commands. The most direct way is to use the buttons on the Formatting toolbar, but you will probably also want to use the Format menu or the shortcut menu, because you can choose several options at once. From the Format menu, you choose the Cells command to open the Format Cells dialog box. From the shortcut menu, you can choose Format Cells to change selected aspects of a cell at once. Since the font, number, alignment, border, and pattern choices are all part of the same dialog box, you only need to use one command to change all of these aspects of a cell's format. In the next exercise, you open the Format Cells dialog box and change the cell formats for your quarterly budgets.

Format the cells on the 1994 1st Qtr sheet

1 Switch to the 1994 1st Qtr sheet.

2 Select cells C11:E20.

3 From the Format menu, choose Cells.

The Format Cells dialog box opens.

4 Click the Number tab, if it is not already selected.

The number options display in the dialog box.

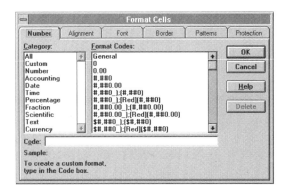

5 In the Category box, select Currency.

6 In the Format Codes box, select the $#,##0_);[Red]($#,##0) format.

This formats your numbers to have a dollar sign.

7 Choose OK, and then select the entire sheet.

Your data is formatted as currency.

8 From the Format menu, choose Cells, and then click the Font tab.

The font choices display.

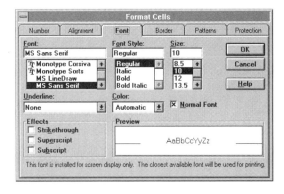

9   In the Font box, scroll downward and select Times New Roman.

10   In the Size box, select 9, and then choose OK.

The dialog box closes and the text in your worksheet changes to 9 point Times New Roman with numbers formatted as currency.

11   Press CTRL+HOME.

Cell A1 becomes the active cell. Your worksheet should look like the following.

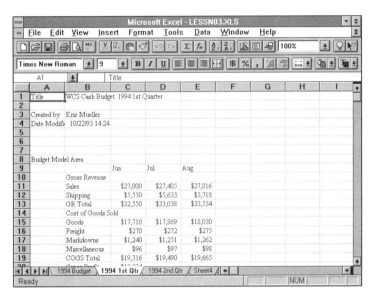

If You Want to Continue to the Next Lesson

1   From the File menu, choose Save.

2   From the File menu, choose Close.

If You Want to Quit Microsoft Excel for Now

▶   From the File menu, choose Exit.

If you see the Save dialog box, click Yes.

Lesson Summary

To	Do this	Button
Format a range of data	Select the range. From the Format menu, choose AutoFormat. Select a table format and choose OK.	
Copy a cell format	Select the cell or range to copy, click the Format Painter button on the toolbar, and select a cell or range to paste the format. *or* Select the cell or range to copy. Click the Copy button on the toolbar. Select the cell or range to paste. From the Edit menu, choose Paste Special. In the Paste Special dialog box, select Formats, and then choose OK.	
Change number formats	Select the cell and then click the Currency Style, Percent Style or Comma Style buttons, or the Increase or Decrease Decimal button on the toolbar. *or* From the Format menu, choose Cells and click the Number tab. Select the cell format and choose OK.	
Change fonts	Select the cell or range and then click the down arrows next to the Font box or the Font Size box to select a font name or size. Click the Bold, Italic, or Underline button on the toolbar. *or* From the Format menu, choose Cell and click the Font tab. Select the name, size, or attribute, and choose OK.	
Change column width to best fit	Double-click the column header border to the left of the column you want to change.	

To	Do this	Button
Change column width or row height	Drag the column header border to the right or the row header border downward.	
Change alignment	Select the cell or range, and then click the Align Left, Center, Align Right, or Center Across Columns button on the toolbar. *or* From the Format menu, choose Cell and click the Alignment tab. Select the alignment you want, and choose OK.	
Add borders or colors	Select the cell or range, and then click the arrows next to the Color, Borders, or Font Color buttons on the toolbar. Select a border or color style. *or* From the Format menu, choose Cells, and click the Border or Patterns tab. Select the style you want and choose OK.	

For more information on	See in the *Microsoft Excel User's Guide*
Automatically formatting a range	Chapter 12, "Formatting a Worksheet"
Copying cell formats	Chapter 12, "Formatting a Worksheet"
Changing cell formats	Chapter 12, "Formatting a Worksheet"

Preview of the Next Lessons

In Part 2, you'll learn how to create and modify graphic representations of your data called *charts*. You'll also learn how to print both charts and worksheets. In the next lesson, "Charting Your Data," you'll learn how to use your data to create attractive charts easily with the ChartWizard.

Review & Practice

In the lessons in Part 1, you learned skills to enter and edit data, write formulas, and format your data. If you want to practice these skills and test your understanding before you proceed with the lessons in Part 2, you can work through the Review & Practice section following this lesson.

Part 1   Review & Practice

Before you move on to Part 2, which covers charting and printing, you can practice the skills you learned in Part 1 by working through the steps in this Review & Practice section. You will open a workbook, enter data, fill in a series, and total the data. You will also create a formula to calculate West Coast Sales' market share for each year and then format the table automatically.

Scenario

The accounting department at West Coast Sales is preparing a ten-year financial history. You've been asked to prepare a sales history for those ten years. You need to be sure that your part of the presentation looks like the other parts that are being prepared in the department.

You will review and practice how to:

- Open a worksheet.

- Enter data.

- Fill a series of data into a range.

- Total columns of data.

- Write a formula.

- Format a table.

Estimated practice time: 10 minutes

Step 1: Open a File and Enter Data

You've received a list of the data for the West Coast Sales 10-year sales history, but you need to enter it into the worksheet, along with the year labels to identify the data. You also need to put your name on the worksheet so that the other people working on the presentation will know that you updated it last.

1 Open the file P1REVIEW.XLS and save it as REVIEWP1.XLS.

2 Fill the series 1983–1993 into column C under the Year label.

3 Enter the following data into the cells in columns D and E.

Company	Industry
$59,774	$1,210,000
$66,174	$1,230,000
$86,814	$1,260,000
$113,490	$1,300,000
$125,280	$1,350,000
$145,452	$1,380,000
$178,922	$1,370,000
$200,340	$1,400,000
$262,850	$1,500,000
$299,468	$1,690,000
$350,200	$2,000,000

4 Type your name in cell C3.

For more information on	See
Opening a file	Lesson 1
Saving a file	Lesson 1
Entering data	Lesson 1
Filling a series of data into a range	Lesson 1

Step 2: Total the Columns and Write a Formula

Now that you have entered the data, you need to total it, so that the presentation includes an overall view of the company vs. the industry's performance over the last ten years. Then you need to add a formula to calculate what percentage of the industry sales comes from West Coast Sales.

1 Add a heading in row 20 for Total Sales.

2 Use AutoSum to total the Company and Industry sales figures.

3 Write a formula in column F that divides the West Coast Sales sales figure by the industry sales figure in each row.

For more information on	See
Totaling columns	Lesson 2
Writing formulas	Lesson 2

Step 3: Format Numbers, Columns, and a Table

Now that you have all of the data in place, a little formatting will finish off the presentation. Format the sales as currency and the sales percentage figures as percents.

1 Use the buttons on the toolbar to format column D as currency with no decimal places.

2 Use the Format Painter button to copy the currency formatting from column D to column E.

3 Use the buttons on the Formatting toolbar to format column F as a percentage with two decimal places.

4 Use the AutoFormat command to format the entire table to the List 1 format.

5 Change the column widths to fit the data.

Your finished worksheet should look similar to the following.

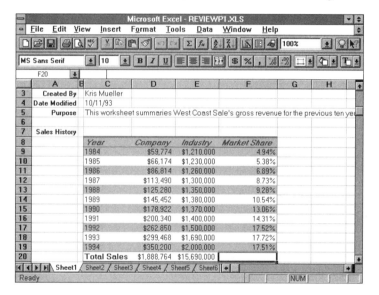

For more information on	See
Formatting cells	Lesson 3
Automatically formatting a table	Lesson 3
Changing column widths	Lesson 3

If You Want to Continue to the Next Lesson

1   From the File menu, choose Save.

2   From the File menu, choose Close.

If You Want to Quit Microsoft Excel for Now

▶   From the File menu, choose Exit.

If you see the Save dialog box, click Yes.

2 Charting and Printing Your Data

Charting Your Data

A chart is like a graph in 1-2-3, except that a chart can be a separate chart sheet or it can be embedded in the worksheet.

A worksheet calculates and presents differences between numbers, similarities between numbers, and changes in numbers over time. But data by itself cannot *illustrate* these concepts. When you make a presentation, or show progress or change in a report, data cannot illustrate your ideas or perceptions as effectively as a graphic representation. With charts, you can make your data visual. You can create a chart to show the changes in your data over time, or how the parts of your data fit together as a whole. You can rearrange your data, even after you have charted it, or add data that you left out. With Microsoft Excel and the *ChartWizard*, you can easily turn your data into dynamic charts for use in your presentations or reports.

You will learn how to:

- Create charts using the ChartWizard.
- Modify, add, and delete chart data.

Estimated lesson time: 30 minutes

If your screen does not match the illustrations in this lesson, see the Appendix, "Matching the Exercises."

Start the lesson

1 Open 04LESSN.XLS.

2 Save the workbook as LESSN04.XLS.

3 Click the Maximize button on the document window, if it is not already maximized.

Creating Charts

You can create charts in two ways: either on the same sheet as your data, or on a separate chart sheet in the same workbook. When you create a chart on the same sheet as your data, you can view both the data and the chart at the same time. When you create a chart on a separate chart sheet in the same workbook, you still have easy access to the chart, but you can print the chart separately.

Creating Charts on a Worksheet

To create a chart on a worksheet, you select the data that you want to use in the chart, and then click the ChartWizard button on the Standard toolbar. The type of chart you can create depends on the data you select. Your selection could include only one *data series* in a chart, either a single row or a single column of data, or several series, multiple rows, or columns. Pie charts, for example, can only use one data series. This means that no matter how many rows and columns you select, a pie chart can only display the first row or column of data. In the following illustration, a pie chart could display one of the selected series, either Gross Revenue, Gross Profit, or Expenses, but not all three.

	Qtr 1	Qtr 2	Qtr 3	Qtr 4	1994 Totals	
Gross Revenue	$99,122	$100,609	$102,118	$103,650	$405,499	— *Single data series*
Cost of Goods Sold	$58,471	$58,997	$59,528	$660,064	$837,060	
Gross Profit	$40,651	$41,612	$42,590	$43,586	$168,439	⌐ *Multiple data series*
Expenses	$33,398	$33,196	$33,231	$33,266	$133,091	⌐
Operating Income	$7,253	$8,416	$9,359	$10,320	$35,348	

A bar chart, however, could show all three selected data series, as could an area chart or a column chart. Most chart types can display several data series, as long as the data is of the same type, as in the example above. All of the selected series are currency, and they are divided into the same categories. When your data series are similar, you are able to see the comparisons in your chart more easily.

Note You can also create charts with dissimilar data series. You'll learn about charts made from different types of data in the One Step Further exercise at the end of this lesson.

After you select the data that you will use, you need to specify a location for your chart. You can select an area as large or as small as you like. You can always change your mind and resize your chart later, as you will learn in Lesson 5, "Modifying Your Charts."

In the next exercise, you select data to use in a bar chart, and then select an area on the worksheet where the chart will appear.

Select the data and range for a chart

1 Switch to the sheet named Summary and select C7:G11.

2 Locate and then click the ChartWizard button on the Standard toolbar.

ChartWizard

Your pointer changes to a cross hair with a small chart symbol when you move it over the sheet. You use this pointer to select an area on your sheet in which the chart will be created.

ChartWizard pointer

3 Drag to select C15:I31.

Now that you have selected an area for your chart, the ChartWizard appears, and displays the cell references for the range that contains your chart data.

Selecting a Chart Type

Microsoft Excel's ChartWizard includes several chart types. Within each of these types or categories of charts, you can choose a variation of the basic chart type that might include gridlines or labels.

Depending on the chart type that you choose, you can get different views of your data. Bar and Column charts compare series of data, for example, sales figures for different regions or for different years. Bar charts show comparison between items, while Column charts can show a comparison over time. Pie charts show the relationship of parts to a whole. Area charts are best for showing the amount of change in values over time. As you use different types of charts, you will get to know which chart types best suit your data. In the next exercise, you create a bar chart.

Select a chart type and variation

1   In the ChartWizard, click the Next button.

Step 2 of the ChartWizard appears, listing the chart types that you can choose from.

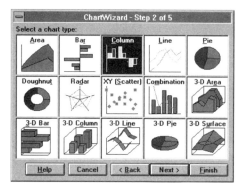

2   Click the Bar chart type in the first row, and then click the Next button.

Step 3 of the ChartWizard appears, showing you the different variations of Bar charts that you can choose from.

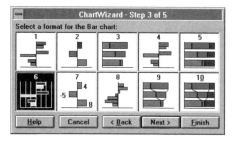

3   Be sure that the sixth format is selected, and then click the Next button.

Step 4 of the ChartWizard appears.

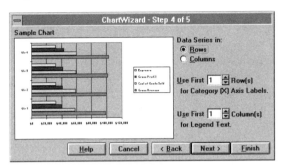

When you create a chart with the ChartWizard, your data is automatically classified into data series and categories. For this particular bar chart, your rows become the data series, while the column headings become categories. Categories are the labels that appear along the *x*-axis, or the horizontal axis. The bars on the chart represent the data series. If you want the columns to become the data series and the row headings to become categories, you can specify this in the ChartWizard.

You can add labels, axis titles, and a chart title to further clarify your chart data. The first column and first row of your data are usually assigned as the legend text and category axis labels. You can specify another row or column instead, if you have more than one level of headings or a row or column that contains neither data nor labels in your selection. You can then choose whether to display a legend or add a chart title. For all but pie and doughnut charts, you can also add category and value axis titles to further explain your categories or values.

In the next exercise, you add labels and a chart title to your bar chart.

Add a chart title and axis titles to your chart

1   Under Data Series In, be sure that Rows is selected, and then click the Next button.

Step 5 of the ChartWizard appears. The sample chart shows the data by quarter.

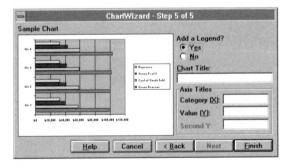

2   Click in the Chart Title text box, and type **Budget Summary Data**

3   In the Axis Titles area, click in the Category [X] box, and type **1994**

4   Click the Finish button.

The ChartWizard closes and your chart appears on the worksheet. Notice that bar charts emphasize the comparison between single items, or a series of items, rather than a difference over time or as related to a whole.

Note   You can also choose the Chart command and then select On This Sheet from the Insert menu to create a chart on the same sheet as your data. Either way, you select an area on the sheet for the chart, and then use the ChartWizard to create the chart.

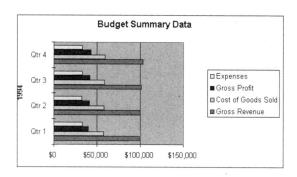

Creating Charts on a Chart Sheet

You've seen how you can use the ChartWizard to create a chart directly on a worksheet. For reports, you probably want to keep the data and the chart together on a sheet. But what if you are working on a presentation, with several charts that will eventually be on separate slides that you intend to print? You can create a new chart sheet and a new chart at the same time. The chart command creates a new chart sheet to hold your chart, and then opens the ChartWizard for you to create the new chart.

In the next exercise, you use the Chart and then the As New Sheet commands on the Insert menu. You then create a doughnut chart to display your Cost of Goods Sold data for the first quarter of 1994.

Create a doughnut chart on a chart sheet

1   Switch to the 1994 1st Qtr sheet, and then select C9:F14.

This is your Cost of Goods Sold data for the first quarter of 1994.

2   From the Insert menu, choose Chart and then choose As New Sheet.

Step 1 of the ChartWizard appears and displays the range that contains your chart data.

3   In the ChartWizard, click the Next button.

Step 2 of the ChartWizard appears and lists the chart types that you can choose from.

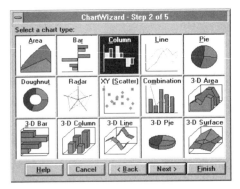

4   Under Select A Chart Type, select the Doughnut chart type, and then click the Next button.

Step 3 of the ChartWizard appears and shows the different variations of Doughnut charts to choose from.

5   Select the sixth variation, and then click the Next button.

Step 4 of the ChartWizard appears . A sample chart appears with some options you can use to alter your data series labels.

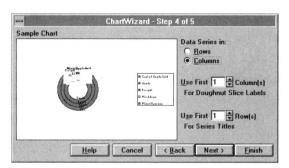

6   In Use First 1 Row[s] For Series Titles, click the up arrow once to display 2, and then click the Next button.

Step 5 of the ChartWizard appears. A sample chart appears with the first two rows as the legend text. You can title your chart and decide whether you want a legend.

7   Under Add A Legend, be sure that Yes is selected.

8   In the Chart Title text box, type **Cost of Goods Sold 1st Qtr. 1994** and then click the Finish button.

The ChartWizard closes and your chart appears on the new chart sheet, Chart1, similar to the following illustration. Notice that a doughnut chart is best at showing relationships between parts and a whole. Doughnut charts are similar to pie charts, except that pie charts can have only one series of data, while doughnut charts can have several.

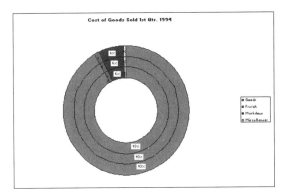

Modifying Chart Data

If you find that your chart includes too much, too little, or the wrong information, you can delete, add, or change the data. You can delete a series from the chart, add a row of data, or switch the order of the data series in your chart.

Before you can make any changes to a chart on a worksheet, you need to activate it. When you activate a chart, the chart is surrounded by a border, and the menu bar changes so that you can change the data or add lines and colors, as you will see in Lesson 5, "Modifying Your Chart."

To delete a series of data, you select the series and press DEL. To add a series of data to a chart embedded on a worksheet, you can simply drag the data to the chart. To add a series of data to a chart on a chart sheet, you use the New Data command on the Insert menu. To move a series to a new location in a chart, you can use the Group command on the Format menu.

In the next exercises, you delete a series of data from your summary chart, add a new series to the chart, and then change the order of the data to see how it affects the chart.

Deleting Data

You can easily delete a data series directly from a chart.

Activate the chart and delete a data series

1 Switch to the Summary sheet, and then double-click the bar chart.

Double-clicking the chart activates it. The chart is surrounded by a border, ready for you to make changes to it.

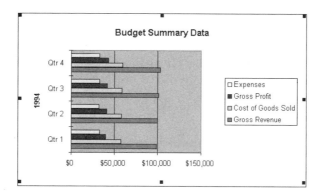

2 Click one of the bars on the chart that represents Expenses.

Clicking one bar in a series selects the entire series. The Expenses series of data is selected.

Note If you click a series and then click one item in the series, that item is selected by itself, instead of the entire series.

---

3 Press DEL.

The entire Expenses series is deleted from your chart. Your chart should look similar to the following.

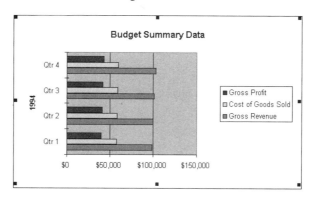

Adding Data

A chart data series is like a graph data range in 1-2-3.

If you are working with a chart on a worksheet, you can add data to a chart by either dragging the data to the chart or by using the New Data command on the Insert menu. When you are working with a chart in a chart sheet, the New Data command on the Insert menu is the easiest way to add data. When you drag data to a chart on a worksheet, you do not need to activate the chart first as you do when using the Insert menu.

In the next exercises, you use both the drag and menu methods to add new data to your chart.

Add new chart data with the mouse

1   On the Summary sheet, select the range C12:G12.

This is the Operating Income data from your summary table. You will drag this data onto your chart.

To drag data between cells in Microsoft Excel, select the range, click over the border of the range, and then drag the data to the destination.

2   Drag the data down over the chart and release the mouse button.

The chart is updated to show the new data. Your chart should look similar to the following.

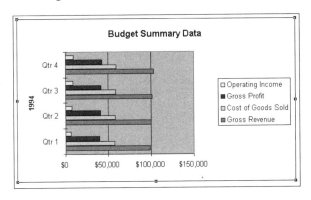

Add new chart data with the menus and the mouse

Using the menu to add data series or points is like respecifying the ranges in /Graph XABCDE in 1-2-3.

1   Double-click the chart to activate it.

2   From the Insert menu, choose New Data.

The New Data dialog box appears, ready for you to enter the range where the new data is stored.

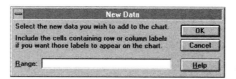

3 In the Summary sheet, click outside the chart, and then drag to select C11:G11.

You might need to drag the New Data dialog box out of the way first. Cells C11:G11 contain the Expenses data that you deleted in the previous exercise.

4 In the New Data dialog box, choose OK.

The dialog box closes and the chart is updated. Your chart should look similar to the following.

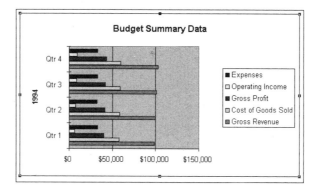

Rearranging Chart Data

If you want to emphasize the differences or similarities between data series, you might want to arrange the series in your chart. For example, if you want to contrast low and high values, you would rearrange the data so that the low and high values are next to each other. If you want to minimize the differences between values, you could arrange the data so that it moves steadily from low to high or high to low. You can easily rearrange the data in your chart to do this.

In the next exercise, you change the order of your data to emphasize the differences between Gross Revenue and the other categories.

Change the order of data in a chart

1   Be sure that the chart is still active and, from the Format menu, choose <u>1</u> Bar Group.

The Format Bar Group dialog box appears, ready for you to make changes to the chart.

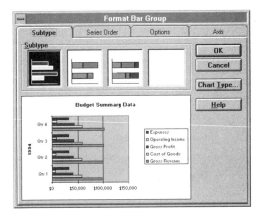

2   In the Format Bar Group dialog box, click the Series Order tab.

The dialog box displays the Series Order options.

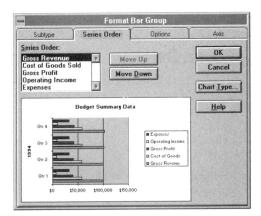

3   In the Series Order list, select Operating Income, and then click the Move Up button twice.

The Operating Income series now appears just above Gross Revenue in your chart.

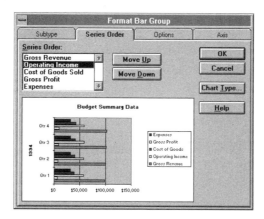

4   In the Series Order list, select Expenses, and then click the Move Up button twice.

The Expenses series moves up in the Series Order list. It now appears just above Operating Income in your chart.

5   In the Series Order list, select Cost of Goods Sold, and then click the Move Down button once.

The Cost of Goods Sold series moves to the bottom of the Series Order list. It will now appear at the top of your chart.

6   In the Format Bar Group dialog box, choose OK.

The dialog box closes and your chart is updated with your changes. Your chart should look similar to the following.

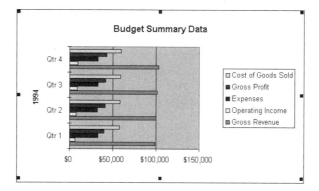

One Step Further

You used Bar charts and Doughnut charts throughout this lesson. Most of the other chart types work similarly to these two, with one or more series of the same type of data. When you need to chart data that is dissimilar or needs to be divided for visual contrast, you can create a chart type per series. Charts that are created with different chart types for different series are usually part bar or column, and part line or area chart. You can track two streams of data (with one or more series each) by using different chart types for different series.

Try creating a chart with different chart types per series to display your Gross Revenue data for second quarter 1994.

Create a combination chart

1   Switch to the sheet named 1994 2nd Qtr, and then select C9:F13.

2   From the Insert menu, choose Chart, and then choose As New Sheet.

Step 1 of the ChartWizard appears.

3   In the ChartWizard, click the Next button.

Step 2 of the ChartWizard appears and displays the possible chart types.

4   Select the Combination chart, and then click the Next button.

Step 3 of the ChartWizard appears and displays the possible chart variations.

5   Select format number 1, and then click the Next button.

The first format is a combination of a column chart and a line chart. Step 4 of the ChartWizard appears and displays the sample chart and some options about your data and data labels.

6   Under Data Series In, select the Rows option.

7   In the Use First 1 Row(s) For Category (X) Axis Labels box, click the up arrow once for 2 rows.

8   Click the Finish button.

The ChartWizard closes and your completed chart appears on the new chart sheet. Your chart should look similar to the following.

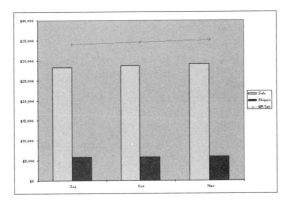

Notice that, unlike the bar chart you created earlier, the combination chart lists the data by category over time. Also, since you used the second variation, the totals data appears as a line on a separate axis.

If You Want to Continue to the Next Lesson

1   From the File menu, choose Save

2   From the File menu, choose Close.

If You Want to Quit Microsoft Excel for Now

▶   From the File menu, choose Exit.

  If you see the Save dialog box, click Yes.

Lesson Summary

To	Do this	Button
Create a chart on a worksheet	Select the data that you want to chart, and then click the ChartWizard button on the toolbar. Select a range for the chart and click Next. Select a chart type and click Next. Select a chart variation. Add a chart title and axis titles as needed, and click Finish.	
Create a chart on a chart sheet	Select a data range. From the Insert menu, choose Chart, and then choose As New Sheet. Click Next. Select a chart type and click Next. Select a chart variation. Add a chart title and axis titles as needed, and click Finish.	
Activate a chart	Double-click the chart.	
Delete a data series	Activate the chart, select the data series, and press DEL.	
Add data to a chart on a worksheet	Select the data, drag it to the chart, and release the mouse button.	
Add data to a chart on a chart sheet	From the Insert menu, choose New Data. Select the data range and choose OK.	

To	Do this	Button
Rearrange chart data	Activate the chart. From the Format menu, choose the Group command for the chart type. In the Group dialog box, click the Series Order tab. In the Series Order list, select the series that you want to move, and then click the Move Up or Move Down button. Choose OK.	

For more information on	See in the *Microsoft Excel User's Guide*
Creating a chart	Chapter 15, "Creating a Chart"
	Chapter 16, "Working With Chart Types and Autoformats"
Modifying chart data	Chapter 17, "Changing Data in a Chart"

Preview of the Next Lesson

In the next lesson, "Modifying Your Charts," you'll learn more about customizing your charts to emphasize data. You'll learn how to add lines and change colors, how to use chart AutoFormats, and how to create your own standard chart type.

Modifying Your Charts

When you chart your data, you might not always end up with exactly what you envisioned the first time. Perhaps you decide that a pie chart would work better than a bar chart, or that a 3-D chart would make your data more dramatic. Maybe the values aren't as visible as you'd like them to be, or you can't quite see the relationships between a series and the value labels.

Microsoft Excel's charting features are flexible so that you can change your chart to match your ideas. In this lesson, you'll learn how to modify your chart, change between chart types, add lines, color, and text, and use chart autoformats to save you steps in creating a set of standardized charts. You'll also learn how to create your own standard chart format, so you can repeat your formatting choices automatically.

You will learn how to:

- Change chart types to make sure that the chart fits your data.

- Make your point clearer with arrows, color, and text.

- Skip repetitive formatting steps by using automatic formatting.

Estimated lesson time: 40 minutes

If your screen does not match the illustrations in this lesson, see the Appendix, "Matching the Exercises."

Start the lesson

1 Open 05LESSN.XLS.

2 Save the workbook as LESSN05.XLS.

3 Click the Maximize button on the document window, if it is not already maximized.

Changing Chart Types

You might decide that a chart you already created would be better with a different chart type. Perhaps a bar chart would work better in 3-D, or with a different chart type for one series. The quickest way to change from one chart type to another is to use the Chart Type command on the shortcut menu. When you select a chart type from the Chart Type dialog box, your chart is automatically updated with the new chart type.

When you change chart types, depending on the chart type that you choose, the resulting chart could appear very different from your original. If you change between similar chart types, from a bar chart to a 3-D bar chart, for example, you will see little difference. When you change between dissimilar chart types, from a bar chart to a pie chart, for example, you will notice a lot of difference. For example, if you change from a bar chart with gridlines to a 3-D bar chart, the gridlines will remain, as will the length of the bars and the effect of the chart. If you change from a bar chart to a 3-D area chart, the gridlines will remain, but the whole effect of the chart will be different.

The following illustrations show the same budget summary data as a bar chart and a 3-D column chart.

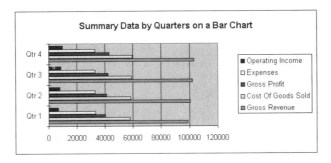

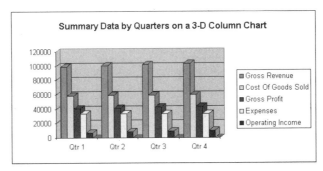

Notice that the bar chart and the column chart show the comparisons between the quarters fairly clearly, and in the same way. Bar charts and column charts are quite similar, and switching between the two does not often change the look very much.

In the following illustration, you see what happens if you show the same summary data as a pie chart.

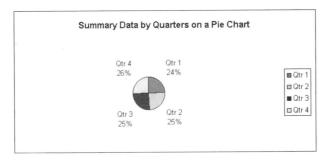

The pie chart type is not really suited to the data you want to show. Notice that your data appears very different in this chart type. The pie chart isn't very useful, since it can only show one series, the Operating Income, over the four quarters. Because pie charts are one-dimensional, you can only show one series or one quarter. If you had used only one quarter's data and shown each budget category, the chart would have made more sense.

After you work with charts a little and experiment with different chart types, you will better understand how the presentation of your data will change depending on the chart type. The bar chart that you created for the summary data in the previous lesson would have more impact on your audience in 3-D bar format. You can change your summary chart from a simple bar to a 3-D bar chart with stacked bars to emphasize the total values, rather than the differences between items in a series. The following illustration shows how your chart will look after you have completed the next few exercises.

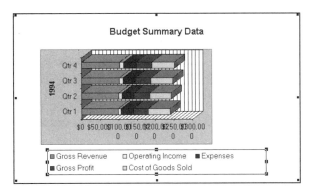

In the next exercise, you change your chart to a 3-D bar chart.

Change a bar chart to a 3-D bar chart

1   Switch to the Summary sheet and double-click the Budget Summary Data bar chart.

The bar chart is activated.

2   With the pointer in an open area, click the right mouse button to display the shortcut menu, and then choose Chart Type.

The Chart Type dialog box opens.

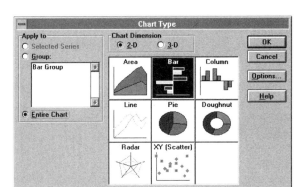

3   In the Chart Dimension area, select 3-D.

4   Click the 3-D bar chart type and choose OK.

Your chart changes from a 2-D bar chart to a 3-D bar chart type. Notice that the formatting options that you chose earlier, such as the legend, and the legend text, remain in effect. Your chart should look similar to the following.

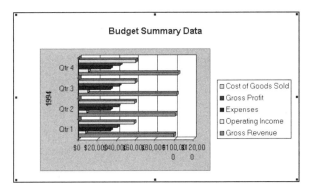

When you change between dissimilar chart types, you might not see all of your data, or you might find that your data does not appear the way you expected. You can change the type of chart with the Chart Type command on the Format menu. If you need to change the order of your data series, as you did in Lesson 4, you can use the Group command on the Format menu. The Group command changes according to the type of chart you are using. For example, for the Summary bar chart, the command would be called the Bar Group command. For the 3-D version of the Summary bar chart, the command would be called the 3-D Bar Group command.

In the next exercise, you change the Summary chart to a stacked 3-D bar chart.

Change chart options

1   With the 3-D bar chart activated, from the Format menu, choose 1 3-D Bar Group.

The Format 3-D Bar Group dialog box opens.

2 Click the Subtype tab, if it is not already selected.

The chart subtype options appear in the dialog box.

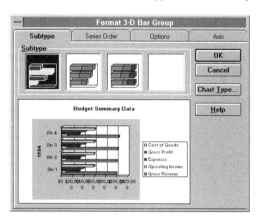

3 Click the second chart subtype, and then choose OK.

The dialog box closes and your chart is updated with your changes.

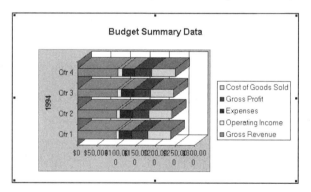

Adding or Deleting Gridlines and Legends

Some chart formats include gridlines and legends, and some do not. If you like a format that doesn't normally have gridlines or a legend, but you want these features, you can easily add them. When you add gridlines to your chart, you make it easier to see and evaluate your data. Legends help explain your data and make the chart more readable. You can also delete gridlines or a legend from a chart if you don't want them.

The Gridlines command is like /Graph Options Grid in 1-2-3.

The Legend command is like /Graph Options Legend in 1-2-3.

You add or delete gridlines by using the Gridlines command on the Insert menu or the Gridlines button on the Chart toolbar. You delete or add a legend by using the Legend command on the Insert menu or by using the Legend button on the Chart toolbar. In the next exercise, you add new gridlines to your chart, delete and add a legend, and then move the legend to the bottom of the chart.

Add gridlines and move the legend

1   From the Insert menu, choose Gridlines.

The Gridlines dialog box opens.

2   In the Value [Z] Axis area, be sure that Major Gridlines is selected, and then select Minor Gridlines.

3   Choose OK.

The dialog box closes and major and minor vertical gridlines appear on your chart. Your chart should look like the following.

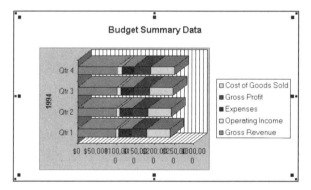

4   Select the legend and press DEL.

The legend is removed form your chart.

Legend

5   Click the Legend button on the Chart toolbar.

A new legend appears on your chart.

6   On the chart, double-click the legend at the right side.

The Format Legend dialog box opens.

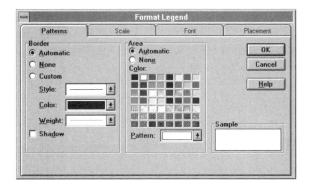

7 In the dialog box, click the Placement tab.

8 In the Type box, select Bottom, and then choose OK.

The dialog box closes and the legend is moved and reshaped to fit along the bottom of the chart. Your chart should look like the following.

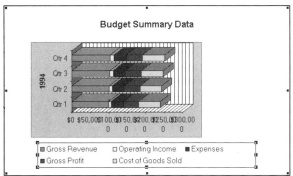

Enhancing Charts

If you want to emphasize a particular data point, or create a unique look for a chart, you can add elements, such as lines, arrows, and different colors to your charts. You can emphasize specific data points with a line or an arrow, or change the color for an entire series or one data point. You can also add text boxes, or change the fonts or attributes used in your chart text.

Suppose you want to point out the progress in the Operating Income value with a *trendline*. Trendlines follow trends in your data and point out the changes in your data graphically. You also want to show the lowest value in your chart by pointing to it with an arrow and labeling it. When you get these elements in place, you can refine them by formatting the label text or adjusting the lines and the colors in your data series until your chart looks similar to the following.

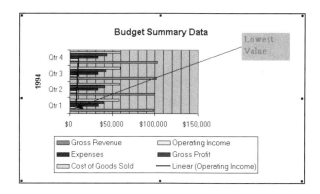

Showing Trends

In some chart types, you need to clearly emphasize progress or change in a particular data series. You've already seen how changing to a specific chart type, such as a column chart instead of a bar chart, can help point out progress in your data. But if you want to point out how a specific series in your data is performing or progressing, you can add a trendline to further clarify the change. For example, if you need to point out the progress of one type of stock in a chart of several types of stocks, you can add a trendline to one data series that will clearly show the changes in that series relative to the others in the chart.

You can add trendlines to bar, column, area, line, and xy (scatter) charts. You cannot add trendlines to pie, doughnut, 3-D, or radar charts. You add trendlines to a specific series, not to the entire chart, so you need to select the series before you can add the trendline. If you remove a series with a trendline, or change the series to a pie, doughnut, 3-D, or radar chart type, the trendline is permanently deleted.

For more information about trendline types, open Help, click the Search button, and search for "trendline".

You can choose from several types of trendlines, depending on the type of trend you are describing. For example, if you were showing the change in stock prices over a period of time, you would use a *linear* trendline. If you were showing an exponential change in a value, you would use an *exponential* trendline.

Since your bar chart is currently in 3-D, you'll need to change it back to a 2-D bar chart before you can add a trendline. In the next exercises, you'll change your summary bar chart back to a 2-D bar chart so you can add a trendline to it. Then, you'll add a simple linear trendline to the Operating Income series.

Change your chart back to a 2-D bar chart

1   Double-click the bar chart to activate it, if it is not already activated.

2   From the Format menu, choose Chart Type.

The Chart Type dialog box opens.

3   In the Chart Dimension box, select 2-D.

4   From the illustrated examples, select the Bar chart and then choose OK.

Your chart changes back to a 2-D bar chart. Notice that the chart is no longer stacked, but looks similar to your original chart with the additional gridlines.

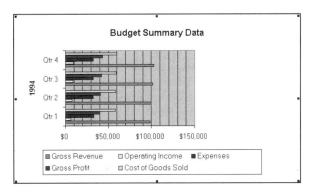

Describe a trend in your chart data

1 Click a bar in the Operating Income series once.

The Operating Income data series is selected.

2 From the Insert menu, choose Trendline.

The Trendline dialog box opens.

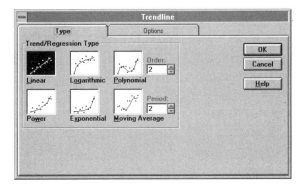

3 Click the Type tab if it is not already selected.

The Trendline dialog box now shows the various types of trendlines that you can choose from.

4 Be sure that the Linear type is selected, and then choose OK.

The dialog box closes and a linear trendline is added to the Operating Income series. Your chart should look like the following.

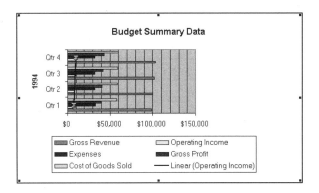

Pointing to Specific Data

If you are creating a presentation or a report and you need to emphasize or point out some specific data, you can add an arrow or a line by using the Drawing button on the toolbar. Once you've placed the line where you want it, you can change the arrow type, if you like.

Note   When you draw an arrow, be sure that you draw toward the object you want to point to, rather than away from it. For example, if you draw an arrow to an object at the bottom of the chart, you would begin drawing the arrow at either the upper-right or upper-left corner of the chart, and stop drawing when you reached the object. The arrow will automatically point to the place where you stopped drawing.

In the next exercise, you create an arrow to point to the smallest value on your chart.

Point to the smallest value

1   Activate the 2-D Bar chart on your sheet, if it is not already activated.

2   Click the Drawing button to display the Drawing toolbar.

3   Click the Arrow button on the Drawing toolbar.

Your pointer changes to a cross hair, ready for you to draw an arrow.

Drawing

Arrow

4   Click near the top right corner of the chart, drag to the Operating Income portion of the 1st quarter bar, and release.

An arrow appears on your chart, pointing to the smallest value. Your chart should look like the following.

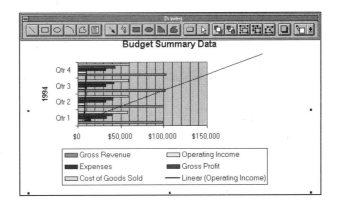

*If the Drawing
toolbar is docked
and has no close
box, you can choose
Toolbars from the
View menu and
deselect the
Drawing toolbar.*

5   Click the close box on the Drawing toolbar to close it.

Explaining Your Chart with Text Boxes

Now that you have added an arrow, you want other people to quickly understand what
the arrow points at. You can either add an explanatory note on your worksheet, or you
can add a text box directly on the chart itself. You can add text boxes to explain or
label any part of your chart. In the next exercises, you add a text box to explain the
data, and then resize the text box to display all of your text.

Add a text box to explain the data

Text Box

1   Click the Text Box button on the Standard toolbar.

Your pointer changes to a cross hair, ready for you to add a text box.

2   Drag the pointer to create a small rectangle, about 1 inch wide by 0.5 inch tall, near
the beginning of your arrow.

A text box is added to your chart.

Note   If your text box is not exactly in the right place, you can always move it later
by dragging it to the correct location.

---

3   Type **Lowest Value**

4   Click outside the text box.

Don't worry if you can see other objects through the text box. You will make the
text box opaque later in this lesson. Your text box should look similar to the
following.

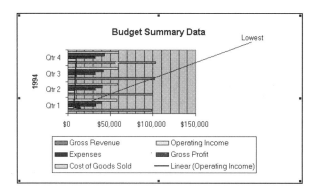

Resize a text box

1   Click the text box once to select it.

2   Move your pointer to the lower-right corner of the text box.

3   Drag the mouse downward and to the right until you can see all of your text in the text box, with a little extra white space in the box.

Changing Your Text and Text Box Formats

If you don't like the font, color, alignment, or other attributes of the text in your chart or your text boxes, you can change them. You format the text just as you format any other text in a worksheet, by selecting it and using the appropriate toolbar button or menu command. If you want to change several aspects of your text at once, you can use the Format Object command on the shortcut menu.

In the next exercises, you change the font and color of your Lowest Value label, make it bold, and then change the background color in the text box.

Change fonts, colors, and attributes of a text box

1   Click the text box to select it.

2   Click the right mouse button.

Be sure that you do not move the mouse before you click. The shortcut menu appears.

3   From the shortcut menu, choose Format Object.

The Format Object dialog box appears.

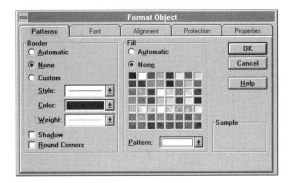

4   Click the Font tab, if it is not already selected, and then in the Font list, select MS Serif.

5   In the Font Style list, select Bold.

6   In the Size list, select 12.

7   Click the down arrow next to the Color list to open the list of colors, and then select the dark blue solid color.

8   Choose OK.

The text in your text box changes to 12 point, bold, dark blue, MS Serif.

9   Press ESC to view your changes.

Your text should look like the following.

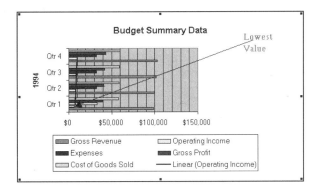

Note   If your text box is too small to display all of your text, select the box and drag the lower-right corner of the box downward until you can see all of the text.

Change colors in a text box

1 Activate the chart, if it is not activated.

2 Select the text box containing the "Lowest Value" text.

3 Click the right mouse button.

The shortcut menu opens.

4 From the shortcut menu, choose Format Object.

The Format Object dialog box opens.

5 In the dialog box, click the Patterns tab.

The Patterns options appear in the dialog box.

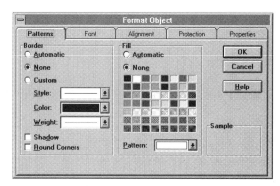

6 In the Fill area, select the light gray square, and then choose OK.

The dialog box closes and your text object is filled with a light gray background.

Emphasizing Data with Colors

If you don't like the colors that are used in your chart, or if you want consistency with another color scheme used in your presentation or report, you can easily change the colors. You can change the color of any object in your chart: gridlines, legend background or text, borders, data series, lines, or even text, as you saw earlier in this lesson. To change a color, you select the object, and then use the Format Object command on the shortcut menu.

Note The Format Object command is like the Group command—it changes depending on what you have selected. If you want to change the color of a text box or an arrow, the command is called Format Object. If you want to change the color of a data series or your gridlines, however, the commands are called Format Series and Format Gridlines, respectively.

In the next exercise, you change the Gross Profit data series to light blue.

Change the color of a data series

1 Double-click the bar chart if it is not activated.

2 Point to any bar in the Gross Profit data series and click the right mouse button.

The shortcut menu opens.

3 From the shortcut menu, choose Format Data Series.

The Format Data Series dialog box opens.

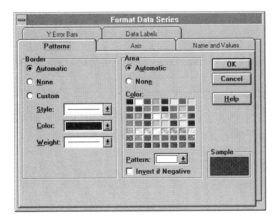

4 Be sure that the Patterns tab is selected.

5 Under Area, select the solid light blue square.

6 Choose OK.

The Gross Profit data series changes to Light Blue. Your chart should look like the following.

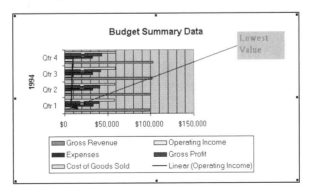

Formatting Charts Automatically

When you create a series of charts for a presentation or report, you want them to have similar properties. Perhaps you have several charts showing similar data, such as yearly figures for different budget categories or growth figures for several offices. When you need to create several similar charts, you can use a chart autoformat or a predefined chart format.

You can use the AutoFormat command on the Format menu to create a standardized chart. You can apply this chart format to several charts so that your series looks alike with the differences in the actual values emphasized by the similarities in the charts.

Important

When you format a chart automatically, you lose any formatting changes that you've already made.

In the next exercise, you change your doughnut chart to a 3-D area chart and apply formatting automatically at the same time.

Format a chart automatically

1 Select the sheet Chart1.

This sheet contains the doughnut chart you created in Lesson 4.

2 With the mouse pointer over the chart, click the right mouse button.

The charting shortcut menu opens.

3 From the shortcut menu, choose AutoFormat.

The AutoFormat dialog box opens.

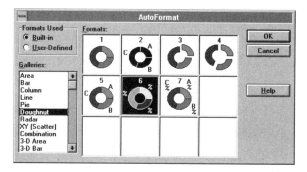

4 In the Galleries list, select 3-D Surface.

You might have to scroll through the list to find it.

5 Under Formats, be sure that the number 1 chart subtype is selected.

6 Choose OK.

Your chart changes to a 3-D Surface chart. Your chart should look like the following.

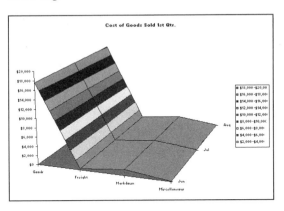

Creating Your Own Custom Chart Format

If your company or department already has a standard look for charts, or if you prefer a chart format other than those available through the AutoFormat command, you can create your own standard format. To create a custom chart autoformat, you use the AutoFormat command on the Format menu. You can make changes to your sample chart and edit the autoformat as well, or you can delete an old autoformat that you no longer need. In the next exercise, you use your 3-D bar chart with a trendline to create a custom autoformat that you can store permanently and reuse at any time.

Create a custom chart format

1 Switch to the Summary sheet and activate the bar chart.

2 Point to an open area, and click the right mouse button to open the shortcut menu.

3 From the shortcut menu, choose AutoFormat.

The AutoFormat dialog box opens.

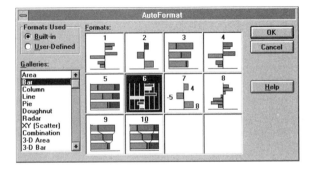

4   In the Formats Used area, select User-Defined.

The AutoFormat dialog box changes to show the Microsoft Excel 4.0 chart format and any formats you have already designed.

5   Click the Customize button.

The User-Defined AutoFormats dialog box opens.

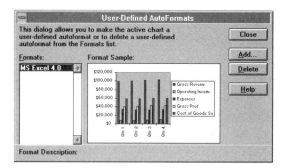

6   Click the Add button.

The Add Custom AutoFormat dialog box opens.

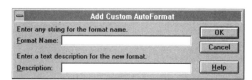

7   In the Format Name box, type **2-D bar trend**

8   In the Description box, type **2-D bar chart with trendline**, and then choose OK.

Your format is added to the gallery of user-defined formats. Now you can use this format by choosing the AutoFormat command.

9   In the User-Defined AutoFormats dialog box, click Close.

The User-Defined AutoFormats dialog box closes.

One Step Further

You can modify most aspects of your charts by using the commands on the Format or shortcut menus. You've seen how to add gridlines, change chart types, and format your charts in other ways. If you are working with 3-D charts, you can change even more options than you can with 2-D charts. You can modify the 3-D view of your chart to change the perspective, elevation, or rotation of your chart. You can make your chart have a sharper perspective—changing more quickly from near to far, or you can change the elevation to look down on the chart or up from the bottom. You can change the rotation so that the gridlines appear on one side or the other. You can even change the rotation so that you look at the back of the chart rather than the front.

Changing your perspective, elevation, or rotation can give your 3-D charts more emphasis and make them stand out in a presentation. Try changing the 3-D view of your area chart to show a more dramatic presentation of the data.

Change the 3-D view format for your area chart

1   Switch to the Chart1 sheet.

2   Click the right mouse button to open the shortcut menu, and then choose 3-D View.

The Format 3-D View dialog box opens.

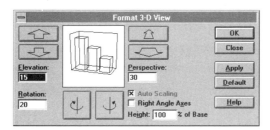

3   In the Elevation box, use the large arrows above the box to change the elevation to 35.

The up arrow increases the elevation. The down arrow decreases the elevation.

4 Click in the Rotation box, and use the rotation arrows to the right of the box to change the rotation to 140.

The rotation arrow on the left increases the degree of rotation. The rotation arrow on the right decreases the degree of rotation.

5 Choose OK.

The dialog box closes and your changes take effect. Your chart should look similar to the following.

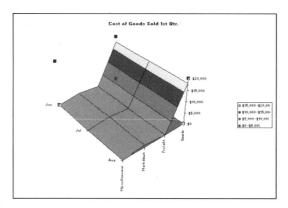

If You Want to Continue to the Next Lesson

1 Double-click the Control-menu box on the Drawing toolbar to close it, if it is open.

2 From the File menu, choose Save.

3 From the File menu, choose Close.

If You Want to Quit Microsoft Excel for Now

▶ From the File menu, choose Exit.

If you see the Save dialog box, click Yes.

Lesson Summary

To	Do this	Button
Change chart types	Activate the chart and click the right mouse button to display the shortcut menu. Choose Chart Type. In the Chart Type dialog box, select the type you want and choose OK.	

To	Do this	Button
Add gridlines	Activate the chart. From the Insert menu, choose Gridlines. Select the gridlines that you want, and then choose OK. *or* Open the Chart toolbar. On the Chart toolbar, click the Gridlines button.	
Add a legend	Activate the chart. From the Insert menu, choose Legend. *or* Open the Chart toolbar. On the Chart toolbar, click the Legend button.	
Position a legend	Double-click the legend in the chart. In the Format Legend dialog box, make your selections and click OK.	
Add a trendline	Click a bar in the series that you want to plot. From the Insert menu, choose Trendline. Select the type you want, and then choose OK.	
Add an arrow	Activate the chart. Display the Drawing toolbar, and click the Arrow button. Drag towards the object to create an arrow, and then release the mouse button.	
Add a text box	On the Standard toolbar, click the Text Box button. Drag to create the text box, and then type your text.	
Change text formats	Select the text you want to change. From the shortcut or Format menu, choose Format Object. Make your selections and then choose OK. *or* Select the text and use the buttons on the Formatting toolbar to change the text formats.	
Change chart colors	Activate the chart, and select the object or series that you want to change. From the shortcut or Format menu, choose Format Object or Format Series. Click the Patterns tab and select the color you want. Choose OK.	

To	Do this	Button
Format a chart automatically	Activate the chart and, from the Format or shortcut menu, choose AutoFormat. Select the chart type and format that you want, and then choose OK.	
Create a custom chart format	Activate the chart and, from the Format or shortcut menu, choose AutoFormat. In the Formats Used area, select User-Defined. Click the Customize button, and then click Add. Type a name and a description, choose OK, and then click close.	

For more information on	See in the *Microsoft Excel User's Guide*
Changing chart types	Chapter 16, "Working with Chart Types and Autoformats"
Enhancing charts	Chapter 18, "Formatting a Chart"
Formatting charts automatically	Chapter 16, "Working with Chart Types and Autoformats"
Adding an arrow	Chapter 18, "Formatting a Chart"

Preview of the Next Lesson

In the next lesson, "Printing Worksheets and Charts," you'll preview your data before you print it. You'll learn about setting up your worksheets, reports, or presentations for printing, and you'll learn how to print chart sheets.

Printing Worksheets and Charts

So far in this book, you've learned to enter data and create formulas, format text, and create charts. Now you want to present the data or charts to someone else. You want your report or presentation to print cleanly, with page breaks in the right places. You also might want a header or a footer to show a date, a page number, or the name of the workbook. In this lesson, you'll learn how to set up your pages with print titles, margins, headers, and footers, and how to preview the pages before you send them to the printer. You'll also learn how to print charts, without cutting off any areas or taking up too much space.

You will learn how to:

- Preview your worksheets.
- Set up pages for printing.
- Print a chart sheet.

Estimated lesson time: 35 minutes

If your screen does not match the illustrations in this lesson, see the Appendix, "Matching the Exercises."

Start the lesson

1   Open 06LESSN.XLS.

2   Save the workbook as LESSN06.XLS.

3   Click the Maximize button on the document window, if it is not already maximized.

Previewing Your Worksheet

You want your pages to print clearly, but you probably don't want to waste a lot of paper checking to see whether the necessary rows and columns appear on the sheet, if the margins are set to the right size, or if the data fits in the columns. Previewing your work shows you what you need to change before you print. In the next exercise, you preview your page layout, and then you print the Cash Budget sheet.

Preview the Cash Budget sheet

1   Be sure the active sheet is the Cash Budget sheet.

Print Preview

You can also use the Print Preview command from the File menu.

2 Click the Print Preview button on the toolbar.

Your sheet appears in the Preview window. Notice that the Purpose statement does not fit on the sheet in the preview window. You need to correct this before you print the worksheet. Your Budget sheet should look like the following.

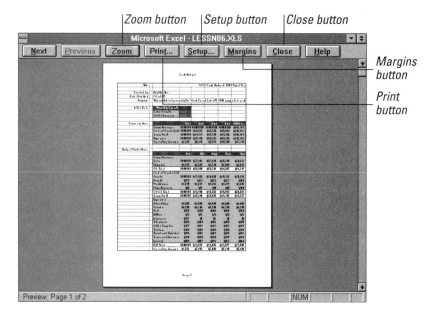

3 Move the pointer over the sheet.

The pointer changes to look like a small magnifying glass.

You can also use the Zoom button to zoom in and out in the preview window.

4 Click near the middle of the Budget sheet.

The sheet zooms in so you can see the budget data. Some of the cells in the budget might contain number signs, rather than actual figures, indicating that you need to widen the columns before printing.

5 Click again to zoom out, and then click the Close button.

The Preview window closes.

Setting Up Pages

When you work with larger worksheets, you are rarely able to print all of your data on one page. In addition, you might want to add information at the top or bottom of your worksheet to identify the date that the sheet was printed or perhaps its filename. If your data requires more than one page, you'll need to adjust page breaks. You can modify your sheets to print the way you want them to, with page breaks in specific places, margins adjusted, titles repeated on every page, and headers and footers.

Fitting Your Data Into a Limited Printing Space

The Page Setup command is like /Print Printer Options, /Print Printer Header, /Print Printer Footer, and /Print Printer Options Margins in 1-2-3.

Sometimes you only need to print part of a sheet. You might need only one section of a database, or just part of the information in your budget. You can print as much or as little of a sheet as you need. At other times, you might have too much information for one page. With the Page Setup command on the File menu, you can adjust the area that is printed and the scale at which it is printed. In the next exercises, you use the Print command on the File menu to print only part of the data, and then change settings in the Page Setup dialog box to make all of your budget information appear on one and then two pages.

Note   In the remaining exercises in this lesson, your computer needs to be connected to an active printer before you can print. If a printer is not available, click Cancel instead of OK in the Print dialog box.

Print part of a worksheet

1   In the Budget sheet, select A7:H16.

This range includes the initial data on your budget, plus the budget summary table.

2   From the File menu, choose Print.

The Print dialog box opens.

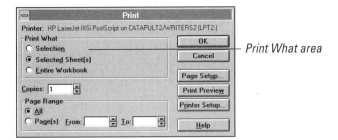

— *Print What area*

3   In the Print What area, click the Selection option, and then choose OK.

A dialog box opens, telling you that your selection is being printed.

Fit the cash budget worksheet onto one page

1   Click cell A1.

2   From the File menu, choose Page Setup.

The Page Setup dialog box opens.

3   In the Page Setup dialog box, click the Page tab.

The Page options appear in the dialog box.

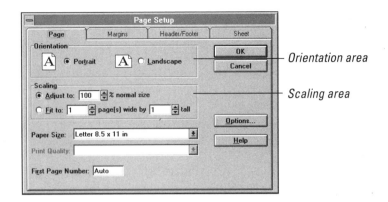

Orientation area

Scaling area

4 In the Orientation area, select Landscape.

Selecting Landscape changes your page from a tall to a wide orientation. Since your budget data covers several columns, you can fit more information onto a wide page than you can onto a long page.

5 In the Scaling area, select the Fit To 1 Page(s) Wide By 1 Tall option.

This scales your worksheet down to fit on only one page. You can change the number of pages to whatever you need.

6 Click the Print Preview button.

The Print Preview window opens and displays your entire budget on one sheet. Your budget should look like the following.

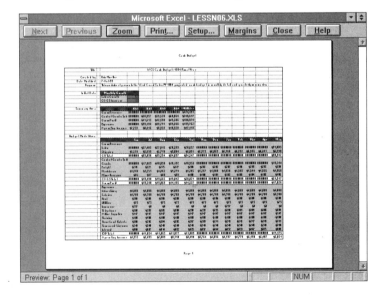

Fit the cash budget worksheet onto two pages

1   In the Print Preview window, click the Setup button.

The Page Setup dialog box opens.

2   In the dialog box, click the Page tab.

The Page options appear in the dialog box.

3   In the Orientation area, select Portrait.

Selecting Portrait changes your page from a wide to a tall orientation.

4   In the Scaling area, select the Fit To 1 Page(s) Wide By 1 Tall option, and change it to Fit To 2 Page(s) Wide By 1 Tall.

This scales your worksheet to fit on two pages. You can change the number of pages to whatever you need.

5   Choose OK.

The Print Preview window opens and displays the first page of your two-page budget. Your budget should look like the following.

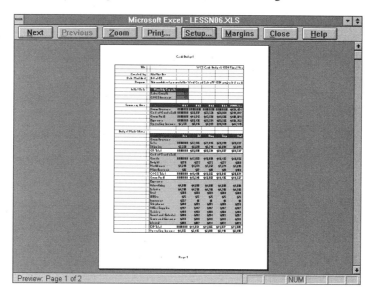

6   Click the Print button and then, in the Print dialog box, choose OK.

7   When the message box closes, from the File menu, choose Page Setup.

8   In the Scaling area, select Adjust To.

This returns scaling to the default setting to prepare for the next exercises.

Adding Print Titles

The Print Titles option is like /Print Printer Options Borders in 1-2-3.

A properly formatted worksheet has row or column headings at the left side or top of every page. You can add *print titles* to repeat the headings and clearly identify the data in your other pages. In the next exercise, you add print titles to your sheet to list the budget categories along the left side of your pages.

Add print titles to your pages

1   From the File menu, choose Page Setup.

The Page Setup dialog box opens.

2   In the dialog box, click the Sheet tab.

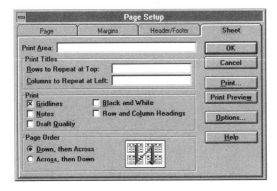

3   In the Print Titles area, click in the Columns To Repeat At Left text box.

4   In your budget sheet, click the column header button for column C.

You might need to move the dialog box out of the way first.

5   Click the Print Preview button in the dialog box.

The Print Preview window opens and displays your worksheet.

6   Click the Next button.

Notice that the budget categories are repeated at the left side of the page. Your worksheet should look similar to the following.

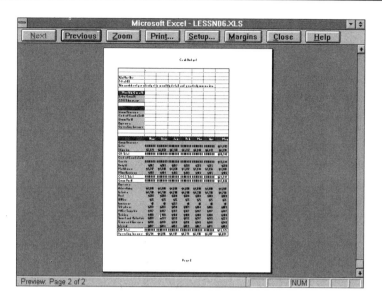

7   Click the Close button.

The Print Preview window closes.

Adjusting Margins

When you print a worksheet, your margins are automatically set at 1 inch for the top and bottom margins, and 0.75 of an inch for the left and right margins. You can adjust the margins with the Page Setup dialog box to any size you like. In the next exercise, you change the margins in your Cash Budget sheet to 1.25 inch for the top and bottom margins, and 1 inch for the left and right margins.

Change your margins

1   From the File menu, choose Page Setup.

The Page Setup dialog box opens.

2   Click the Margins tab on the Page Setup dialog box.

The Margins options appear.

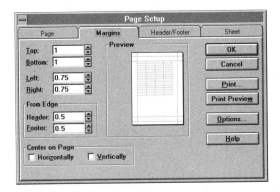

3   In the Top box, click the up arrow once.

The margin changes to 1.25 inches.

4   In the Bottom box, click the up arrow once.

The margin changes to 1.25 inches.

5   In the Left box, click the up arrow once.

The margin changes to 1 inch.

6   In the Right box, click the up arrow once.

The margin changes to 1 inch.

7   Click the Print Preview button.

The Print Preview window opens, displaying the cash budget with your changes.

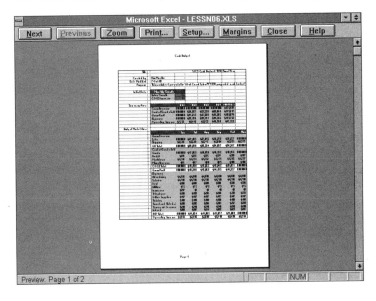

8   Click the Close button.

The Print Preview window closes.

Breaking Your Worksheet into Pages

When you print a large document, page breaks are inserted automatically at the cell nearest the margin. You might not always like where your pages break, however, since the automatic page breaks do not always follow your spreadsheet design. If you want to insert your own page breaks at specific rows, you select a row and use the Page Break command on the Insert menu. The page break is inserted above the selected row. To remove a page break that you added manually, you select the row below the page break, and use the Remove Page Break command on the Insert menu.

You might also find that your pages are not printing in the order that you want. If your document is more than one sheet wide, pages automatically print down your worksheet, and then across. You can change the printing order by using the Sheet tab in the Page Setup dialog box.

In the next exercise, you add a page break and then alter the printing order to print across, and then down.

Insert a page break and change the printing order

In this exercise, you create a horizontal page break by selecting a row before inserting the break. You can also create a vertical page break by selecting a column, with the break appearing to the left of the selected column. If you select a single cell, both a horizontal and a vertical page break are inserted.

1   Click the row header for row 18 in the Cash Budget sheet.

This row contains the Budget Model Area title and is a good place for a page break if you want to keep the two tables intact.

2   From the Insert menu, choose Page Break.

A dotted line appears above row 18, showing the page break you inserted.

3   From the File menu, choose Page Setup.

The Page Setup dialog box opens.

4   In the dialog box, click the Sheet tab.

The Sheet tab appears.

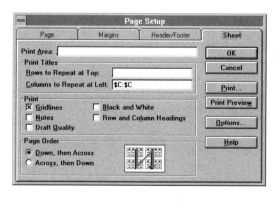

5   In the Page Order area, select Across, then Down.

This changes your page numbering to go across the pages and then down.

6   Click the Print Preview button in the dialog box.

The Print Preview window opens. Your screen should look like the following.

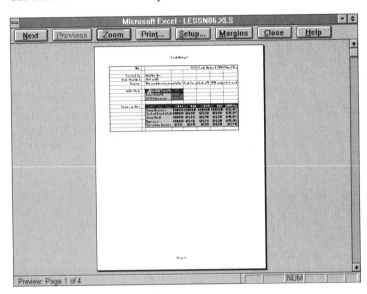

7   Click the Close button.

Adding Headers and Footers

Microsoft Excel automatically adds the name of your file to the header area and the page number to the footer area of anything that you print. If you want a title or the date to appear at the top or bottom of your pages, you can change the header or footer on your document. You can also delete the header or footer.

Using Standard Headers and Footers

Microsoft Excel provides standard header and footer options that you can select in the Page Setup dialog box. With these built-in formats, you can add the company name, the filename with or without the extension, the date, the page number, or your own name. You can also mark documents as confidential, or add a document title. In the next exercise, you'll remove all of the information from the header, and move the page number and filename into the footer.

Modify a header and a footer

1   From the File menu, choose Page Setup.

The Page Setup dialog box opens.

2   Click the Header/Footer tab in the dialog box.

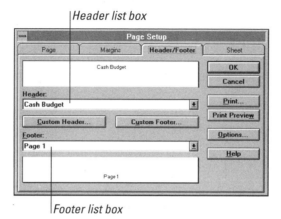

Header list box

Footer list box

3   Click the down arrow next to the Header list box.

4   In the Header list, scroll upward and select (none).

Selecting (none) removes the header.

5   Click the down arrow next to the Footer list box.

6   In the Footer list, scroll and select LESSN06.XLS, Page 1.

This option places the filename and the page number at the bottom of the page. Your header and footer options should look like the following.

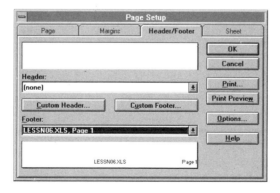

7   Click the Print Preview button in the dialog box.

The Print Preview window opens and displays your document with the new footer. Your document should look like the following.

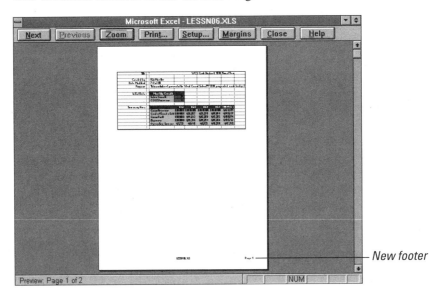

New footer

8   Click the Close button.

The Print Preview window closes.

Creating Custom Headers and Footers

You can create your own headers and footers by using the Custom Header and Custom Footer buttons in the Page Setup dialog box. You can add the page number, date, time, filename, or sheet name, plus any other text that you want to include. In the next exercise, you add the document title, the date, and your name to the header with the Custom Header button.

Add a custom header

1   From the File menu, choose Page Setup.

The Page Setup dialog box opens.

2   Click the Header/Footer tab in the dialog box.

The Header/Footer options appear.

If you have worked with headers and footers in Microsoft Excel 4.0, the Custom Header and Custom Footer dialog boxes should look familiar. They are the same as in Microsoft Excel 4.0.

3   Click the Custom Header button.

The Header dialog box opens.

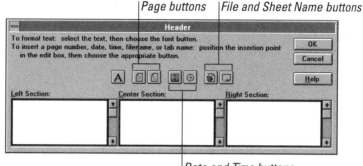

Page buttons |*File and Sheet Name buttons*

Date and Time buttons

4   Click in the Left Section box, and then type your name.

Whatever you place in this box appears at the left margin of the header.

5   Click in the Center Section box, and then type **1994 Cash Budget**

Whatever you place in this box appears at the center of the header.

Date

6   Click in the Right Section box, and then click the Date button.

Whatever you place in this box appears at the right margin of the header. Your dialog box should look like the following.

Font button

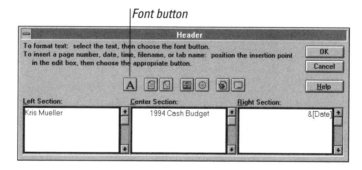

7   Select the text in the Center Section box, and then click the Font button.

The Font dialog box appears.

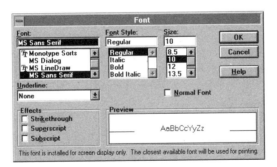

8 In the Font Style list, select Bold. In the Size list, select 12, and then click OK.

The Font dialog box closes.

9 In the Header dialog box, click OK.

The dialog box closes and the Page Setup dialog box changes to reflect the new header. Your dialog box should look like the following.

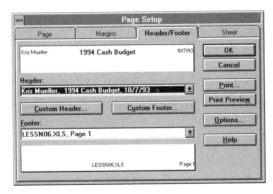

10 Click OK.

The Page Setup dialog box closes.

Printing a Worksheet

The Print command is like /Print Printer Go in 1-2-3.

Now that you've set up your pages, you can print them. To print your worksheet, you can either use the Print button on the Standard toolbar, or the Print command on the File menu. When you use the Print button, your worksheet is printed immediately to the default printer using the current print options.

When you use the Print command, you can make additional choices before you print, such as number of copies or selected pages to print. You can also use the Print buttons in the Print Preview window or the Page Setup dialog box to view your printing options and then print your worksheet. You can print a selected range, a selected sheet, or your entire workbook. You can print multiple copies or a specific page range in your worksheet. In the next exercise, you use the Print command to print two copies of the selected sheet.

Print your worksheet

1   From the File menu, choose Print.

The Print dialog box opens.

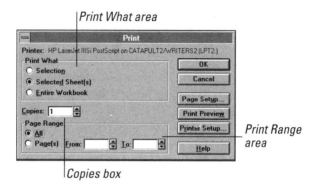

Print What area

Print Range area

Copies box

2   In the Print What area, be sure that the Selected Sheet(s) option is selected.

3   In the Copies box, click the Up arrow once to change the number to 2.

4   Click OK.

The dialog box closes and another opens, informing you that two copies of your worksheet are being printed on your printer.

Printing a Chart Sheet

When you create a chart on a separate sheet, you can print that sheet separately and make page setup decisions for that sheet alone. With a chart sheet, you can also decide how to scale the chart when you print it, and whether to print it in color or in black and white. You can reduce a chart to fit the page size or enlarge it to fill the full page. You can also size the chart on the screen to create a custom chart size. In the next exercise, you scale your bar chart to fit your page and then print it in black and white.

Print a chart sheet

1   Select the Chart 1 sheet.

2   From the File menu, choose Page Setup.

The Page Setup dialog box opens.

3   In the dialog box, click the Chart tab.

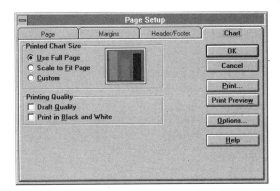

4 In the Printed Chart Size area, select Scale To Fit Page, if it is not already selected.

5 In the Printing Quality area, select Print In Black And White, if it is not already selected, and then click the Print button in the dialog box.

The Print dialog box opens.

6 Click OK.

A dialog box opens, telling you that your chart is printing.

One Step Further

The gridlines on a spreadsheet can sometimes detract from your data. If you are creating a report or a presentation, you might not want to have column and row gridlines on your sheets when you print them. You can turn off your gridlines in the Page Setup dialog box so that they don't appear when you print.

Try turning off the gridlines on your Summary sheet so that the data and chart will appear on a plain white background.

Turn off gridlines

1 Switch to the 1994 2nd Qtr sheet.

2 From the File menu, choose Page Setup.

The Page Setup dialog box opens.

3 Click the Sheet tab.

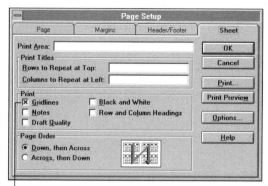

Gridlines check box

4   In the Print area, clear the Gridlines check box.

5   Click the Print Preview button.

The Print Preview window opens with the Summary sheet open. Notice that your data and chart are now on a plain white background with no gridlines.

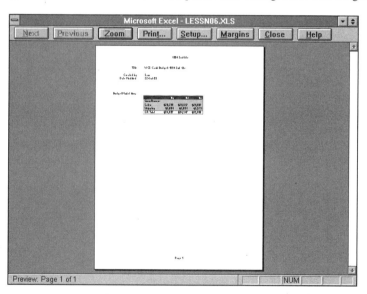

6   Click the Print button.

The Print dialog box appears.

7   In the Print dialog box, choose OK.

If You Want to Continue to the Next Lesson

1   From the File menu, choose Save.

2   From the File menu, choose Close.

If You Want to Quit Microsoft Excel for Now

▶   From the File menu, choose Exit.

   If you see the Save dialog box, click Yes.

Lesson Summary

To	Do this	Button
Preview your worksheet	Click the Print Preview button on the Standard toolbar. *or* From the File menu, choose Print Preview.	
Print part of a worksheet	Select the range you want to print. From the File menu, choose Print. In the Print What area, click the Selection option, and then choose OK.	
Fit your worksheet onto specified pages	From the File menu, choose Page Setup. Click the Page tab and, in the Scaling area, type the number of pages wide by the number tall. Choose OK.	
Add print titles	From the File menu, choose Page Setup. Click the Sheet tab. In the Print Titles area, select Columns or Rows. Select the range that includes the titles in the worksheet, and then choose OK.	
Change margins	From the File menu, choose Page Setup. Click the Margins tab. In the Top, Bottom, Left, and Right margin boxes, type the margins you want. Choose OK.	
Add a page break	Select the row below or the column to the right of where you want the page break to occur. From the Insert menu, choose Page Break.	
Change the printing order of pages	From the File menu, choose Page Setup. Click the Sheet tab and, in the Page Order box, select a printing order. Choose OK.	

To	Do this	Button
Add or delete a standard header or footer	From the File menu, choose Page Setup. Click the Header/Footer tab. In the Header or Footer list box, select the style you want, or click None to remove the header or footer. Click OK.	
Add a custom header or footer	From the File menu, choose Page Setup. Click the Header/Footer tab. Click the Custom Header or Custom Footer button and type the information that you want. Click OK and then click OK again.	
Print a worksheet	From the File menu, choose Print. Select the options you want and click OK. *or* Click the Print button on the Standard toolbar.	
Print a chart sheet	From the File menu, choose Page Setup. Click the Chart tab and change the scaling, if necessary. Click the Print button in the dialog box. Click OK. *or* Click the Print button.	

For more information on	See in the *Microsoft Excel User's Guide*
Printing	Chapter 14, "Printing"
Printing a Chart Sheet	Chapter 18, "Formatting a Chart"

Preview of the Next Lessons

In Part 3, you'll learn how to manage your data by sorting and filtering it to find specific information. You'll create reports that make your data clear to others and you'll link data between different files to save time and effort in using the same data for different purposes. In the next lesson, "Organizing Your Workbooks," you'll learn how to copy and move sheets within and between your workbooks, add cell notes and text boxes to your sheets, add summary information to your files, and find files quickly in Microsoft Excel.

Review & Practice

In the lessons in Part 2, you learned skills to help you chart your data, modify your charts, and print your data and charts. If you want to practice these skills and test your understanding before you proceed with the lessons in Part 3, you can work through the Review & Practice section following this lesson.

Part 2   Review & Practice

Before you move on to Part 3, which covers sorting, organizing, and linking your data, and creating reports, you can practice the skills you learned in Part 2 by working through the steps in this Review & Practice section. You will create a 3-D column chart on a separate chart sheet, add gridlines and a text block to explain the data, and then print the worksheet and the chart.

Scenario

As part of the 10-year financial history for West Coast Sales, you need to create a chart showing how WCS's share of the market has increased over the decade. You've got the skills now to create a chart that can show the changes, as well as the skills to make sure that the information is clear and well presented. You need to print the data and the chart when you are finished so that two of your co-workers can review them and make suggestions.

You will review and practice how to:

- Create a chart on a separate chart sheet.

- Add gridlines and text to a chart.

- Add a header and footer to a chart.

- Preview and print a worksheet and chart sheet.

Estimated practice time: 15 minutes

Step 1: Create a Chart on a Separate Chart Sheet

Use the Year, Company, and Industry data on your 10-year sales history sheet to create a new 3-D column chart on a separate sheet.

1   Open the file P2REVIEW.XLS and save it as REVIEWP2.XLS.

2   Use the Chart command and the ChartWizard to create a 3-D column chart on a separate sheet.

Do not include the totals row or the market share column in your chart data.

3   Use the first column of your data (the year column) for the category axis labels.

For more information on	See
Creating a chart on a separate chart sheet	Lesson 4

Step 2: Modify Your Chart

Modify your completed 3-D column chart by adding and rearranging some chart elements to create a cleaner look.

1   Activate the chart and change the chart subtype to the fourth subtype, the subtype with one series in front of another.

2   Add gridlines to all of the major axes in the chart.

3   Move the legend to the bottom of your chart.

4   Add a text box to the top of your chart, insert the following description, and center the text.

This chart compares WCS sales growth to the industry as a whole over the last 10 years.

For more information on	See
Modifying a Chart	Lesson 5

Step 3: Preview the Document and Add a Header and Footer

Add a custom header and footer, and then select both sheets and preview them before printing.

1   Use the Page Setup dialog box and the Custom Header and Custom Footer buttons to add the following header and footer information.

Header: West Coast Sales, date, Confidential.

Footer: Page X, sheet name, filename.

2   Use the Print Preview button to preview your worksheet and then the chart sheet.

Your chart sheet should look similar to the following.

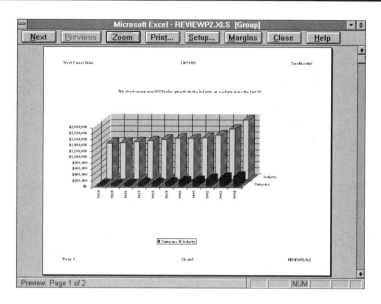

For more information on	See
Adding Headers and Footers	Lesson 6
Previewing Your Document	Lesson 6

Step 4: Print the Sheets

Print two copies of your sheets for your co-workers to review.

▶ Change the number of copies to two, and print your document.

For more information on	See
Printing a Worksheet	Lesson 6

If You Want to Continue to the Next Lesson

1   From the File menu, choose Save.

2   From the File menu, choose Close.

If You Want to Quit Microsoft Excel for Now

▶   From the File menu, choose Exit.

   If you see the Save dialog box, click Yes.

Part

3 Managing Your Data

Organizing Your Workbooks

When you organize your workbooks logically, other people are better able to understand and use them. Even if you don't share your workbooks, it makes sense to organize them well for your own convenience. Copying or moving sheets into logical positions is one aspect of organizing your workbooks.

Documenting your workbooks is another aspect of organizing them. You can add cell notes and text boxes to annotate your sheets and explain specific formulas or values. You can also fill in summary information for your files, to make them easier to find and identify later.

In this lesson, you'll learn how to manage your workbooks by copying and moving sheets, how to document your work by adding text boxes and cell notes, and how to search for files.

You will learn how to:

- Copy and move sheets to make your workbooks more manageable.

- Document your work with cell notes, text boxes, and summary information.

- Find files quickly by searching for summary information.

Estimated lesson time: 35 minutes

If your screen does not match the illustrations in this lesson, see the Appendix, "Matching the Exercises."

Start the lesson

1 Open 07LESSN.XLS.

2 Save the workbook as LESSN07.XLS.

3 Click the Maximize button on the document window, if it is not already maximized.

Managing Your Workbooks

While you create a workbook, you might know what information you want to include, but not the best way to organize it. For example, if you are building a workbook that contains several detail sheets and one summary sheet, you might want the summary sheet first if you work mostly with the summary, or last if you work mostly with the details. With Microsoft Excel, you can easily begin your workbook without getting the order of the sheets exactly right the first time. You can always add or remove sheets, or copy or move them around in your workbook. For example, if you have set up a sheet for each of the districts or regions in your company, you can add a sheet if a new district opens. You learned how to add and delete sheets in Lesson 1. Now you'll learn how to copy and move sheets to put them in the best possible order for your work.

Copying Sheets

If you have a sheet in one workbook that you also need to use in another, you have two choices. You can link the sheet to the other workbook, as you will learn in Lesson 12, "Linking Your Data," or you can put a copy of the sheet in the other workbook. You can also copy a sheet within the same workbook if, for example, you are building a workbook with several similar sheets. If you need to update the information from the original sheet frequently, linking the sheet will ensure that the information in your sheet is current. If you don't need to maintain the same information in each sheet, copying the sheet will probably suffice.

In the next exercise, you'll open the file 07LESSNA.XLS and copy the Fax Inventory sheet to your LESSN07.XLS practice file.

Copy a sheet to another file

1   Open the file 07LESSNA.XLS and save it as LESSN07A.XLS.

    You now have two files open named LESSN07.XLS and LESSN07A.XLS.

2   In LESSN07A.XLS, be sure that the Fax Inventory sheet is the active sheet.

3   From the Edit menu, choose Move Or Copy Sheet.

    The Move Or Copy dialog box opens.

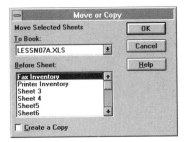

4   Click the down arrow next to the To Book box, and then select LESSN07.XLS.

5   In the Before Sheet list, select Sheet 2.

    This places the copy before Sheet 2 in your workbook.

6   Select the Create A Copy check box.

    If this check box is not selected, the sheet would be moved instead of copied, which would remove it from the original workbook.

7   Choose OK.

    The Fax Inventory sheet is copied to your practice file, LESSN07.XLS, just after the Copier Inventory sheet, and before Sheet 2. Microsoft Excel automatically displays the new worksheet. Your workbook should look similar to the following.

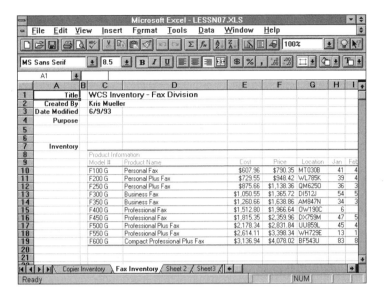

If you need to build another sheet with several characteristics similar to an existing sheet, you don't need to copy the individual items from one sheet and paste them onto another. You can simply copy the entire sheet and then make any changes that you want. To copy a sheet within a workbook, you can either use the same command that you used to copy a sheet between workbooks, or you can use your mouse. In the next exercises, you'll copy the Fax Inventory sheet, and then rename and modify the copy to be a totals sheet for your inventory.

Copy a sheet within a workbook

1   Point to the tab of the Fax Inventory sheet, and hold down CTRL while pressing the mouse button.

Your mouse pointer changes to look like a small sheet with a plus sign on it.

2   Drag the pointer until it appears immediately before the Copier Inventory sheet.

The pointer has a small triangle that shows where the sheet will be copied. Your pointer should be immediately before the Copier Inventory sheet.

3   Release the mouse button.

The Fax Inventory sheet is copied and then dropped into place immediately before the Copier Inventory sheet. Notice that it is automatically renamed Fax Inventory (2), as in the following.

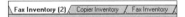

Rename and modify a sheet

1   Double-click the Fax Inventory(2) sheet tab.

The Rename Sheet dialog box opens.

2   In the Name box, type **Inventory Totals**, and then choose OK.

The dialog box closes and your sheet is renamed.

3   In cell C1, select the text Fax Division, and then type **Totals**, and press ENTER.

4   Select the range C10:U19, and then press DEL.

All of the contents for cells C10:U19 are removed from the cells, leaving only the categories and headings for your inventory data.

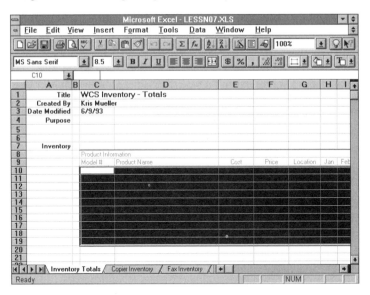

Moving Sheets

Just as you can copy sheets either within or between workbooks, you can also move them. The difference is that copying leaves the original sheet intact, while moving results in the existence of only one sheet at the new location. If you have a sheet in one workbook that belongs in another, you can move it with the Move Or Copy Sheet command. In the next exercise, you'll move an inventory sheet from the LESSN07A.XLS file to your LESSN07.XLS file.

Move a sheet between files and close a file

1   From the Window menu, choose LESSN07A.XLS.

   The LESSN07A.XLS workbook becomes active.

2   Click the Printer Inventory sheet tab.

3   From the Edit menu, choose Move Or Copy Sheet.

   The Move Or Copy dialog box opens.

4   Click the down arrow next to the To Book box, and then select LESSN07.XLS.

5   In the Before Sheet list, select Copier Inventory.

   This places the Printer Inventory sheet before the Copier Inventory sheet in your workbook.

6   Be sure that there is no X in the Create A Copy check box. If there is an X, click the check box to remove it.

7   Choose OK.

   The Printer Inventory sheet is moved to your practice file, immediately before the Copier Inventory sheet. Your workbook looks similar to the following.

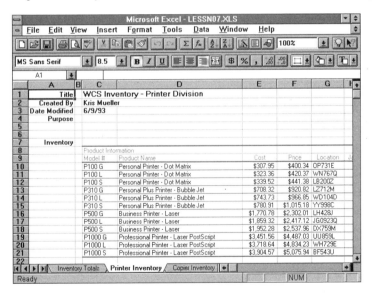

8   From the Window menu, choose LESSN07A.XLS.

9   From the File menu, choose Close.

10   In the Save Changes dialog box, click Yes.

If you only need to move sheets within a workbook, you can simply drag them with the mouse. When you do this, your pointer displays a small sheet symbol next to it. This pointer is similar to the one you saw when you copied a sheet. As you saw in the last section, a plus sign in the sheet symbol indicates that you can copy a sheet within your workbook. The pointer, without the plus sign, indicates that you can move the sheet to any position within your workbook.

In the next exercise, you'll arrange the inventory sheets in alphabetical order by moving the Printer Inventory sheet so that it appears after the Fax Inventory sheet.

Move sheets within a workbook

1   Point to the sheet tab for the Printer Inventory sheet, and hold down the mouse button.

Your pointer should look similar to the following.

2   Drag the sheet to the right of the Fax Inventory sheet until the little arrow points to where the sheet will be inserted, as in the following.

3   Release the mouse button.

The Printer Inventory sheet takes its place after the Fax Inventory sheet, as in the following.

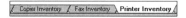

Documenting Workbooks

Although it's important to have your worksheets in the best order, it's more important to be able to identify the information on a sheet right away. You've already seen how to use names to clarify formulas, and to add titles and text to explain charts, but what about your worksheets themselves? You need to be sure that whoever uses your workbooks will be able to understand how you put your formulas together, and what data you used to generate a chart or report. With *cell notes* and *text boxes*, you can leave a trail of information for other people to use. With the *summary information* dialog box, you can be sure that people will know what the workbook contains, even before they open it.

Adding Cell Notes

Sometimes, a cell contains a reference to another sheet or a formula that points to data in another location. Or, perhaps a value you use represents a certain number or percentage that is used as initial data throughout a sheet. For example, on the Budget sheet you created earlier, the Sales Growth and Cost of Goods Sold Increase figures are initial data, values that the rest of the sheet depends on. The values in the Sales and Expenses budget items increase over the year according to the Sales Growth and Cost of Goods Sold Increase percentages. If you leave such items undocumented, another user might be confused, or might even delete them by mistake. If you want to be sure that another user knows what a particular item is on your sheet, you should add a note to the appropriate cell, explaining what the data is for or what data the formula uses.

You can add cell notes with the Note command on the Insert menu. You can add several notes at a time. In the next exercise, you'll add cell notes to the Price, Totals, and Values headings on the Inventory Totals sheet to explain how these formulas are constructed.

Document the price, totals, and values formulas

1 Click the Inventory Totals sheet tab.

You might have to scroll forward through the sheet tabs to find it. You will add the notes to the totals sheet first.

2 Select cell F9, the cell that contains the heading Price.

3 From the Insert menu, choose Note.

The Cell Note dialog box opens.

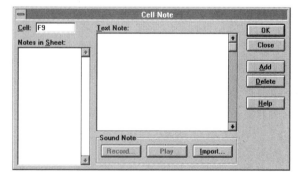

4 In the Text Note box, type **Price equals Cost * 130%**, and then click the Add button.

5 Click cell T9 in the sheet.

This cell holds the Totals heading.

6 Select the text in the Text Note box, and then type **This number represents the entire inventory over the whole year, including projections for September through December.**

7 Click the Add button.

8 Double-click the Cell box, and then click cell U9 in the sheet.

This cell holds the Values heading.

9 In the Text Note box, select the text, and then type **Value equals price * totals**, and then click the Add button.

10 Choose OK.

The Cell Note dialog box closes and note indicators (red dots in the top-right corner of each cell) are added to cells F9, T9, and U9. Your sheet should look like the following.

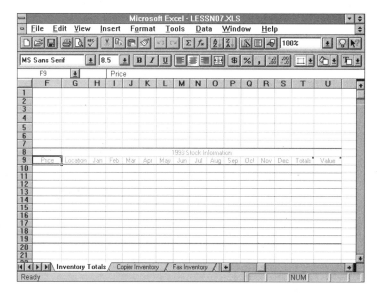

If you have several sheets in a series with the same data and you want to be sure that the cell notes you added to one sheet appear on the others, you can simply copy the cells containing the notes to the other sheets. In the next exercise, you'll copy the entire heading row from the Inventory Totals sheet to the Copier, Fax, and Printer Inventory sheets.

Copy the cell notes to the other sheets

Copy

1 On the Inventory Totals sheet, select C9:U9, and then click the Copy button on the toolbar.

2 Click the Copier Inventory sheet tab, and select cell C9.

3 From the Edit menu, choose Paste Special.

The Paste Special dialog box opens.

4 In the Paste Special dialog box under Paste, select Notes, and then choose OK.

The dialog box closes, and the notes are added to cells C9:U9.

5 Repeat steps 2 through 4 for both the Fax Inventory and Printer Inventory sheets.

The cell notes from the Inventory Totals sheet are copied to the Fax Inventory and Printer Inventory sheets.

Adding Notes with Text Boxes

When you have finished creating a new worksheet, you might want to add some text that explains what the sheet is for, or what the different sections of the sheet are. Although you can type the text into a cell on the sheet, it might not be visible all of the time if you have a lot of text. The amount of visible text is determined by the column width, and you might not want to make the column wider. Instead of typing your text into a cell, you can add a text box. With a text box, you can type as much text as you need and manipulate the size of the text box, without affecting the rest of the worksheet.

In the next exercises, you'll add a text box to explain the product codes on the Copier Inventory sheet, and then copy the text box and modify it on the other inventory sheets.

Explain the inventory product codes

1 Click the Copier Inventory sheet tab.

2 Click the Text Box button on the Standard toolbar.

Your pointer changes to a thin plus sign when in the worksheet area.

Text Box

3 Drag to create a box that approximately covers cells D27:I31.

A text box appears, ready for you to enter text.

4 In the text box, type the following:

X00 SPACEBAR SPACEBAR **Basic copier** ENTER

X10 SPACEBAR SPACEBAR **Basic copier plus extra trays** ENTER

X20 SPACEBAR SPACEBAR **Basic copier plus extra trays, AutoFeed, AutoSort**

5 Click anywhere outside of the text box.

Copy the text box to the other inventory sheets

Copy

Paste

1 Click the text box once to select it, and then click the Copy button on the toolbar.

2 Click the Fax Inventory sheet tab, and then click the Paste button on the toolbar.

The text box is pasted onto the Fax Inventory sheet. Placement is not important at this point; you'll move it into position and modify the text later.

3 Click the Printer Inventory sheet tab, and then click the Paste button on the toolbar again.

The text box is pasted onto the Printer Inventory sheet as well. Next, you'll adjust the text box's position and update the text to match the printer codes.

Move and modify the text box

1 Drag the text box by its border downward over the range D27:G31.

2 Double-click inside the text box to activate the insertion point.

3 Select all of the text in the text box, and type the following:

G SPACEBAR SPACEBAR **Basic printer model** ENTER

L SPACEBAR SPACEBAR **Basic printer model plus extra trays** ENTER

S SPACEBAR SPACEBAR **Basic printer model plus extra trays and extended service contract**

Your worksheet should look similar to the following.

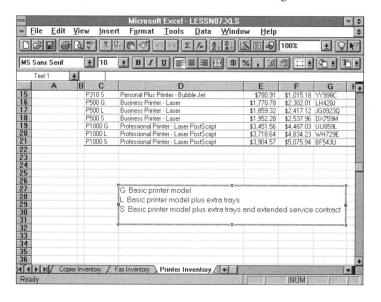

4 Click the Fax Inventory sheet tab.

5 Drag the text box by its border down over the range D27:H31.

6 Click the text box to activate the insertion point.

7 Select all of the text in the text box, and type the following:

X00 SPACEBAR SPACEBAR **Basic fax** ENTER

X50 SPACEBAR SPACEBAR **Basic fax plus automatic redial, memory feed**

Your worksheet should look similar to the following.

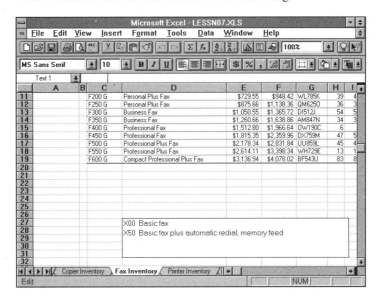

8 Click outside the text box to prepare for the next exercise.

Updating Summary Information

Now that you've placed your pages in the correct order and documented your information for future users, how can you be sure that the file itself will be identifiable? If you have files with similar names or similar data on the sheets, it's often difficult to determine which file you need. By taking the time to fill in and update the summary information for a file, you'll make it easier for yourself and for others.

You can update the summary information when you first save a file, or when you use the Summary Info command on the File menu. In the Summary Info dialog box, you can specify a title for your worksheet, a subject, an author, some keywords, and some comments about the file. In the Comments section, you can add information such as the last person who updated the file. In the next exercise, you'll update the summary information for your file to add a more detailed description and other information.

Add a description and keywords to your file

1 From the File menu, choose Summary Info.

The Summary Info dialog box opens.

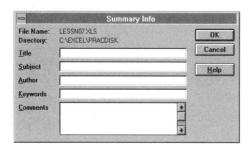

2 In the Title box, type **WCS Inventory for 1994 - All Divisions**

3 In the Subject box, type **Copier, Fax, and Printer inventories**

4 In the Author box, type your name.

5 In the Keywords box, type **Inventory**

6 In the Comments box, type **Includes projections for September thru December 1994.**

7 Choose OK.

The Summary Info dialog box closes and saves your new summary information.

Finding Files

Organizing doesn't do any good if you still can't locate your file when you need it. You can look through lists of filenames, but you might have trouble identifying the file you want. With the Find File command on the File menu, however, you can specify a file name and a directory. With the Advanced Search button, you can specify a title, a subject, an author name, some keywords, or other information from your file to help you find the file.

In the next exercise, you'll use the Find File command to locate a Microsoft Excel inventory file, and then preview it.

Note If you have already used the Find File command to search for a file, Microsoft Excel will automatically search for that file again when you choose the Find File command. If you see a dialog box that says it is searching through your directories, wait for a moment. The expanded Find File dialog box will open with the search results. At that point, click the Search button and continue with step 2.

Find a file and open it

1 From the File menu, choose Find File.

The dialog box opens.

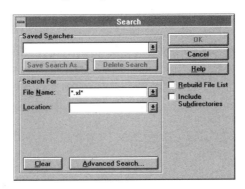

2 In the File Name box, type ***.XLS**

This will search for any files with an XLS extension.

3 In the Location box, type **c:\excel\practice**

This is the directory that contains your practice files. If your practice files are in another directory, type that directory instead.

4 Click OK.

A dialog box opens, showing the status of the search. The Find File dialog box expands to display the list of found files and a preview window.

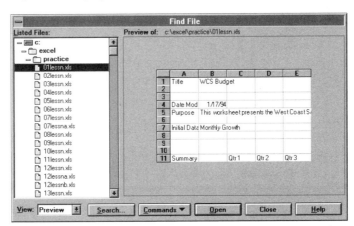

5 In the View box, select File Info.

The Find File dialog box displays information about the files instead of a preview.

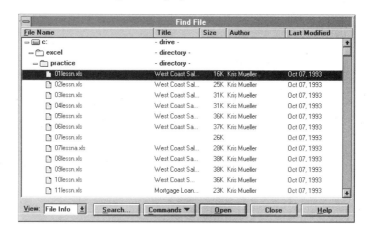

Search for a file by its subject

1 In the Find File dialog box, click the Search button.

The Search dialog box opens.

2 In the dialog box, click the Advanced Search button.

The Advanced Search dialog box opens.

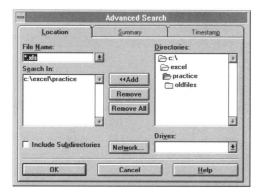

3 In the dialog box, select the Summary tab.

The Summary options appear in the Advanced Search dialog box, as in the following illustration.

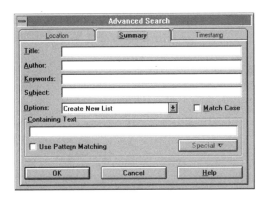

4   In the Containing Text box, type **inventory**

5   Click the down arrow next to the Options list box and select Search Only In List. Then choose OK.

6   In the Search dialog box, choose OK.

The Find File dialog box opens again and displays the results of your search.

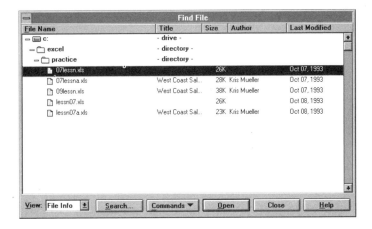

7   In the list, select the file 07LESSNA.XLS.

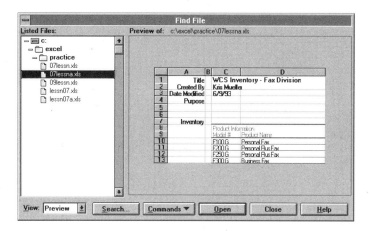

8   Click the down arrow next to the View list box and select Preview.

A preview of the 07LESSNA.XLS file appears.

9   In the Find File dialog box, click the Close button.

The Find File dialog box closes.

One Step Further

If you decide that you don't need a particular note, you can delete it easily, leaving the others intact. If you want to keep a paper record of your cell notes, you need to print them separately. Cell notes do not print when you print the rest of your worksheet.

Try deleting a note and then printing all of your cell notes for the worksheet.

Delete a cell note and print the rest

1   Switch to the Copier Inventory sheet and, from the Insert menu, choose Note.

The Cell Note dialog box opens.

2   In the Notes In Sheet list, select F9, and then click the Delete button. Click OK to confirm the deletion.

The note is removed from the list.

3   Choose OK to close the dialog box.

The note marker is removed from your sheet in cell F9.

4   From the File menu, choose Print.

The Print dialog box opens.

5   Click the Page Setup button.

The Page Setup dialog box opens.

6 Click the Sheet tab.

The Sheet tab opens. The dialog box should look similar to the following.

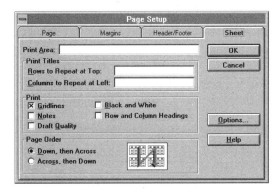

7 In the Print area, click the Notes check box to put an X in the box.

8 Choose OK, and then choose OK again in the Print dialog box.

The Page Setup and Print dialog boxes close and your notes print.

If You Want to Continue to the Next Lesson

1 From the File menu, choose Save.

2 Hold down SHIFT, and then from the File menu, choose Close All.

If You Want to Quit Microsoft Excel for Now

▶ From the File menu, choose Exit.

If you see the Save dialog box, click Yes.

Lesson Summary

To	Do this	Button
Copy a sheet to another file	Select the sheet to copy. From the Edit menu, choose Move Or Copy Sheet. In the Move Or Copy dialog box, select a destination filename and select where to add the new sheet. Select the Create A Copy check box, and then choose OK.	
Copy a sheet within a workbook	Hold down CTRL and drag the sheet tab to another location in your workbook.	
Rename a sheet	Double-click the sheet tab. In the Name box, type the new name and choose OK.	

To	Do this	Button
Move a sheet to or from another workbook	Select the sheet to move. From the Edit menu, choose Move Or Copy Sheet. In the Move Or Copy dialog box, select a destination filename and select where to add the new sheet. Clear the Create A Copy check box and choose OK.	
Move a sheet within a workbook	Drag the sheet tab to another location in your workbook.	
Add a cell note	Select a cell, and then from the Insert menu, choose Note. Type your note in the Text Note box, and then click Add. Choose OK.	
Add a text box	Click the Text Box button on the Standard toolbar and drag to create the text box. Type your text, and then click outside the text box.	
Update summary information	From the File menu, choose Summary Info. Type the information you want, and then choose OK.	
Find a file	From the File menu, choose Find File. In the dialog box, click the Search button. In the Search dialog box, type the information that you want to search for, and then click Search.	

For more information on	See in the *Microsoft Excel User's Guide*
Copying and moving sheets	Chapter 7, "Working in Workbooks"
Adding cell notes	Chapter 38, "Troubleshooting and Annotating a Worksheet"
Adding text boxes	Chapter 13, "Creating Graphic Objects on Worksheets and Charts"
Updating summary information	Chapter 6, "Managing Workbook Files"
Finding a file	Chapter 6, "Managing Workbook Files"

Preview of the Next Lesson

In the next lesson, "Sorting and Managing Lists," you'll learn how to sort your data by different criteria and how to filter your data to show only the information you need. Then you'll create subtotals in a few quick steps.

Sorting and Managing Lists

One of the things you'll probably do often in Microsoft Excel is sort and manage lists of data. The data in the following illustration is organized into a list, with column headings that define *fields* and rows that contain *records*. A field is a specific piece of information in your list of data, such as Emp ID, Last Name, First Name, and Position. A record contains all of the information about a specific item in your list. In the illustration, a record contains all of the personnel information for one person, including the employee ID number, last name, first name, position, department, division, salary, start date, and birth date. An entire list of data organized into fields and records, such as the employee list in the illustration, is referred to as a *database*.

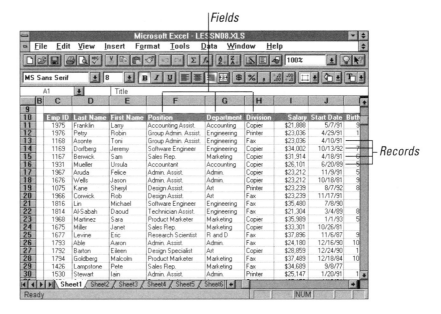

Fields

Records

Whenever you have a database of people, places, or products, you need a way to filter out everything except the specific information that you need at the moment. You also need to be able to sort the data by specific criteria. If you were preparing a report on how many employees are in the administration department, for example, you would need to be able to display only the administration department in your list. Microsoft Excel provides two useful tools for locating specific information in a list: *filtering* and *sorting*. With these tools, you can easily sort and filter the data in your worksheet.

In this lesson, you'll learn how to filter your data with AutoFilter to pull out only the data that you need. You'll also learn to sort your data easily with multiple sorting levels.

You will learn how to:

- View only the data that you need with automatic filtering.

- Sort data by specific criteria.

Estimated lesson time: 20 minutes

*If your screen does
not match the
illustrations in this
lesson, see the
Appendix, "Matching
the Exercises."*

Start the lesson

1 Open 08LESSN.XLS.

2 Save the workbook as LESSN08.XLS.

3 Click the Maximize button on the document window, if it is not already maximized.

Filtering Lists to Show Only the Data You Need

When you work with a database, you need to be able to find information quickly. Perhaps you have a list of client phone numbers, or product codes and descriptions. If you need to find all of the phone numbers in one area code, or all of the product codes that stand for printers, you probably don't want to look through the whole list and pick out the names manually. You can use the field names in your database to filter your data automatically to show only the records you need.

To do this, you select any cell in your list, and then use the AutoFilter command to turn on automatic filtering. When you filter a list automatically, you can select any cell and the entire list around the cell is selected, just like when you use the AutoSum button to total a range automatically. Then you filter the data, using field names to show only the records you need. When you have finished filtering data, you turn off automatic filtering. In the next exercises, you use the AutoFilter command to prepare your data for filtering, and then you select the criteria you want to use to filter your data.

Prepare your data for filtering

1 Select cell C10.

You could select any cell in your list to select the entire range.

2 From the Data menu, choose Filter, and then choose AutoFilter.

The range adjacent to your selected cell is assumed to be the database you want to filter. Filtering arrow buttons appear next to your column labels, similar to the following illustration.

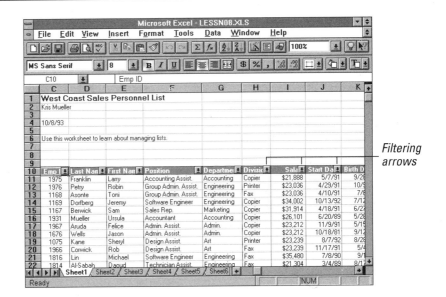

Filtering arrows

Note You might see a dialog box asking whether you want to use the top row as your heading. Choose OK to proceed.

3 Click the filter arrow in cell H10, the Division column label.

You select the division column label so that you can filter out all but one division in the list. A list of criteria drops down, showing the options that you can choose from.

There are four choices that always appear in your list of criteria. The All, Custom, Blanks, and NonBlanks options let you show all of the records, only records that meet custom criteria, all blank records, or all records that contain information. In addition to these four choices, any other word, code, or number that appears in the column you select for filtering will appear once in the criteria list. You can select any one of the standard choices or the choices from your data list to be the criterion for filtering your data.

When you select an item in the criteria list, all of the other data is filtered out of your worksheet. In the next exercises, you'll filter out all of the employees except those in the Copier division, and then all but the accounting employees in the Copier division.

Filter out everything but the Copier division

▶ From the list, select Copier.

Every row is filtered out of your database except for records in the Copier division. The other records still exist, but they are hidden for the moment. Notice that the visible row numbers from 11 to 124 are no longer continuous and that the filter arrow for the Division column appears blue on your worksheet, while the others are still black. Your worksheet should look like the following.

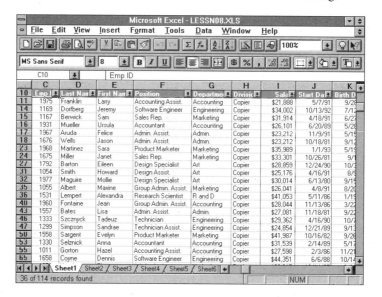

Filter out all but the accounting department in the Copier division

▶ Click the filter arrow in cell G10, and then select Accounting from the list.

The Accounting personnel in the Copier division are displayed in your worksheet.

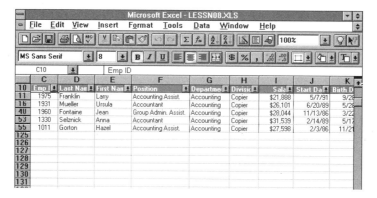

You can redisplay your data by selecting All in any columns that had filtered criteria. Or, you can use the Filter command on the Data menu and then choose Show All. In the next exercise, you restore your data to include all departments and all divisions, and then extract only the group administration assistants from your list.

Restore your data and extract all group administration assistants

1 From the Data menu, choose Filter, and then choose Show All.

All departments and divisions appear in the worksheet again.

2 Click the filter arrow in cell F10, and then select Group Admin. Assist. from the list.

Only the group administration assistants appear in your worksheet.

Finding Data Using Custom Filters

Although you can usually find the information you need by selecting a single item from a filter list, sometimes you need to find records that match a custom set of criteria. If you need to find every person in your list who started on or before November 9, 1991, for example, you can select Custom from the Start Date filter list and then place ">= 11/9/91" in the Custom AutoFilter dialog box. You use *operators* such as an equal sign (=), greater than sign (>), and less than sign (<) to determine your custom criteria. In the next exercise, you find all employees who have the title "Admin. Assist." or "Group Admin. Assist." in your data.

Find all administration assistants and group administration assistants

1 Click the filter arrow in cell F10, and then select Custom.

The Custom AutoFilter dialog box opens.

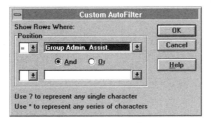

2 In the Position area, be sure that "=" is selected in the top operator box.

3 Click the down arrow next to the criteria box, and then select Admin. Assist.

4 Click the Or option button.

5 Click the down arrow next to the lower operator box, and then select "=."

6 Click the down arrow next to the lower criteria list box, and then select Group Admin. Assist.

The Custom AutoFilter dialog box should look similar to the following.

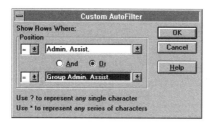

7   Choose OK.

Your data is filtered to show only administration assistants and group administration assistants.

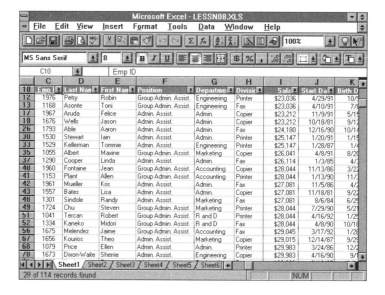

Turn off the filter

1   From the Data menu, choose Filter, and then choose Show All.

2   From the Data menu, choose Filter, and then choose AutoFilter.

The filter arrows on the column labels disappear.

Sorting Data

When you want to display or print your list of records in a particular order, you need to sort your data. Sorting works somewhat like filtering—you select the range that you want to sort, and then you use names to define how you want to sort your data. You can sort your data by any field name in the database. The field name or criteria that you use to sort by is referred to as a *sort key*. To sort a range, you can select any cell within the range, and then use the Sort command. When you choose the Sort command, the range around the active cell is automatically selected for sorting.

In the next exercise, you sort your personnel list by division, so that you first see all of the employees in the Copier division, then the Fax division, and then the Printer division.

Sort the personnel list by division

1   Select cell C10, if it is not already selected.

You can select any cell in the database to select the entire database for sorting.

2   From the Data menu, choose Sort.

The Sort dialog box opens.

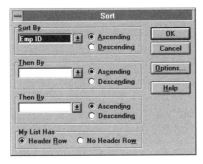

3   In the Sort By area, click the down arrow, and then select Division from the list.

Because you want all of the other fields to be sorted within the Division field, you use Division as the first sort key.

4   Be sure that the two Then By boxes are blank, and then choose OK.

Your list sorts alphabetically by division, with the Copier division first, Fax division next, and Printer division last.

Note   Unlike filtering, sorting your database moves the rows to new positions. If you do not want to rearrange your data, use the Undo Sort command from the Edit menu to restore the database to its original order.

Sometimes you might want to use more than one sorting criteria, or sort key. Your data is sorted by division, but what order is it in within the division? You can use multiple sort keys to be sure that your data displays in the correct order. You can also change the sort order to sort in *descending* order, from Z to A, rather than in *ascending* order, from A to Z. In the next exercise, you sort your data again, but this time in ascending order by division, and descending order by salary.

Sort the personnel list by division and then by salary

1 From the Data menu, choose Sort.

The Sort dialog box opens.

2 Be sure that Division is still in the Sort By box.

3 Click the down arrow next to the first Then By box, select Salary, and then select the Descending option.

4 Choose OK.

Your data is sorted first by divisions alphabetically, and then by salaries from highest to lowest salary within each division. Your worksheet should look like the following.

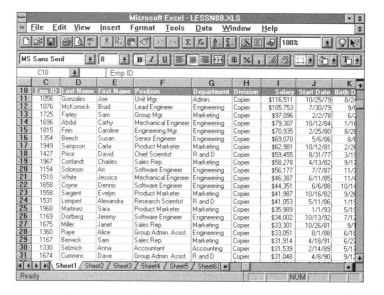

One Step Further

Although the Sort dialog box allows you to sort on only three keys, you might want to sort a long or complex list by more than three sort keys. If you need more sort keys to sort your list adequately, you can sort your data more than once. To make a sort with more than three keys successful, you need to sort by the minor categories first, and then by the major categories.

In the personnel list you've been working with in this lesson, you have columns for Last Name, Position, Division, and Department. To sort the records in the order of Division, Department, Position, and Last Name, you would need to perform two sorts. For the first sort, you would use the minor categories: Department, Position, and Last Name. Then, for the second sort, you would use the major category: Division.

By performing two sorts, you can sort by all four criteria, as long as you perform the sorts in the correct order. In other words, if you want your information to be sorted by department within each division, by position within each department, and by last name within each position, you would put Department in the Sort By box, then Position in the first Then By box, and Last Name in the second Then By box the first time you sort, and then place Division in the Sort By box for the second sort. Whatever you sort by in the second sort will take precedence over what you sort by in the first sort.

Try sorting the personnel list by Division, Department, Position, and Last Name.

Sort by Division, Department, Position, and Last Name

1   Select cell C10, and then from the Data menu, choose Sort.

The Sort dialog box opens.

2   In the Sort By area, select Department.

3   In the first Then By box, select Position, and select the Ascending option button.

4   In the second Then By box, select Last Name.

5   Choose OK.

Your data sorts alphabetically by Department, then Position, then Last Name. Your list should look similar to the following.

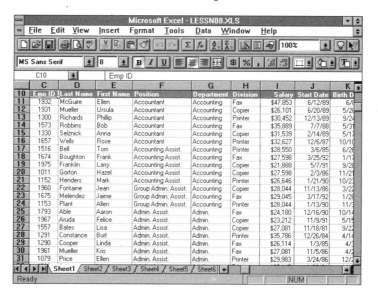

6   From the Data menu, choose Sort again.

The Sort dialog box opens.

7   In the Sort By area, select Division.

8   In the first Then By box, select (none).

9 In the second Then By box, select (none), and then choose OK.

Your data is sorted by Division, with the previously sorted Department, Position, and Last Name categories still in order under the new sort. Your list should look similar to the following.

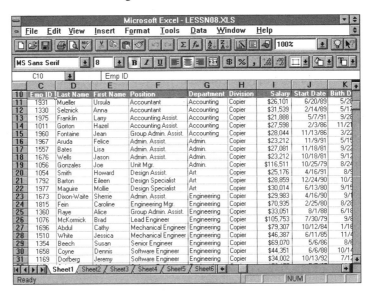

If You Want to Continue to the Next Lesson

1 From the File menu, choose Save.

2 From the File menu, choose Close.

If You Want to Quit Microsoft Excel for Now

▶ From the File menu, choose Exit.

If you see the Save dialog box, click Yes.

Lesson Summary

To	Do this
Filter data	Select any cell in your database. From the Data menu, choose Filter, and then choose AutoFilter. Use the filter arrows to choose your criteria.
Filter data using multiple criteria	From the Data menu, choose Filter, and then choose AutoFilter. Click the filter arrow and select Custom. In the Custom AutoFilter dialog box, select the operators and criteria that you want, and then choose OK.
Show all data	From the Data menu, choose Filter, and then choose Show All.
Turn off AutoFilter	From the Data menu, choose Filter, and then choose AutoFilter.
Sort data	Select any cell in your database, and then from the Data menu, choose Sort. In the Sort dialog box, select the criteria you want, and then choose OK.

For more information on	See in the *Microsoft Excel User's Guide*
Filtering lists and sorting data	Chapter 21, "Sorting and Filtering Data in a List"

Preview of the Next Lesson

In the next lesson, "Creating Reports," you'll learn how to outline your worksheet to see different levels of detail and how to consolidate your data to present an overview, rather than the detail information for a report.

Creating Reports

If you use Microsoft Excel in a business or organizational setting, you will need to share the information in your workbooks with other people. Presenting your data to others usually involves the use of a report. Microsoft Excel makes it easy to produce clear and logical reports by providing ways for you to summarize or consolidate your data. Reports rarely consist of every detail; rather, reports show an overview, a trend, or a synopsis, with supporting data in the background. In this lesson, you'll learn how to create subtotals to find the information you need when you need it, how to modify your worksheet outlines to summarize the information you want, and how to consolidate your data to produce a concise but accurate picture of it.

You will learn how to:

- Create quick summary reports.

- Outline your data to show the level of detail that you need.

- Create reports by consolidating several worksheets with similar data.

Estimated lesson time: 25 minutes

If your screen does not match the illustrations in this lesson, see the Appendix, "Matching the Exercises."

Start the lesson

1 Open 09LESSN.XLS.

2 Save the workbook as LESSN09.XLS.

3 Click the Maximize button on the document window, if it is not already maximized.

Creating Summary Reports

When you're preparing a report or organizing your data, you often need to summarize information. Whether it's a question of how many copiers were sold, how much the sales totaled, or how many products are made in a particular division, you need to add space in your worksheet for the totals and then design a formula to summarize your information. With Microsoft Excel 5, you can add subtotals automatically, without manually adding space for them or entering a formula.

You also need a way to show only as much information as is necessary in your report. Rather than showing all of the detail in your worksheet, you can determine the level of detail that will appear in your report when you use subtotals and worksheet outlining. You can show all of the information, show only subtotals and grand totals, or show only grand totals, depending on the purpose of your report.

Inserting Subtotals in a List of Data

With Microsoft Excel, you can create subtotals for your data automatically. Instead of manually inserting rows and formulas, you can use the Subtotals command to insert the rows and formulas for you.

You can create several types of subtotals. You can count the number of items in a list, add up the amounts, average the amounts or number of items, find the maximum or minimum numbers in your list, or perform more complex statistical functions, such as standard deviation. In your inventory list, for example, you could find out how much the average cost of a copier is, or how many different copiers the Copier division produces.

Before you use the Subtotals command, you will usually need to sort your data to be sure that you are adding the subtotals at logical points in your worksheet. Because your inventory list is already sorted by product name, you won't need to sort your data for this exercise. In the next exercise, you create subtotals on the Copier Inventory sheet to see the total cost for each type of copier.

Show the total cost for each type of copier

1   Click the Copier Inventory sheet tab, and then select cell C9.

You can select any cell in your database, just as when you sort or filter your data.

2   From the Data menu, choose Subtotals.

The Subtotal dialog box opens.

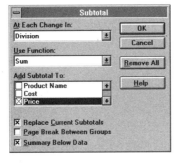

3   Click the down arrow next to the At Each Change In box, and select Product Name.

This provides a subtotal for each type of copier.

4   In the Use Function box, be sure that Sum is selected.

5   In the Add Subtotal To box, remove any check marks in any of the category boxes, and place a check mark in the Cost check box.

You'll need to scroll through the list to see every item.

6 Choose OK.

Subtotals are added to your worksheet under the Cost heading in column F, showing the total cost for each category of copier. Your worksheet should look similar to the following.

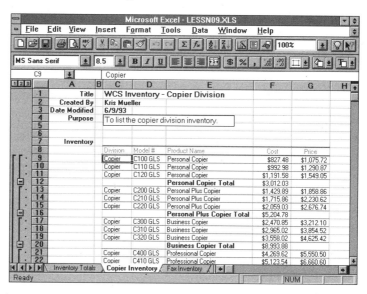

If you've just created a set of subtotals, and you decide that you don't need them after all, you can use the Remove All button in the Subtotal dialog box to remove them. In the next exercise, you'll use the Remove All button to remove the subtotals you just created in your copier inventory.

Remove the subtotals you just created

1 From the Data menu, choose Subtotals.

The Subtotal dialog box opens.

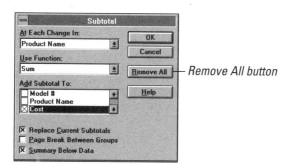

— *Remove All button*

2   In the Subtotal dialog box, click the Remove All button.

The subtotals are removed. Your worksheet should look like it did before you added subtotals.

Creating Nested Subtotals

If you are creating a more complex report that uses a lot of information from your inventory list, you can create multiple, or *nested*, subtotals to supply that information. As long as you turn off the Replace Current Subtotals check box in the Subtotal dialog box, you can create as many nested subtotals as you need.

In the following exercises, you sort the database by division, and then by product name, and then use subtotals on the Inventory Totals sheet to find out the average cost and price for each product in each division.

Sort by division and then by product name

1   Click the Inventory Totals sheet tab, and then select cell C9.

2   From the Data menu, choose Sort.

The Sort dialog box opens.

3   In the Sort By area, be sure that Division and Ascending are selected.

4   In the Then By area, select Product Name, and be sure that Ascending is selected.

5   Choose OK.

The Sort dialog box closes and your data is sorted by Division and then by Product Name.

Average the cost and price of each product

1   From the Data menu, choose Subtotals.

The Subtotal dialog box opens.

2   In the At Each Change In box, select Product Name.

3   In the Use Function box, select Average.

4   In the Add Subtotal To box, be sure that nothing is selected, and then click the Cost and Price check boxes.

5   Choose OK.

Subtotals are added to average the cost and price for each product. Your worksheet should look similar to the following.

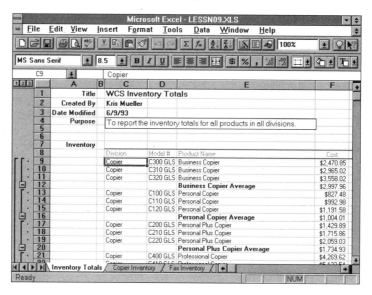

Notice that the subtotals appear in whatever columns you select in the Add Subtotal To box. When you select one or more items in this box, you are telling Microsoft Excel to subtotal the information in those columns and to place the results in the columns as well.

Average the cost and price of all products per division

1   Select cell C9, and then from the Data menu, choose Subtotals.

The Subtotal dialog box opens.

2   In the At Each Change In box, select Division.

3   In the Use Function box, be sure Average is selected.

4   In the Add Subtotal To box, be sure only the Cost and Price check boxes are selected.

5   Clear the Replace Current Subtotals check box, and then choose OK.

Subtotals are added to average the cost and price of products for each division. Your worksheet should look similar to the following.

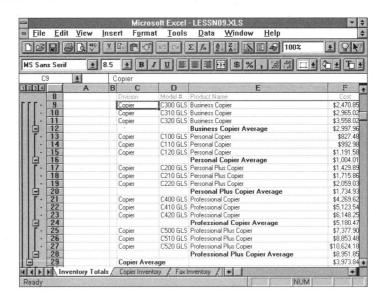

Working with Summary Report Outlining

When you create a report, you may not need to use every detail that's recorded in your worksheet, or even in your subtotals. Often, you need more of an overall or summary view of your data. You can display a wide scope of information, without minor details, by creating an outline of the worksheet.

When you created your subtotals, Microsoft Excel automatically *outlined* your worksheet. Each division and its products were grouped together, and each product name and its cost and price were grouped together, as in the preceding picture.

The lines that you see in the margin to the left and the numbers above the lines are outlining symbols that allow you to control how much detail you see in your report. In the Inventory Totals sheet, you now have four levels of outlining. You can create up to eight vertical and eight horizontal levels of outlining per worksheet. The first level is the highest level, consisting of only the grand total count of products per division and the grand total sum of products in stock over the whole year. The second level breaks it down a little more, into subtotal counts and the grand total count. The third level adds the subtotals for the stock sums, and the fourth level shows all of the details in your worksheet.

You can collapse your outline by clicking the row level symbols, the numbered buttons at the top of the outlining area. The row level symbols are numbered 1, 2, 3, and 4, to correspond with the levels of detail in your worksheet. If you want to see only the grand totals, you click the first row level button. If you want to see all details, you click the fourth row level button.

In the next exercise, you collapse your outline to show only the Cost and Price averages for each Division, and then restore it partially to show the Cost and Price averages for each product, but not the details for each individual product.

Collapse and then restore the outline to show some details

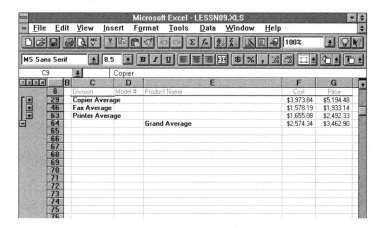

Level 2 outline

1   Locate and click the level 2 outline button.

Your worksheet changes to show only the Cost and Price averages for each Division.

2   Click the level 3 outline button.

Your worksheet changes to show the Cost and Price averages for each Product Name. Your worksheet should look similar to the following.

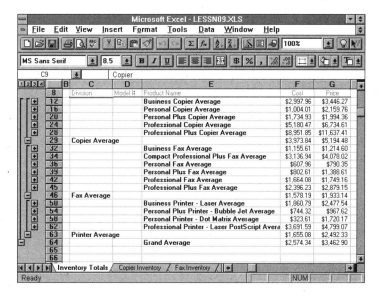

In the previous exercise, you worked with entire levels of your outline. You can also show or hide portions of a level. For example, under the Copier division, you have five copier totals. You can show all details for any one of these totals, or for all of them by using the show detail symbol. In the next exercise, you show and then hide all of the details for the Personal Plus Copier.

Show and then hide all details for the Personal Plus Copier

1 Locate and then click the show detail symbol for the Personal Plus Copier on your worksheet (the plus sign in the outlining area to the left of the Personal Plus Copier).

The details for only the Personal Plus Copier appear. The other copiers are still only shown as subtotals. Your worksheet should look like the following.

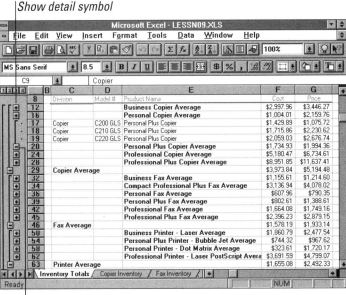

Show detail symbol

Hide detail symbol

2 Click the hide detail symbol for the Personal Plus Copier.

The Personal Plus Copier information is hidden again. Your worksheet should now show only the subtotals, with no detail information.

Outlining a Sheet Without Subtotals

If you need to create a report that shows summary information without the details, but you have a worksheet that already was summarized manually, you can still outline your worksheet with the Auto Outline command. To outline your data, you must have formulas to total your data, either below or to the right of your data. These formulas determine how many levels your outline will have, and where the divisions will be. They can also determine the orientation of your outline. When you created subtotals before, they were below your data, and so your outline was vertically oriented. If the formulas in your data are to the right of your data, the outline will be horizontal instead. In the next exercises, you use automatic outlining to turn your Fax Inventory sheet into a summary report, and then you hide some of the data.

Change your fax inventory data into a summary report

1 Switch to the Fax Inventory sheet.

2 Select cells C9:G21.

These cells contain the cost and price information for each of the products in the Fax division.

3 From the Data menu, choose Group And Outline, and then choose Auto Outline.

Your data is outlined in three levels. You can manipulate this worksheet to show as much or as little data as you need to, just like the Inventory Totals worksheet. Your worksheet should look similar to the following.

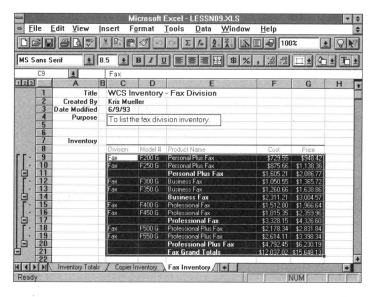

Hide data in the Fax Inventory outline

1 Click the hide detail button immediately to the left of the Fax Grand Totals row.

All of the individual product data is hidden. Only the Fax Grand Totals are visible, as in the following illustration.

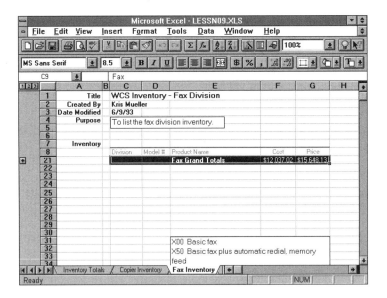

2   Click the show detail button next to the Fax Grand Totals row.

Microsoft Excel displays all of the detail data again.

Removing Worksheet Outlining

If you do not want to use the outlining that has been applied to an existing worksheet, or you changed your mind about the outlining that you created, you can remove the outlining. To do so, you select a cell within the range that was outlined, and then use the Clear Outline command to remove the outlining. You can also use this command to remove the outlining from a subtotaled list. When you clear the outline in a subtotaled list, only the outlining symbols are removed; the subtotals remain.

In the next exercise, you'll use the Clear Outline command to remove your outlining from the Fax Inventory sheet. You'll also remove the subtotals to prepare for the exercises on consolidating data.

Remove the outlining and subtotals from the Fax Inventory sheet

1   Select cell G9.

You can select any cell within the outlined range to remove the outlining.

2   From the Data menu, choose Group And Outline, and then choose Clear Outline.

The outline and all of the outlining symbols are removed.

3   Hold down CTRL, select rows 11, 14, 17, 20, and 21, and then press DEL.

You must remove the subtotals so they are not added into the consolidated report.

Creating Consolidated Reports

Suppose you have three sheets of inventory data and you need to produce a report that summarizes all of them. You already saw how you can place all of the data in one sheet and then use subtotals and outlining to create a report in which you can show or hide levels of detail. Another way to create a report is to *consolidate* all of the data onto one sheet, summarizing as you go. Consolidating pulls all of the detail data together from separate sheets or separate ranges, summarizes the information, and then places the summary onto a sheet that you specify.

When you consolidate data, you need to select a summary destination, a function (such as Sum) to use in consolidating the data, and the detail data that you want to consolidate. The destination can be another sheet or another workbook. The function you use depends on the type of data and the type of report that you are creating. For the inventory data, you would want to use Sum to summarize the inventory totals. You can consolidate data from other sheets or from another workbook. When you consolidate data, however, you need to be sure that the data on each sheet has the same column and/or row headings. Otherwise, you will end up with a list of details, rather than the summary you want. In this case, you'll take the data from the three division sheets in the inventory workbook.

In the next three exercises, you'll select a destination for your consolidated inventory and select a function for your consolidation, select the data that you want to consolidate, and then add labels and finish consolidating all of your inventory data onto one sheet.

Select a destination and a consolidating function

1 Switch to the Inventory Report sheet.

This sheet is mostly-blank, ready for you to add the consolidated data from the Printer sheet.

2 Select cell C8, and then from the Data menu, choose Consolidate.

The Consolidate dialog box opens.

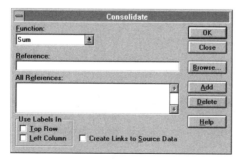

3 In the Function box, be sure that Sum is selected.

Select information to consolidate

1   Click in the Reference text box, and then click the Printer Inventory sheet tab.

2   Drag the Consolidate dialog box out of the way, and then drag to select cells E8:G20.

   The sheet name is placed in the Reference text box. Cells E8:G20 contain all of the printer inventory data and the row of headings.

3   Click the Add button.

4   Click the Fax Inventory sheet tab.

5   On the Fax Inventory sheet, drag to select cells E8:G19.

6   Click the Add button.

7   Click the Copier Inventory sheet tab.

8   On the Copier Inventory sheet, drag to select cells E8:G23.

   These cells contain all of the Copier Inventory data and the row of headings.

9   Click the Add button.

   The three consolidation ranges appear in the dialog box. Your dialog box should look similar to the following.

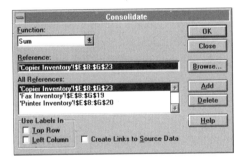

Add labels and finish consolidating the inventory data

1   In the Use Labels In area, select both check boxes.

   You want to use the labels in both the top row and left column of your data.

2   Choose OK.

   The Consolidate dialog box closes and your printer, copier, and fax data is consolidated on your worksheet. You might need to adjust the column widths before you can see all of your data. Your Inventory Report sheet should look similar to the following.

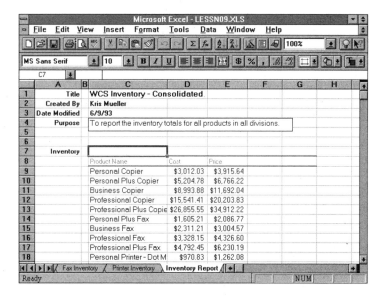

One Step Further

If you find that you would prefer to show the items in a subtotaled list in a different order, ascending instead of descending order, for example, you can sort your list. To sort a subtotaled list, you simply hide the detail rows, and then sort the subtotal rows. When you sort a subtotaled list, the hidden detail rows are automatically moved with the subtotal rows.

Important   If you do not hide the detail rows before sorting a subtotaled list, your subtotals will be removed and all of the rows in your list will be reordered.

Try sorting the subtotaled data in your Inventory Totals sheet by Division in descending order.

Sort a subtotaled list

1   Switch to the Inventory Totals sheet, and select cell C8.

2   Click the level 2 outline symbol in the outlining area to hide all but the Division subtotal rows.

3   From the Data menu, choose Sort.

The Sort dialog box opens.

4   In the Sort By box, select Division, and then select Descending.

5   Click OK.

If You Want to Continue to the Next Lesson

1 From the File menu, choose Save.

2 From the File menu, choose Close.

If You Want to Quit Microsoft Excel for Now

▶ From the File menu, choose Exit.

 If you see the Save dialog box, click Yes.

Lesson Summary

To	Do this
Add subtotals	Click in any cell in your database. From the Data menu, choose Subtotals. In the At Each Change In box, select which category you want to subtotal. In the Use Function box, select a formula. In the Add Subtotal To box, select the column in which you want the subtotals to appear, and then choose OK.
Remove all subtotals	From the Data menu, choose Subtotals. In the Subtotal dialog box, click the Remove All button.
Add a nested subtotal	Click in any cell in your database. From the Data menu, choose Subtotals. In the At Each Change In box, select which category you want to subtotal. In the Use Function box, select a formula. In the Add Subtotal To box, select the column in which you want the subtotals to appear. Be sure that there is no X in the Replace Current Subtotals check box, and then choose OK.

To	Do this
Collapse an outline	Click the hide detail symbol for the level that you want to collapse.
Expand an outline	Click the show detail symbol for the level that you want to expand.
Outline a worksheet	Select the range that you want to outline. From the Data menu, choose Group And Outline, and then choose Auto Outline.
Remove an outline	Select any cell in the range that is outlined. From the Data menu, choose Group And Outline, and then choose Clear Outline.
Consolidate data from several sheets	Select a destination sheet. From the Data menu, choose Consolidate. In the Function box, select a function. Click in the Reference text box and then drag to select the first range that you want to consolidate. Click the Add button and continue selecting and adding ranges until you have selected all of the ranges. Choose OK.

For more information on	See in the *Microsoft Excel User's Guide*
Creating subtotals	Chapter 22, "Summarizing Data in a List"
Outlining a worksheet	Chapter 33, "Outlining a Worksheet"
Consolidating data	Chapter 26, "Consolidating Data"

Preview of the Next Lesson

In the next lesson, "Creating Customized Reports with Pivot Tables," you'll learn how to modify a special kind of summary table, called a pivot table, to create a detailed analytical report.

Creating Customized Reports with Pivot Tables

Pivot tables have replaced Crosstab tables in Microsoft Excel version 5.

When you are creating a report, you often need to view your data in different ways. Perhaps you have a list of sales by person, and you need to list sales by region. Or maybe you have a simple personnel list, and you need to see totals by department or division. Rather than creating a report with subtotals, you can use a *pivot table* to aggregate the data in your list and show only the categories you choose. Then you can decide which categories to show summaries for, and which functions to use in the summaries. Instead of the list, you can create a report in which you can add, remove, or substitute fields easily, without affecting your original data.

In this lesson, you create a simple pivot table and adjust the data that appears in the table. Then, you change how your data is summarized. You also learn how to format cells in a table and how to format the entire table automatically.

You will learn how to:

- Summarize your data with a pivot table.

- Change your data's organization without restructuring the worksheet.

- Format your data to present a professional look.

Estimated lesson time: 55 minutes

If your screen does not match the illustrations in this lesson, see the Appendix, "Matching the Exercises."

Start the lesson

1 Open 10LESSN.XLS.

2 Save the workbook as LESSN10.XLS.

3 Click the Maximize button on the document window, if it is not already maximized.

Creating a Pivot Table

Your personnel list, as it appears now, has eight database fields, represented by labels across the top of the list (Last Name, Position, and so on), and it contains several records. If you want to report subtotals only, you can use the subtotals or outlining commands to create a summary report. But, if you want to create a report that combines all of the data and shows an aggregate of only certain subsets of the data, it would be much easier to use a pivot table instead.

With a pivot table, you can take an entire list of data and show summaries for parts of the data, in any orientation that you like. With your personnel list, you could create a pivot table that shows all departments in each division, and averages the number of employees. Or your pivot table could show the maximum or minimum salaries in each division, department, and position. The possibilities in a pivot table are limited only by the type of data you are working with.

You can also easily hide certain positions, departments, or divisions within the list. When you create a pivot table, you create *pivot table fields*, fields that act as qualifiers, showing only a summary of the data that fits your criteria, not the entire contents of the database field. So, you can simply alter the Department field to contain only the Accounting department, or all but the Art department.

To create a pivot table, you simply select the database you want to use, and then use the PivotTable command on the Data menu. After you've decided which fields to include, you can decide where the pivot table will be placed in your workbook. Usually, it's best to create your pivot tables on a separate sheet in your workbook. You will then have enough space to work with your table without overlapping other information on a sheet.

In the next exercise, you'll use the data in your personnel list to create a pivot table that shows the totals for salaries by position in each department.

Create a pivot table from your personnel list

1 Be sure the Personnel List sheet is the active sheet, and then select cell C10.

You can select any cell in your database to use the entire database in your pivot table.

2 From the Data menu, choose PivotTable.

The PivotTable Wizard opens.

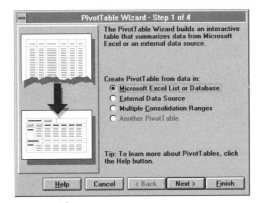

3 Click the Next button.

Step 2 of the PivotTable Wizard appears, with your database area already entered in the Range box.

4   Choose the Next button.

Step 3 of the PivotTable Wizard appears, ready for you to design your table.

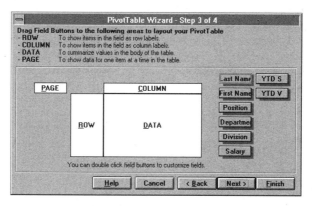

5   Drag the Position button from the right side of the dialog box into the Row area.

Moving the Position button into the Row area means that each position will be listed in a separate row in your pivot table.

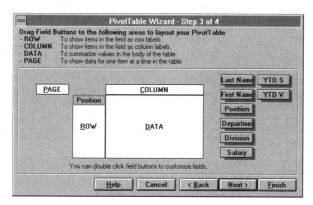

6   Drag the Division button from the right side of the dialog box into the Column area.

Each division will appear in a separate column in your pivot table.

7   Drag the Salary button from the right side of the dialog box into the Data area.

Notice that the Salary button changes to read "Sum Of Salary." The salaries for each position in each department will be summarized in the data area of your pivot table. Your prototype table should look like the following.

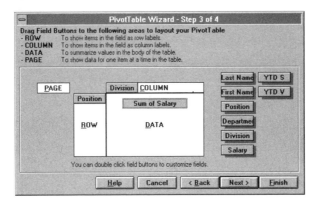

8 Click the Next button.

Step 4 of the PivotTable Wizard appears.

9 Click in the PivotTable Starting Cell box, click the Personnel Report sheet tab, and then select cell C8.

You might need to move the dialog box out of the way to select cell C8.

10 In the PivotTable Options area, be sure that all of the options, including the Grand Totals For Columns and Grand Totals For Rows options are selected, and then click the Finish button.

The pivot table appears on your Personnel Report sheet, starting in cell C8. Notice that the Query And Pivot toolbar opens so that you can make changes to your table. Your worksheet should look similar to the following.

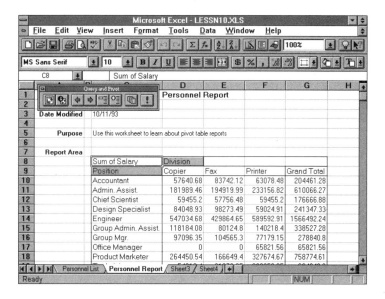

Modifying a Pivot Table

The first time you create a pivot table for a report, you might not always be certain which data you will need. Pivot tables make it easy to modify the data you've included. If you were creating a worksheet by hand, you would have to do a lot more restructuring and probably a lot of data entry to rearrange, add, or remove data. The Query And Pivot toolbar includes tools that you can use to modify your pivot table without using any menu commands.

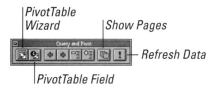

With the PivotTable Wizard and PivotTable Field buttons, you can modify either your entire table or only a specific field. With the Show Pages button, you can separate your data onto different pages according to which field you select. You can use the Refresh Data button to update your pivot table if the *source data*, the data in your original list, changes. You can also use the shortcut menu to modify the pivot table, add data, or refresh the data in your pivot table. You'll use the buttons on the Query And Pivot toolbar and the shortcut menu in the next section to modify the pivot table you just created.

With the PivotTable Wizard and the shortcut menu, you can quickly add or remove data from your table. Any data that appears in your original worksheet is available to use in your pivot table, even if it does not currently appear in the pivot table itself.

Adding Data

The pivot table in the LESSN10.XLS file already has one column header, one row header, and one formula to total the salaries for each position in each department. In the next exercise, you'll add another data field to your pivot table to summarize how much sick leave is available to all of the people in each position in each department.

Add sick leave summaries to your pivot table

1 Select cell D10 and then click the right mouse button.

Since you want to add a new data field to your pivot table, you need to select a cell in the data area. The shortcut menu appears.

2 In the shortcut menu, choose Add Data Field, and then choose YTD S.

YTD S stands for year-to-date sick leave. The Sum Of YTD S data field is added to your pivot table.

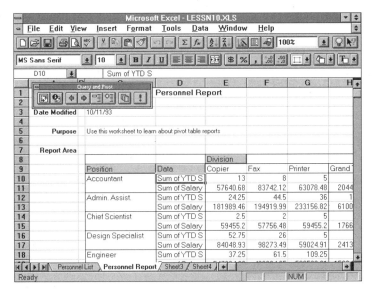

Note   You can also add data from another database application using the Microsoft Query tool. For more information about using data from another database application in a pivot table, refer to *Querying Databases with Microsoft Excel.*

You can easily add data to your table or rearrange it. If you have more than one column or row header, you can drag it to another position on your worksheet without using the PivotTable Wizard. Of course, you can always use the PivotTable Wizard to move your data around. If you have a large table and you need to divide it into segments, you can use the Page orientation in the PivotTable Wizard. When you change a field to the Page orientation, you separate each item in that field onto a different page in your report. These pages are not separate sheets in your workbook, but separate views of your pivot table. In the next exercises, you'll add the Department field to the Page area of your table. You'll view the different departments, and then move the Department field to a row orientation.

Place departments on separate pages

PivotTable Wizard

1   Select cell C8, and then click the PivotTable Wizard button on the Query And Pivot toolbar.

You could also use the PivotTable command on the shortcut menu. The PivotTable Wizard opens, ready for you to make changes to the organization of your table.

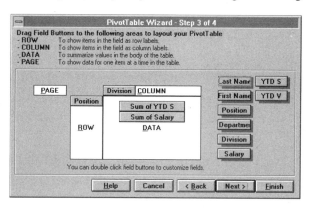

2   Drag the Department field button into the Page area in the PivotTable Wizard.

The Department field button appears in the Page area. When you change something to a Page orientation, the pivot table displays only one category from that field in your pivot table at a time. You can view the other items in the field by selecting them in a list, but you will not see them all at the same time. The dialog box should look similar to the following illustration.

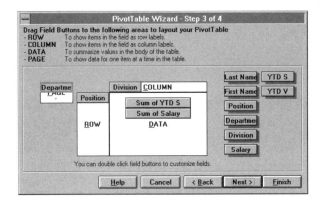

3 In the PivotTable Wizard, click the Finish button.

The PivotTable Wizard closes and the Department field appears in a Page orientation in your table.

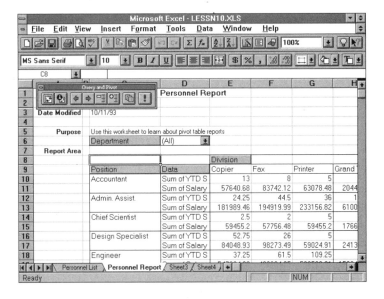

View different departments

1 Click the down arrow next to the Department name.

The Department list opens.

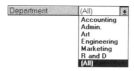

2 In the list, select Engineering.

The pivot table changes to show the Sum Of Salary and Sum Of YTD S for the Engineering department by position in each division.

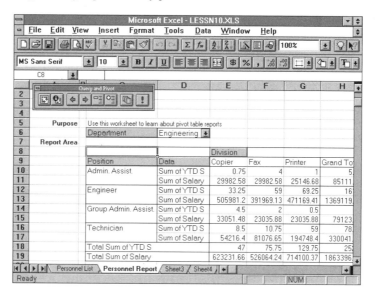

3 Click the down arrow next to the Department name.

The Department list opens again.

4 In the Department list, select (All).

The pivot table changes to show the summaries for all departments by position in each division. Your worksheet should look similar to the following.

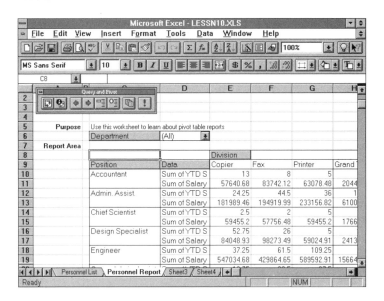

5 Click the down arrow next to the Department name.

The Department list opens again.

6 In the Department list, select Accounting.

The pivot table changes to show the summaries for the Accounting department by position in each division, as it did at the beginning of this exercise.

Change the department field to a row header

1 On your Personnel Report sheet, drag the Department button downward just above and to the left of the Position button.

Notice that when you click and drag in the Page area, your mouse pointer changes to look like a pointer dragging three pages.

After you drag in the row area, the pointer changes to look like a pointer dragging two row headers with details to the right of them.

2   Release the mouse button.

The Department button moves from the Page area to a row header. It now appears in the column before the Position field. Now, each department is listed in a row with the different positions listed below. Your pivot table should look similar to the following.

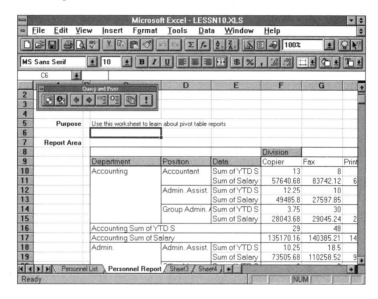

Hiding, Showing, and Removing Data

Removing data from your pivot table is even easier than adding data. Don't worry about removing data from your table permanently; you can always add it back. You will not lose information if you remove a field from your pivot table. If you want the data to remain in your table, but you don't want it to be visible, you can hide it. You can also hide details under a particular row or column heading. You can hide or show data with the PivotTable Field dialog box. In the next exercise you'll hide the details under the Accounting department, so that instead of seeing each position, you'll see a summary of all of the positions in that department.

Hide the Accounting department details

▶   Double-click cell C10.

Cell C10 contains the Accounting label. The positions in the Accounting department disappear, and are replaced by a summary total as in the following illustration.

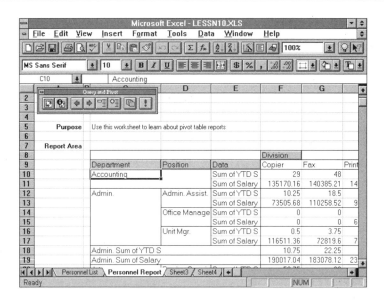

If you are working with sensitive data, such as a personnel list, you might want to hide certain information in your table, without actually deleting it from your worksheet. In the next exercise, you'll move the Department button back to a Page orientation, and then hide all but the Engineering and R and D department information.

Hide the accounting, admin., art, and marketing data

1   Drag the Department button back to cell C6.

The Department field is changed to a Page orientation, rather than a Row orientation.

2   Click the down arrow next to the Department button, and select (All) from the list if it is not already selected.

The list of departments appears. Note that all three divisions are showing.

3   Double-click the Department button itself.

The PivotTable Field dialog box opens.

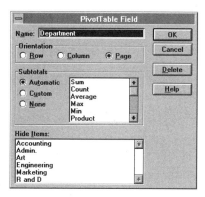

4   In the Hide Items list, select Accounting, Admin., Art, and Marketing, and then choose OK.

5   Click the down arrow next to the Department button.

The list of divisions now shows only Engineering and R and D.

Show all departments again

1   Double-click the Department button.

The PivotTable Field dialog box opens.

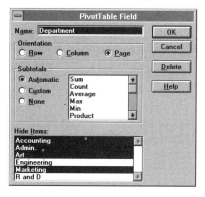

2   In the Hide Items box, click Accounting, Admin., Art, and Marketing to show them again.

3   Choose OK.

All departments are visible in your table again. Your pivot table should look similar to the following.

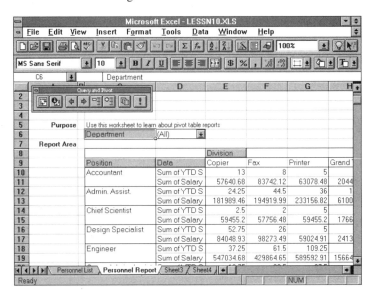

If you need to see the details that are used in the summaries for each data field, you can pull out the information used in a specific data field. To see the detail data, you simply double-click the data field, and a new sheet will open with the detail information on it. The information will be a copy of the original database information, but without the other data from the database. In the next exercise, you'll view the detail information that makes up the total of the salaries for all engineers in the Copier division.

Show all details for the total of engineers' salaries in your table

▶   Double-click cell E19.

A new sheet appears, with the detail engineers' salary information from your database listed.

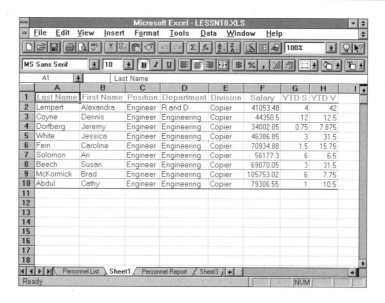

One of the advantages to working with pivot tables is that you can add or remove data from the pivot table without affecting the original database information. If you decide that you don't need to see a particular data field, you can simply remove it from your pivot table. You can always add the information back later, if you decide that it's necessary after all. In the next exercise, you'll remove the year-to-date sick leave data from your pivot table.

Remove sick leave data from your pivot table

1   Switch to the Personnel Report sheet.

2   Select cell D10, and then click the right mouse button.

The shortcut menu appears.

3   From the shortcut menu, choose PivotTable.

The PivotTable Wizard opens to Step 3 so that you can modify your pivot table.

4   Drag the Sum Of YTD S button out of the pivot table area.

The Sum Of YTD S field is removed from the Data area.

5   In the PivotTable Wizard, click the Finish button.

The PivotTable Wizard closes and the YTD S data is removed from the table. Your table should look similar to the following.

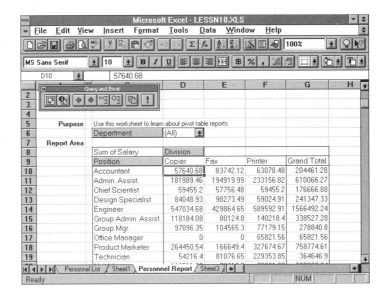

Changing Summary Functions

So far you've seen only two functions used in your pivot table: Sum and Count. You can use several other functions depending on the type of data you are using. For number data, the default function is Sum, but you can also use Average, Max, Min, and other functions that apply to your data. For text data, the default function is Count, but again, you can change the function as necessary. In the next exercise, you'll add year-to-date vacation time summaries to the Data area, and then change the summary functions from Sum to Max and Min to see the maximum and minimum amounts of vacation time for each position in each division.

Change summary functions

1 Select cell D10, and then click the right mouse button.

The shortcut menu appears.

2 From the shortcut menu, choose Add Data Field, and then choose YTD V.

The Sum Of YTD V data field appears in your pivot table.

3 Click cell D10, the Sum Of YTD V field, and then click the right mouse button.

The shortcut menu appears again.

4 From the shortcut menu, choose PivotTable Field.

The PivotTable Field dialog box opens.

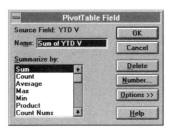

5   In the Summarize By list, select Max, and then choose OK.

The PivotTable Field dialog box closes and the YTD V description changes to
"Max Of YTD V."

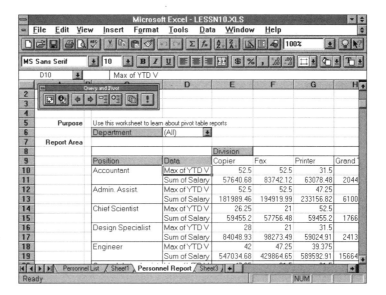

Show the minimum values for year-to-date vacation time

1   Select cell D10, and then click the right mouse button.

The shortcut menu appears.

2   From the shortcut menu, choose Add Data Field, and then choose YTD V.

The Sum Of YTD V data field appears in your pivot table, just below the Max Of
YTD V.

3   Select cell D11, and then click the right mouse button.

The shortcut menu appears.

4   From the shortcut menu, choose PivotTable Field.

The PivotTable Field dialog box opens again.

5 In the Summarize By list, select Min, and then choose OK.

The Sum Of YTD V field is replaced by the Min Of YTD V field. Now both the minimum and maximum values for year-to-date vacation time appear in your pivot table. Your table should look similar to the following.

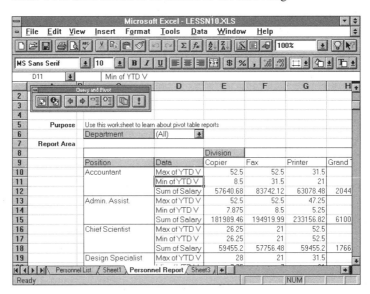

Removing Grand Totals

When you created your pivot table, you decided to add grand totals to both the rows and columns in your pivot table. These grand totals make it easy to see the summaries for your entire data. But if you only need to see the row or column totals, or perhaps you don't need to see the grand totals at all, you can easily remove the totals with the PivotTable Wizard. In the next exercise, you'll use the PivotTable Wizard to remove the grand totals from both the rows and the columns of your pivot table.

Remove the grand totals from your pivot table

1 Select cell C8, and then click the right mouse button to open the shortcut menu.

2 From the shortcut menu, choose PivotTable.

The PivotTable Wizard appears with Step 3 active.

3 Click the Next button.

Step 4 of the PivotTable Wizard appears.

4 In the PivotTable Options box, clear the Grand Totals For Columns and Grand Totals For Rows options.

5 Click the Finish button.

The grand totals are removed from your pivot table. Your table should look similar to the following.

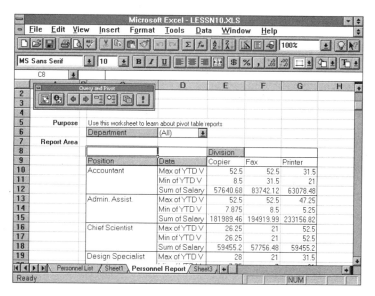

Formatting Your Pivot Table Report

When you have finished setting up your pivot table and are ready to include it in a report, you might want to add number formatting or colors, or other types of formatting. You want the report to make sense and to be interesting to look at. You can format your tables automatically, just as you can any other data in a worksheet, with the AutoFormat command. When you want to automatically format a pivot table, however, you don't have to select the entire range you want to format. If you select only one cell in the pivot table, the entire table will be automatically selected and formatted. You can also apply number formats to make currency figures look like currency, or percentages look like percentages. You can format your data fields with the PivotTable Field command. In the next exercises, you format your entire table automatically, and then format your data fields individually.

Format your pivot tables

1 Select cell C10.

2 From the Format menu, choose AutoFormat.

The AutoFormat dialog box opens.

3 In the Table Format list, select Classic 2, and then choose OK.

Your pivot table is formatted with purple column headers and light gray row headers. It should look similar to the following.

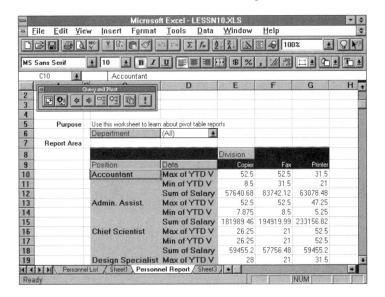

Format the numbers

1 Select cell E12.

You will format only the Sum Of Salary data for now.

2 Click the right mouse button to open the shortcut menu.

3 From the shortcut menu, choose PivotTable Field.

The PivotTable Field dialog box opens.

4 In the PivotTable Field dialog box, click the Number button.

The Format Cells dialog box opens.

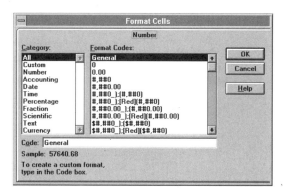

5 In the Category list, select Currency, and then select the $#,##0.00_);($#,##0.00) format.

6 Choose OK, and then choose OK again.

All of the data in the Sum Of Salary field changes to be formatted as currency.

If you change some of the data on your worksheet after you've created your pivot table, you can easily update, or *refresh*, the data in your table. In the next exercise, you'll change some data on your personnel list and then refresh your pivot table.

Refresh your data

1 Switch to the Personnel List sheet.

2 Select cell E11, the cell that contains Larry Franklin's position.

3 In cell E11, type **Accountant** and press ENTER.

4 In cell H11, the cell that contains Larry Franklin's salary, type **28800** and press ENTER.

5 Switch to the Personnel Report sheet.

6 On the Query And Pivot toolbar, click the Refresh Data button.

Your data is refreshed. Your table should look similar to the following.

Refresh Data

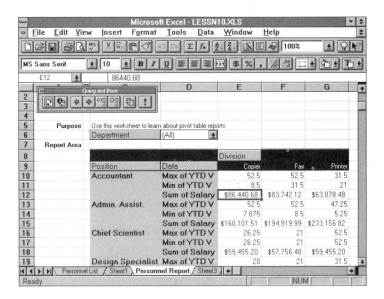

One Step Further

Just as you can chart data on any worksheet, you can chart the data in your pivot tables to enhance your reports. When you work with charts and pivot tables, however, you need to be careful about how much information you put into the table. You should probably limit your pivot table to no more than two rows and two columns of fields for a successful chart. If you have more than that, your chart might become difficult to understand. You also need to remove any grand totals or subtotals (besides the summary functions in the data area) from your pivot table before charting the data. If you leave the grand totals or subtotals intact, your chart will not reflect the actual relationships between the data; rather, it will show the relationship between the data and the grand totals or subtotals.

Note In this exercise, you create a chart from a pivot table with only one data field. To create a chart from a multiple-level pivot table, you still need to remove the totals, but you don't need to remove data from your table. For more information about multiple-level pivot tables, refer to the *Microsoft Excel User's Guide*, Chapter 24, "Creating a Pivot Table."

You've already removed the grand totals from your pivot table, but you need to remove the year-to-date vacation summaries before you are ready to chart the remaining data. Try removing the two YTD fields, and then create a 3-D bar chart to show the total salaries for each position by division on a separate sheet.

Remove the YTD V fields

1 Click cell D12, and then click the right mouse button to open the shortcut menu.

2 From the shortcut menu, choose PivotTable.

Step 3 of the PivotTable Wizard appears.

3 Drag Max Of YTD V and Min Of YTD V out of the pivot table area.

4 Click the Finish button.

The pivot table now displays only the Sum Of Salary field.

Chart a pivot table

1 Drag to select C8:F20.

This range includes the headings and the data for the pivot table, except for the Department button. Since your pivot table already shows all departments, you don't need to include the department information in your selection.

2 From the Insert menu, choose Chart, and then choose As New Sheet.

The ChartWizard opens.

3 Click the Next button.

4 In Step 2, select the 3-D Bar chart type, and then click the Next button.

5 Click the Next button.

6 Click the Finish button.

A new chart sheet opens with a 3-D bar chart showing the total salaries for each position in each division for each department. Your chart should look similar to the following.

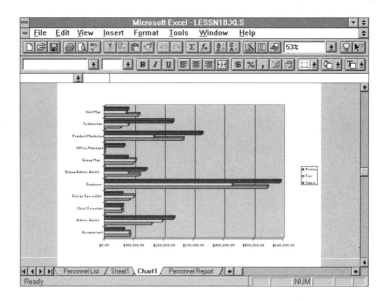

If You Want to Continue to the Next Lesson

1 From the File menu, choose Save.

2 From the File menu, choose Close.

If You Want to Quit Microsoft Excel for Now

▶ From the File menu, choose Exit.

If you see the Save dialog box, click Yes.

Lesson Summary

To	Do this	Button
Create a pivot table	Select a cell or a range for your pivot table. From the Data menu, choose PivotTable. In the PivotTable Wizard, click the Next button. Drag to select the range that contains the data for your pivot table, and then click the Next button. Drag the fields you want to the Row, Column, and Data areas of the table. Click the Next button and be sure that Grand Totals For Rows and Grand Totals For Columns are selected. Click the Finish button.	

To	Do this	Button
Add data to a pivot table	Click a cell in the pivot table, and then from the shortcut menu, choose Add Data Field. Choose the data field that you want to add.	
Hide or show data in a pivot table	Double-click the PivotTable field that you want to change. In the PivotTable Field dialog box, select the items that you want to hide, or select hidden items to show again, and then choose OK.	
Remove data from a pivot table	Drag the field away from the pivot table area.	
Move data around in a pivot table	Click the PivotTable Wizard button on the Query And Pivot toolbar, or from the shortcut menu, choose PivotTable. Drag the fields you want into the positions you want in the PivotTable Wizard. Click the Finish button.	
Change summary functions	Select the data field that you want to change. From the shortcut menu, choose PivotTable Field. In the PivotTable Field dialog box, select the summary function that you want, and then choose OK.	
Remove grand totals	Select a cell in the pivot table, and then from the shortcut menu, choose PivotTable. Click the Next button to move to step 4 of the PivotTable Wizard. In the PivotTable Options box, clear the Grand Totals For Columns and Grand Totals For Rows options. Click the Finish button.	
Format a pivot table automatically	Select a cell in the pivot table, and then from the Format menu, choose AutoFormat. Select a format, and then choose OK.	
Format numbers in a pivot table	Double-click the data field that contains the numbers that you want to format. From the shortcut menu, choose PivotTable Field. In the PivotTable Field dialog box, click the Number button. In the Format Cells dialog box, select the number format that you want, and then choose OK. Choose OK again to close the PivotTable Field dialog box.	

For more information on	See in the *Microsoft Excel User's Guide*
Creating a pivot table	Chapter 24, "Creating a Pivot Table"
Modifying a pivot table	Chapter 25, "Customizing a Pivot Table"
Formatting a pivot table	Chapter 25, "Customizing a Pivot Table"

Preview of the Next Lessons

In Part 4, you'll learn how to analyze data by looking at alternative outcomes, and to link data both within workbooks and between different applications. In the next lesson, "Comparing Alternatives," you'll learn how to process your data with analytical functions. You'll also learn how to do some forecasting with your data, find a specific value with the Goal Seek command, and look at various alternatives.

Review & Practice

In the lessons in Part 3, "Managing Your Data," you learned skills to help you sort and manage lists of data; organize your workbooks; and create reports with worksheet outlining, consolidation, and pivot tables. If you want to practice these skills and test your understanding before you proceed with the lessons in Part 4, you can work through the Review & Practice section following this lesson.

Part 3   Review & Practice

Before you move on to Part 4, which covers analyzing and sharing your data, you can practice the skills you learned in Part 3 by working through the steps in this Review & Practice section. You will organize your workbook, sort and filter the data, and add subtotals and modify a pivot table.

Scenario

The Copier division keeps a sales journal that lists each product marketer and how many sales he or she has made during the last week. You need to create a report that shows the total amount and total quantities that each product marketer sold. Different members of the department have already worked on the files, but you've just been assigned to the sales report as part of your regular duties. First, you'll organize the workbooks that are used in generating the report, so that all of the information is in one place. Then you'll create two versions of the report, so you can offer more than one format to the product managers.

You will review and practice how to:

- Copy and move sheets to make your workbooks more manageable.

- Document your work with cell notes, text boxes, and summary information.

- Sort data by specific criteria.

- View only the data that you need with automatic filtering.

- Create quick summary reports with subtotals.

- Change your data's organization without restructuring the worksheet.

Estimated practice time: 20 minutes

Step 1: Open Files and Organize Your Workbook

Open the two workbooks that contain your copier sales journal data, and then copy the totals sheet into the main file. Also, add a note to explain the C/N code, which could be confusing to other users.

1 Open the file P3REVIEW.XLS, and save it as REVIEWP3.XLS.

2 Open the file P3REVWA.XLS, and save it as REVWP3A.XLS.

3 Use the Move Or Copy Sheet command on the Edit menu to copy the Copier Sales Total sheet from REVWP3A.XLS to REVIEWP3.XLS. Place the sheet before the first sheet in the REVIEWP3.XLS workbook.

4   On the Copier Data sheet, use the Note command on the Insert menu to add a note in the C/N column heading cell that reads **The C/N code stands for Client/New Contact**.

For more information on	See
Moving and copying sheets	Lesson 7
Adding notes to explain data	Lesson 7

Step 2: Filter and Sort the Data on Your Data Sheet

You need to tell someone how many Air orders there are, so you'll first filter the data to do a quick check. Then, you'll remove the filters so you can continue to create your report. The data needs to be sorted by last name, to keep each product marketer's orders separate, and then you need to track whether the order is for a current or new client.

1   Use the AutoFilter command to filter out all of the data except the orders to be shipped by Air.

2   Use the AutoFilter command again to turn off the filters.

3   Use the Sort command to sort the data first by the product marketer's name, then by C/N.

For more information on	See
Filtering your data	Lesson 8
Sorting your data	Lesson 8

Step 3: Summarize Your Data with Subtotals

Your report needs to include the quantity of products each product marketer sold, and the amount he or she sold them for. You'll use subtotals to show the total amount and total number of products sold by each product marketer.

1   Use the Subtotal command to add subtotals to the Quantity and Amount columns.

2   Adjust the column widths as necessary to show all of your data.

3   Format the list using the List 3 format and automatic formatting.

Your sheet should look similar to the following.

```
┌─────────────────────────────────────────────────────────────────────────────┐
│ ─                    Microsoft Excel - REVIEWP3.XLS                    ▼ ▲│
│ ─  File  Edit  View  Insert  Format  Tools  Data  Window  Help          ▲│
├─────────────────────────────────────────────────────────────────────────────┤
│ □ ☞ ⊞ ⊜ ▣ ✓  ✗ ⓑ ⓒ ✎  ⬡ ⬠  Σ ƒ  ⬆ ⬇  ⬡ ⊞ ⧉ 100%        ⬇ ⬓▶│
├─────────────────────────────────────────────────────────────────────────────┤
│ MS Sans Serif      ⬇ 10  ⬇  B I U  ☰ ☰ ☰ ⊞  $ % , ⬚ ⬚  ⬚ ⬇ ⬚ ⬇ ⬚ ⬇│
├─────────────────────────────────────────────────────────────────────────────┤
│   E7        ⬇       C/N                                                      │
├─────────────────────────────────────────────────────────────────────────────┤
│ ⬚⬚⬚  B│     C      │  D    │ E │  F      │   G     │   H     │   I    │  J  ▲│
├─────────────────────────────────────────────────────────────────────────────┤
│     7 │Product Marke│Company│C/N│Product #│ Quantity│  Price  │ Amount │Ship E│
│ ┌  8 │Cane, Nate   │ 261   │ C │C230 GLS │       1 │$4,620.80│$4,620.80│Air  │
│ │· 9 │Cane, Nate   │ 341   │ C │C400 GLS │       1 │$5,544.96│$5,544.96│Ground│
│ │·10 │Cane, Nate   │ 195   │ C │C110 GLS │       2 │$1,289.58│$2,579.16│Air  │
│ │·11 │Cane, Nate   │ 362   │ N │C520 GLS │       1 │$13,797.63│$13,797.63│Ground│
│ ⊟ 12 │Cane, Nate Total│    │   │         │       5 │         │$26,542.55│     │
│ ┌ 13 │Morton, Sara │ 341   │ C │C320 GLS │       1 │$4,620.80│$4,620.80│Ground│
│ │·14 │Morton, Sara │ 195   │ C │C100 GLS │       2 │$1,074.65│$2,149.30│Air  │
│ │·15 │Morton, Sara │ 362   │ C │C210 GLS │       1 │$1,289.58│$1,289.58│Ground│
│ │·16 │Morton, Sara │ 261   │ N │C300 GLS │       1 │$3,208.89│$3,208.89│Air  │
│ │·17 │Morton, Sara │ 261   │ N │C300 GLS │       1 │$3,208.89│$3,208.89│Air  │
│ │·18 │Morton, Sara │ 341   │ N │C500 GLS │       1 │$9,581.69│$9,581.69│Air  │
│ ⊟ 19 │Morton, Sara Total│  │   │         │       7 │         │$24,059.15│     │
│ ┌ 20 │Sammler, Mark│ 362   │ C │C310 GLS │       1 │$3,850.67│$3,850.67│Ground│
│ │·21 │Sammler, Mark│ 261   │ C │C400 GLS │       1 │$5,544.96│$5,544.96│Air  │
│ │·22 │Sammler, Mark│ 341   │ C │C100 GLS │       1 │$1,074.65│$1,074.65│Air  │
│ │·23 │Sammler, Mark│ 195   │ N │C120 GLS │       3 │$1,547.50│$4,642.50│Ground│
│ │·24 │Sammler, Mark│ 362   │ N │C520 GLS │       1 │$13,797.63│$13,797.63│Ground▼│
├─────────────────────────────────────────────────────────────────────────────┤
│ ⏮◀▶⏭\ Copier Sales Total \ Copier Data / Copier Pivot /  ◀│          ▶│
├─────────────────────────────────────────────────────────────────────────────┤
│ Ready                                           │        │NUM│           │
└─────────────────────────────────────────────────────────────────────────────┘
```

For more information on	See
Creating reports with subtotals	Lesson 9

Step 4: Modify Your Pivot Table Report

The person who worked on the report before you included too much information in the pivot table. You need to switch to the Copier Pivot sheet and remove the Sum Of Price and Count Of Product # fields from the Pivot table so that only the Sum Of Quantity and Sum Of Amount fields show, echoing the data in the previous sheet. Then you need to format the entire table and the Sum Of Amount field so that they look more like the rest of the report.

1 On the Copier Pivot sheet, use the PivotTable command on the shortcut menu to modify the pivot table.

2 Remove the Sum Of Price and Count Of Product # fields.

3 Format the entire pivot table in the List 3 format with the AutoFormat command.

4 Format the numbers in the Sum Of Amount field to show as currency.

Your sheet should look similar to the following.

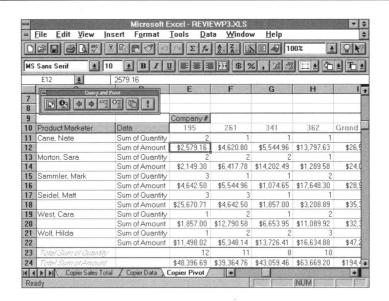

For more information on	See
Modifying pivot tables	Lesson 10

If You Want to Continue to the Next Lesson

1   From the File menu, choose Save.

2   Hold down SHIFT, and then from the File menu, choose Close All.

If You Want to Quit Microsoft Excel for Now

▶   From the File menu, choose Exit.

   If you see the Save dialog box, click Yes.

4 Analyzing and Sharing Your Data

Comparing Alternatives

As you work with your data, you might find yourself wondering "What if that payment were $50.00 less?" or "What if the interest rate changes?" or "What if the payment period is only one year instead of three?" Doing such analyses manually can be difficult and time consuming. You can carry out these "what-if" explorations easily, however, with Microsoft Excel 5. With Microsoft Excel's what-if analysis tools, you can place different input data in your worksheet formulas and compare the results. To find out how much a value must change to produce a specific result, you can use goal seeking. You can use a data table to see a list of possible values that depend on one or two changing factors. If you need to know all of the possibilities, or the entire scenario for your data, you can use Scenario Manager. In this lesson, you'll learn how to use these tools to help you find out "what happens if..."

You will learn how to:

- Find a value using goal seeking.

- Compare different solutions to an equation using a data table.

- Save different groups of values using Scenario Manager.

Estimated lesson time: 35 minutes

If your screen does not match the illustrations in this lesson, see the Appendix, "Matching the Exercises."

Start the lesson

1   Open 11LESSN.XLS.

2   Save the workbook as LESSN11.XLS.

3   Click the Maximize button on the document window, if it is not already maximized.

Seeking a Specific Goal

When you are looking for answers to what-if questions, you might want to find out what the result of a formula would be if only one variable changed. For example, you might need to find out how much sales would have to increase to reach a specific operating income goal, or how much of a down payment you would have to make to purchase a house. When you need to find a value by changing only one variable, you can use *goal seeking*. In this process, you enter your goal value, select the variable that you want to change, and then let the program find the value that will allow you to reach your goal. With goal seeking, you can test values and enter them into your worksheet when you find the ones you need.

For example, suppose you want to buy a house. In the LESSN11.XLS file, the Down Payment sheet has information about a specific house price, closing costs, a down payment, and a loan amount. The house price is set, the down payment is 10 percent of the house price, and the closing costs are 3 percent of the loan amount. The loan amount depends on the price of the home and how much the bank is willing to lend. If your loan amount is fixed, you can use goal seeking to determine the exact closing costs, down payment, and house price you can afford.

In the next exercise, you use goal seeking to find out how much the down payment, closing costs, and house price would be for a $110,000 loan.

Seek a down payment amount

1   Be sure the Down Payment sheet is the active sheet.

2   Select cell D15, and from the Tools menu, choose Goal Seek.

Cell D15 contains the formula that calculates the loan amount, =D9-D12. You'll substitute a value for this formula, and see how much the house price in cell D9 has to change to produce the new value. The Goal Seek dialog box opens.

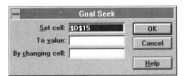

3   Click the To Value text box, and type **110000**

4   Click the By Changing Cell box, and then select cell D9.

You might need to drag the Goal Seek dialog box out of the way before you select the cell. You'll reach your goal of a $110,000 loan by changing the house price in cell D9.

5   Choose OK.

The Goal Seek Status dialog box appears, telling you that a value has been found. The value appears in cell D9 for you to preview, but it has not been entered in the cell. Notice that cells D11, D12, and D13, which depend on the value in cell D9, have changed as well. You might need to move the Goal Seek Status dialog box to see the figures. Your screen should look like the following illustration.

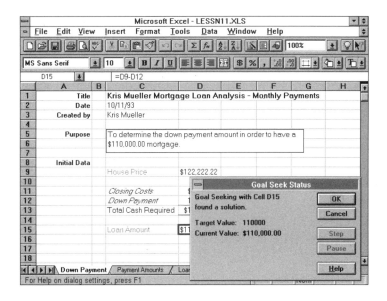

6 Choose OK.

The value is entered in cell D9, and cells D11, D12, and D13 are updated with the new values.

Note If you want to restore the original values in your sheet after seeking a goal, you can use the Undo command on the Edit menu or the Undo button, provided that you have not taken any other actions.

Looking at Alternatives with Data Tables

After you have entered formulas on your worksheet, you might want to perform what-if analyses to see a range of possible values for your formulas. *Data tables* can provide a shortcut by calculating all of the values in one operation. A data table is a range of cells that shows the results of substituting different values in one or more formulas.

Perhaps you have several possible combinations of data that you'd like to compare. For example, you might need to compare loan payments for different interest rates or for different terms. Or, you might need to compare the effect of different sales growth figures on your operating income. Rather than using goal seeking, which produces only one value, you could use a data table to compare several values. You can create data tables to list as many values as you need for one or two variables. For example, you could find out what the loan payment would be for interest rates between 6 and 9 percent, or you could see the effect of 2, 3, 4, or 5 percent sales growth on your operating income.

There are two types of data tables: *one-input tables* and *two-input tables*. With a one-input table, you enter different values for one variable and see the effect on one or more formulas. With a two-input table, you enter different values for two variables and see the effect on one formula.

Creating a One-Input Data Table

The Table command is similar to /Data Table 1 or /Data Table 2 in 1-2-3, except that data tables in Microsoft Excel are recalculated when you change the source data.

To set up a one-input data table, you list the values down a single column or across a single row. Then you create the formula that will determine the values and fill in the table. To create a data table, you use the Table command on the Data menu.

Before you can set up a data table to find values, however, you need to determine the formula you use. In this case, you want to find the actual payment amount for the loan. In the next exercise, you add a formula to your worksheet that calculates payments based on a varying interest rate, with a constant term and loan amount. You use the Function Wizard to create a formula that calculates the payments for a loan based on its interest rate, term, and present value.

Enter the formula for the data table

1   Switch to the Payment Amounts sheet, and then select cell D13.

2   Click the Function Wizard button on the toolbar.

Function Wizard

The Function Wizard dialog box opens.

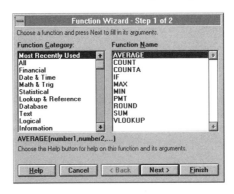

3 In the Function Category list, select Financial.

4 In the Function Name list, select PMT, and then click the Next button.

PMT is a standard function for calculating payments in loans. The next step in the Function Wizard dialog box appears.

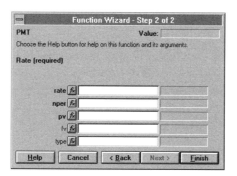

5 In the rate text box, type **$D$8/12**

The rate label refers to the monthly interest rate for the loan. Cell D8 contains the yearly percentage rate. To find the monthly percentage rate, you must divide the yearly rate by 12.

6 Click in the nper text box, and then type **$D$9**

The nper label refers to the total number of payments in your loan, or the term in cell D9.

7 Click in the pv text box, and then type **–$D$10**

The pv label refers to the present value of your loan. Since you have not made any payments, the present value of your loan (from your perspective) is negative.

8 Click the Finish button, and then press ENTER.

The PMT function is entered into cell D13 and returns the monthly payment of $922.70, based on an 8.5-percent interest rate. Your worksheet should look like the following illustration.

Interest Rate	8.50%	
Number of Months	360	
Loan Amount	$120,000.00	
	Monthly Payment	**Interest Paid**
	$922.70	
6.00%		
6.25%		
6.50%		
6.75%		
7.00%		

In this exercise, you set up a data table so that the interest rates in column C (the *input values*) are each substituted in the formula in cell D8 (the *input cell*), and the resulting monthly payments appear in the cells below the formula in cell D13. When the input values are in a column, as in this case, you enter the formula that refers to the input cell in the row above the first input value and one cell to the right of the column of input values. This is why you entered your formula in cell D13 in the previous exercise. If the input values are in a row, you enter the formula one cell below and to the left of them.

In the exercise, you create a data table with one variable to fill in the payment amounts for loans at percentages between 6 and 9 percent.

Create a one-input data table

1   Select cells C13:D26.

2   From the Data menu, choose Table.

The Table dialog box appears.

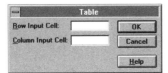

3   Place the insertion point in the Column Input Cell box, and then select cell D8.

Cell D8 contains the original interest rate.

4   Choose the OK button.

The values in cell C14:C26 are each substituted in the input cell formula and the table is filled in with the results. Your worksheet should look like the following illustration.

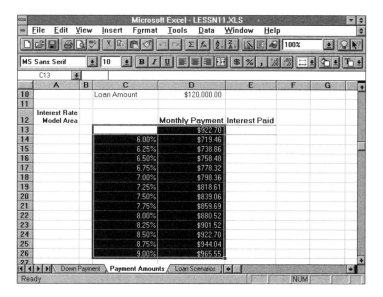

Adding Formulas to Existing Data Tables

Now that you have the data table in place, you can compare the values and make some decisions. But what if you need to find out how the different values will affect another formula? How will the different interest rates affect the overall amount of interest paid, for example? You can add a formula to a data table and see exactly how the values in the data table affect the results of the formula. In the next exercise, you add a formula to see the interest paid over the life of the loan.

Calculate the total interest paid

1 In cell E13, type =**($D$13*$D$9)–$D$10**

Cell D13 contains the monthly payment amount, cell D9 contains the total number of months, and cell D10 contains the loan principle amount. This formula calculates the total amount of interest you would pay, beyond repayment of the basic principle.

2 Click the Enter box or press ENTER.

Microsoft Excel calculates the total interest paid based on a 10-percent interest rate.

3 Select cells C13:E26.

4 From the <u>D</u>ata menu, choose <u>T</u>able.

5 Click in the Column Input Cell box, and then select cell D8.

6 Choose the OK button.

Each value in column C is substituted in the input cell, and the data table is filled in with the results of the formulas.

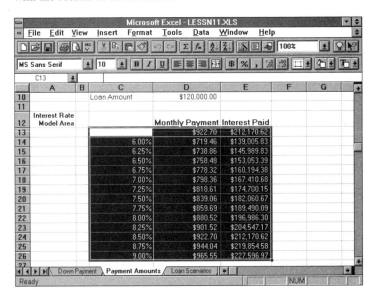

Creating a Two-Input Data Table

If you want to see how changes in two variables affect one formula, you can use a two-input data table. For example, you could see how your loan payments change depending on both the interest rate and the term of the loan. In the next exercise, you create a data table with two variables to calculate the loan payments.

Calculate loan payments based on both interest rate and term

Copy

1 Select cell D13, and then click the Copy button on the toolbar.

Because you need to use the same formula to find the payments, and because you created it with absolute values, you can save time by copying and pasting the formula into the new data table area.

Paste

2 Select cell C30, and then click the Paste button on the toolbar.

The PMT function and all of its arguments are pasted into cell C30.

To find the loan payments based on both interest rate and term, you would set up a data table so that interest rates entered in column C are substituted in one input cell (D8), and loan terms entered in row 30 are substituted in a second input cell (D9).

To create a data table with two variables, you need to put one set of values in a single column, and one set in a single row. For example, you'd place the interest rates in column C and the terms in row 30. With two variables, you can use only one formula in your data table, and you must enter the formula in the cell at the intersection of your row and column of possible values. You already placed the formula in cell C30 in the previous exercise. When you perform calculations using the Table command, the resulting monthly payments are entered in the cells below row 30 and to the right of column C.

Fill in a two-input data table

1 Select cells C30:I43.

2 From the Data menu, choose Table.

3 Be sure the insertion point is in the Row Input Cell box, and then select cell D9.

The values for the number of months are in a row. Cell D9 contains the term of the loan, or number of months.

4 Place the insertion point in the Column Input Cell box, and then select cell D8.

The values for the interest rate are in a column. Cell D8 contains the value of the interest rate.

5 Choose the OK button.

6 If necessary, scroll to display cells C29:I43.

Microsoft Excel substitutes each value in the input cells and fills in the data table with the results of the formulas. Your two-input data table should look like the following illustration.

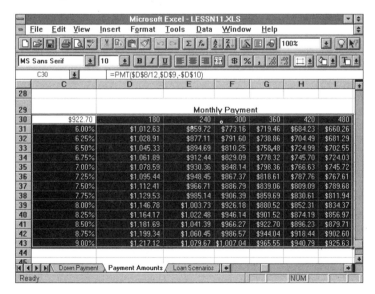

Editing and Deleting Data Tables

If you decide that the data table does not give you the information that you need, you can edit the input values or formulas in the top row or the left column of a data table. Microsoft Excel recalculates the table after you edit any cells that affect the table results. If you decide that you don't need the data table at all, you can delete the entire table. In the next exercises, you change the loan amount in your data table to $135,000.00, and then delete the data table.

Change the loan amount

1   Select cell D10, type **135000,** and then press ENTER.

2   Scroll downward to view both tables.

Your tables are updated to reflect the new loan amount. Your tables should look like the following.

	Monthly Payment	Interest Paid
	$1,038.03	$238,691.95
6.00%	$809.39	$156,381.56
6.25%	$831.22	$164,238.56
6.50%	$853.29	$172,185.06
6.75%	$875.61	$180,218.67
7.00%	$898.16	$188,337.01
7.25%	$920.94	$196,537.67
7.50%	$943.94	$204,818.25
7.75%	$967.16	$213,176.35
8.00%	$990.58	$221,609.58
8.25%	$1,014.21	$230,115.57
8.50%	$1,038.03	$238,691.95
8.75%	$1,062.05	$247,336.40
9.00%	$1,086.24	$256,046.59

	Monthly Payment					
$1,038.03	180	240	300	360	420	480
6.00%	$1,139.21	$967.18	$869.81	$809.39	$769.76	$742.79
6.25%	$1,157.52	$986.75	$890.55	$831.22	$792.55	$766.45
6.50%	$1,175.99	$1,006.52	$911.53	$853.29	$815.61	$790.37
6.75%	$1,194.63	$1,026.49	$932.73	$875.61	$838.91	$814.53
7.00%	$1,213.42	$1,046.65	$954.15	$898.16	$862.46	$838.93
7.25%	$1,232.36	$1,067.01	$975.79	$920.94	$886.23	$863.56
7.50%	$1,251.47	$1,087.55	$997.64	$943.94	$910.23	$888.40
7.75%	$1,270.72	$1,108.28	$1,019.69	$967.16	$934.44	$913.44
8.00%	$1,290.13	$1,129.19	$1,041.95	$990.58	$958.85	$938.67
8.25%	$1,309.69	$1,150.29	$1,064.41	$1,014.21	$983.46	$964.09
8.50%	$1,329.40	$1,171.56	$1,087.06	$1,038.03	$1,008.26	$989.68
8.75%	$1,349.26	$1,193.01	$1,109.89	$1,062.05	$1,033.24	$1,015.43
9.00%	$1,369.26	$1,214.63	$1,132.92	$1,086.24	$1,058.39	$1,041.34

Note   Curly brackets { } around the formulas in the data table indicate that the cells contain an *array*. Because the resulting values in a data table are an array, you cannot edit or clear them individually. If you try to edit the data table values, a message appears telling you that you cannot change part of a table. If you want to edit data table results, you can convert the results into a range of constant values. To do this, use the Values option in the Paste Special dialog box.

You can also copy values from a data table. When you do this, only the values are copied, not the formulas for those values. To recalculate, move, or delete a data table, you must first select the entire table, including the formulas and the input values. In the next exercise, you delete the entire data table.

Delete a data table

1   Select C30:I43.

2   Click the right mouse button anywhere within the selected range, and from the shortcut menu, choose Clear Contents.

Using Scenario Manager to Analyze Data

Occasionally, you might need to examine possible results on a larger scale than either goal seeking or data tables can manage. If you need to see a collection of input values to substitute into your worksheet, and you need to maintain several sets of these collections, you can use Scenario Manager. For example, if you want to find out the result that a different down payment and a different interest rate would have on your purchase price, but you want to see each result separately, you could create separate scenarios to store different combinations of data. Or, if you want to see whether hiring another salesperson or increasing advertising would have the greatest effect on your sales growth, you could compare the scenarios. With Scenario Manager, you can set up each collection of data separately to examine when making your decision.

To set up separate scenarios, you need to begin with a worksheet that already contains the data and formulas that you want to use. Then you can use the Scenario Manager to name the scenarios and to substitute different values in the cells you specify. In the next exercises, you create three scenarios to compare three combinations of price, interest rate, and down payment for a home.

Create a scenario

1   Switch to the Loan Scenarios sheet.

2   From the Tools menu, choose Scenarios.

The Scenario Manager dialog box opens.

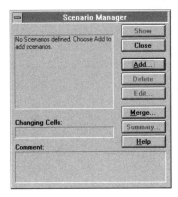

3 Click the Add button.

The Add Scenario dialog box opens.

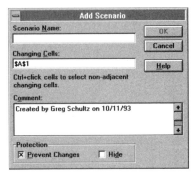

4 In the Scenario Name text box, type **Low Rate**

5 With the insertion point in the Changing Cells box, delete the existing cells, and select cells D8:D10 in the worksheet.

You might need to move the dialog box out of the way first.

6 Choose OK.

The Scenario Values dialog box opens.

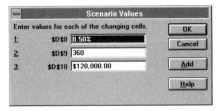

7 In box number 1, type **6%**, and then choose OK.

The Scenario Manager appears again.

Create additional scenarios

1 Click the Add button.

The Add Scenario dialog box opens, displaying the set of changing cells previously specified.

2 In the Scenario Name box, type **Low Rate, Low Term**, and then choose OK.

The Scenario Values dialog box opens.

3 In box number 1, type **7%**. In box number 2, delete the existing number, type **240**, and then click the Add button.

The Add Scenario dialog box appears again.

4 In the Scenario Name box, type **Low Rate, Low Term, Low Amount**, and then choose OK.

The Scenario Values dialog box opens.

5 In box number 1, type **7%**. In box number 2, delete the existing number and type **240**. In box number 3, delete the existing number, type **110000**, and then choose OK.

The Scenario Manager dialog box reappears with all three scenarios listed.

6 Click Close.

Show a scenario

Use Scenario Manager to show the scenarios you created in the preceding steps.

1 From the Tools menu, choose Scenarios.

2 In the Scenarios box, select Low Rate.

3 Click the Show button.

Microsoft Excel substitutes the values from the Low Rate scenario in your worksheet. You might need to move the Scenario Manager dialog box out of the way first.

4 Click Close.

Editing Scenarios

After you create a scenario, you can change or add input values. You use the Scenarios command to edit the values. In the Scenario Manager dialog box, select the name of the scenario you want to edit, and then choose the Edit button.

Edit a scenario

1 From the Tools menu, choose Scenarios.

The Scenario Manager dialog box opens.

2 In the Scenarios list, select Low Rate, Low Term, Low Amount, and then click the Edit button.

3 In the Scenario Name box, type **Low Rate, Low Term, High Amount**, and then choose OK.

The Scenario Values dialog box opens.

4 In box number 3, replace the existing number with **140000**, and then choose OK.

5 Click the Show button.

The new scenario appears in your worksheet.

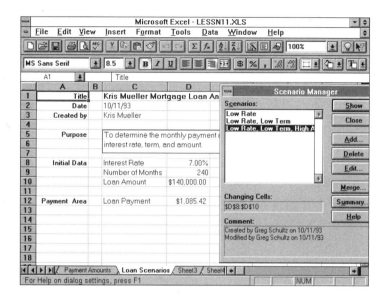

6   Click Close.

The Scenario Manager dialog box closes.

One Step Further

If you want to see your scenario data all at once, you can create a report that lists the scenarios you created as well as any input values and any *result cells* that you want to display. A result cell is any cell on your worksheet that is recalculated when you apply a new scenario. Microsoft Excel creates the summary report on a separate worksheet.

In the next exercise, you use Scenario Manager to add one more scenario, and then you create a summary report, specifying the cell containing the loan payment (cell D12) as the result cell.

1   From the Tools menu, choose Scenarios.

2   Add a scenario named "High Rate, High Term, High Amount."

3   Enter the values 9.25%, 360, and 140000 for box numbers 1, 2, and 3, respectively.

4   Choose OK.

5   In the Scenario Manager dialog box, be sure the High Rate, High Term, High Amount scenario is selected, and then click the Summary button.

6   In the Result Cells box, type **$D$12** if it is not already there.

7   Choose OK.

A new sheet called Scenario Summary appears with a summary of your scenarios already formatted and outlined. Your scenario report should look like the following illustration.

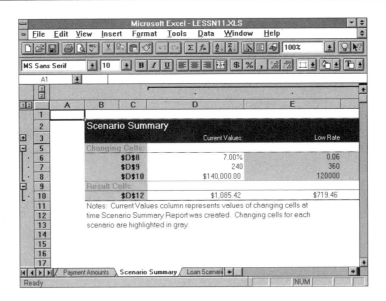

If You Want to Continue to the Next Lesson

1 From the File menu, choose Save.

2 From the File menu, choose Close.

If You Want to Quit Microsoft Excel for Now

▶ From the File menu, choose Exit.

If you see the Save dialog box, click Yes.

Lesson Summary

To	Do this
Find a specific value to make a formula reach your goal	Select the cell containing the formula that you want to use to reach a specific value. From the Tools menu, choose the Goal Seek command, and specify the variable cell whose value you want to change to reach your goal.

To	Do this
Create a one-input data table	Enter the input values in a row or column. Enter a formula above and to the right of the input values (if they are in a column), or below and to the left (if they are in a row). This formula depends on an input cell. Select the range of cells containing the input values, the formula, and the cells that will contain the table values, and then choose the Table command from the Data menu. When prompted, enter the name or reference of the row or column input cell.
Create a two-input data table	Enter the input values in a row and column. Enter a formula at the intersection of the row and column of input values. Select the range of cells containing the input values, the formula, and the cells that will contain the table values, and then choose the Table command from the Data menu. When prompted, enter the name or reference of the row or column input cell.
Edit a data table	Select the formula or the input value that you want to change, and type the new formula or input value.
Delete a data table	Select the entire table. Click the right mouse button in the selected range to display the shortcut menu, and then choose Clear Contents.
Create a scenario	From the Tools menu, choose Scenarios. Click the Add button. In the Scenario Name box, type a name. In the Changing Cells box, drag to select the cells that will change. Choose OK. In the Scenario Values dialog box, type the values that you want, and then choose OK. Click Close.
Show a scenario	From the Tools menu, choose Scenarios. Select the scenario that you want, and then click the Show button.
Edit a scenario	From the Tools menu, choose Scenarios. Select the scenario that you want, and then click the Edit button. Make your changes in the dialog boxes, and then choose OK.

For more information on	See in the *Microsoft Excel User's Guide*
Seeking a specific goal	Chapter 27, "Solving What-If Problems"
Finding alternatives with data tables	Chapter 27, "Solving What-If Problems"
Creating scenarios	Chapter 28, "Managing What-If Scenarios"

Preview of the Next Lesson

In the next lesson, "Linking Your Data," you'll learn how to use the same data in more than one file by using links between worksheets. You'll learn how to create the links, update them when your data changes, and restore links that are broken.

Linking Your Data

When you are creating a worksheet, you often need to use data stored in a different worksheet or workbook. You can copy and paste the data, but what if the data changes frequently? If you copy and paste, you'll need to do it again when the data changes. There's a solution to this problem: *linking*. You can create a link between a *dependent* worksheet, the worksheet that will use the data, and a *source* worksheet, the worksheet in which the original data resides. Your dependent worksheet will then be updated whenever the data changes in the source worksheet. With Microsoft Excel, you can easily create links between a dependent worksheet and a source worksheet, and Microsoft Excel 5 can update the data automatically when it changes.

In this lesson, you'll learn how to create links that allow you to use the same data for more than one worksheet, how to update the linked data if the original data changes, and how to change links or restore lost or broken links.

You will learn how to:

- Create links so you can use the same data in more than one worksheet.
- Update the data when the source information changes.
- Change or restore broken links.

Estimated lesson time: 20 minutes

Start the lesson

If your screen does not match the illustrations in this lesson, see the Appendix, "Matching the Exercises."

1 Open 12LESSN.XLS.

2 Save the workbook as LESSN12.XLS.

3 Open 12LESSNA.XLS.

4 Save the workbook as LESSN12A.XLS.

5 Click the Maximize button on the document window, if it is not already maximized.

Creating Links

Suppose that the Copier division at West Coast Sales is starting a new marketing campaign in January, and you need to include some of the marketing campaign data in the copier division budget. The campaign information resides in one workbook and the division information is in another. Instead of copying the information from the campaign workbook to the division workbook, or retyping the information in the division workbook, you can create a link between the two workbooks. To do this, you begin with the dependent (copier division) workbook, which receives the linked data, and use a formula to point to the information in the source (marketing campaign) workbook, which contains the original data. The formula that you use to link between the source and dependent data takes the form (at its simplest) of an external cell reference. You simply tell the dependent worksheet the location where the data resides in the source worksheet, and Microsoft Excel does the rest.

The following illustrates the link between the dependent (copier division) workbook and the source (marketing campaign) workbook.

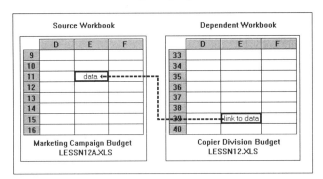

In the next exercise, you create a link between the marketing campaign workbook in the LESSN12A.XLS file and the copier division workbook in the LESSN12.XLS file so you can track the campaign expenses with the other division expenses.

Create a link

1 Be sure the active file is LESSN12.XLS.

2 On the Copier Division Budget sheet, click cell E39, and then type =

You'll create a link in this cell to point to the Campaign Allocation amount in the marketing campaign sheet.

3 From the <u>W</u>indow menu, choose LESSN12A.XLS.

The marketing campaign sheet becomes the active sheet.

4 On the Marketing Campaign Budget sheet, click cell E11, and then press ENTER.

When you press ENTER, the link formula is completed, and you are returned to the Copier Division Budget sheet in the LESSN12.XLS workbook. Notice that the campaign allocation amount appears in cell E39.

5 Be sure that cell E39 is still the active cell.

In the formula bar, the formula in cell E39 refers to cell E11 on the Marketing Campaign Budget sheet in the file LESSN12A.XLS. Cell E39 shows the data in that cell, $62,000.00. Your worksheet should look like the following.

Formula linking to source worksheet

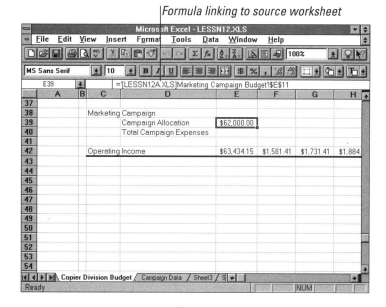

The formula that you create to link the data from the source sheet to the dependent sheet in step 4 uses only an equal sign and the external cell reference, ='[LESSN12A.XLS]Marketing Campaign Budget'!$E$11. Just as with any other formula, the equal sign begins the formula, and the cell reference tells the formula which cells to use.

The cell reference for a linking formula contains more than just a cell location, however; it also includes the filename and sheet name of the source worksheet, and sometimes the path name, if the source workbook is in a different directory from the dependent workbook. For external cell references, such as this one in the linking formula, workbook names are always surrounded by square brackets [ ], and the cell reference is always preceded by an exclamation point.

Note   Cell references in linking formulas are automatically created as absolute references because you don't usually want them to change if you move the formula in your dependent workbook.

Now that you have one link, you can easily add several more links to the same sheet. You can simply copy the first link formula into the other cells but, since the formula includes absolute references, you'll need to update the cell references to point to the correct cells. You can also point to the cells you want to reference; however, copying and then updating the formula will generally save you time and help you avoid typing errors. In the next exercise, you copy the link formula into the other campaign area cells in the copier division workbook, and then update the references to point to the correct cells.

Add links for the rest of the campaign information

1 Select cell E39, and drag the fill handle on the cell across to cell H39.

The same formula and value appear in cells F39 to H39.

38		Marketing Campaign				
39			Campaign Allocation	$62,000.00	$62,000.00	$62,000.00	$62,000
40			Total Campaign Expenses				

2 Double-click cell F39.

You'll update the reference in cells F39 to H39 to point to the correct cells in the source workbook.

3 In the formula, delete the E, then type **F** and press ENTER.

The formula is updated to point to cell F39, and the cell now displays the value $62,250.00.

4 Double-click cell G39.

5 In the formula, delete the E, then type **G** and press ENTER.

6 Double-click cell H39.

7 In the formula, delete the E, then type **H** and press ENTER.

The updated references should look like the following.

38		Marketing Campaign				
39			Campaign Allocation	$62,000.00	$62,250.00	$62,750.00	$63,000.00
40			Total Campaign Expenses				

In the next exercise, you create the other links you need in your copier division workbook. First you'll copy the formula to the other cells, and then you update the references.

Link the campaign expenses data to the copier division worksheet

1 Drag to select E39:H39.

2 Drag the fill handle on cell H39 down to cell H40, and then release it.

The formulas in E39:H39 are filled into cells E40:H40.

3 Double-click cell E40.

4 In the formula, delete 11, then type **20** and press ENTER.

5 Repeat steps 3 and 4 for cells F40, G40, and H40.

Your references are changed to point to the Total Campaign Expenses and Campaign Funds Remaining rows on your Marketing Campaign Budget sheet. The updated references should look similar to the following.

38	Marketing Campaign				
39		Campaign Allocation	$62,000.00	$62,250.00	$62,750.00	$63,000.00
40		Total Campaign Expenses	$50,075.00	$49,725.00	$52,750.00	$52,450.00
41						

Updating Links

If the data in your source workbook changes while the dependent workbook is closed, the information is updated in your dependent workbook the next time you open it. If both workbooks are open, the update takes place immediately. If you make a change to the source data, but you don't open the dependent workbook, a dialog box will appear the next time you open the dependent workbook, asking whether you want to update the data. You can also update a link with the Links command on the Edit menu. In the next exercise, you make a change in the source workbook and then view the updated dependent workbook.

Note Microsoft Excel 5 has automatic updating, as you will see in the next exercise, which can save you a lot of time when you are working with small workbooks. But automatic updating can slow down your calculations if you are working with large workbooks. If you want to turn off automatic updating, use the Options command on the Tools menu, and then in the Options dialog box, switch to the Calculation page. In the Calculation area, select the Manual option, and then choose OK.

Update a link

1 From the Window menu, choose Arrange.

The Arrange Windows dialog box opens.

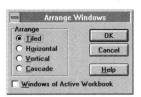

2 In the dialog box, select Horizontal, and then choose OK.

Arranging your windows will allow you to see both windows at once. You'll learn about arranging your windows in Lesson 14, "Customizing Your Workspace."

3 Click the window for LESSN12A.XLS.

4 On the Marketing Campaign Budget sheet, select cell E11.

5 Type **62500**, and then press ENTER.

6   Select E11 again, and drag the fill handle from cell E11 to H11.

All of the cells now show the value $62,500.00 and your links are updated automatically. Cells E39:H39 on the Copier Division Budget sheet show the values $62,500.00. Your worksheet should look similar to the following.

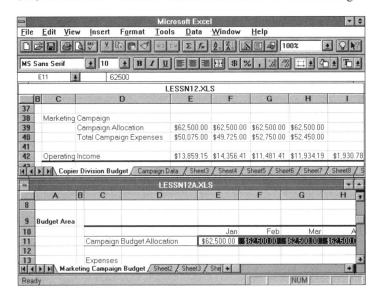

Changing and Restoring Links

The Links command is like /Edit Links in 1-2-3.

If you move the source workbook file to another directory, rename it, or delete it, the links to your data will be broken. If you have a backup copy of your source file, or if your file is in another directory, you can easily change the link so that your data will appear in the dependent workbook as before. If you need to move a file into a new directory, be sure that you also move any other files that are linked to it to the same directory.

If you break a link between a source and dependent file, you can restore the link with the Links command on the Edit menu. Whether you are restoring a link to a source workbook that was moved to another directory, or changing a link to point to a new source workbook, you can use the following steps. In the next exercise, you change the links to your copier campaign data to point to a backup file.

Note   If you want to delete a source file and remove any links to it, you can select the linked cells on the dependent worksheet and clear the linking formulas. If you want to retain the information, but not the link, you can copy the cells on the dependent worksheet that contain the linked information, and then use the Paste Special command to paste only the values in place of the links.

Change a link to a backup copy of a file

1   In the LESSN12.XLS window, click the Maximize button.

2   Be sure that the Copier Division Budget sheet in LESSN12.XLS is the active sheet.

3   Select cell E39, and then from the Edit menu, choose Links.

The Links dialog box opens.

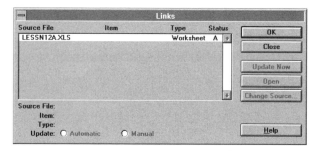

4   In the dialog box, select the file LESSN12A.XLS.

5   Click the Change Source button.

The Change Links dialog box opens.

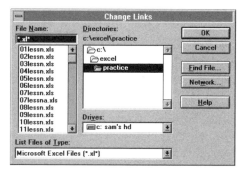

6   In the File Name list, scroll downward and select 12LESSNB.XLS.

7   Choose OK.

The dialog boxes close.

8   Open the file 12LESSNB.XLS.

9   From the Window menu, choose LESSN12.XLS.

Your workbook is updated with the data from the backup file. Your workbook should look similar to the following.

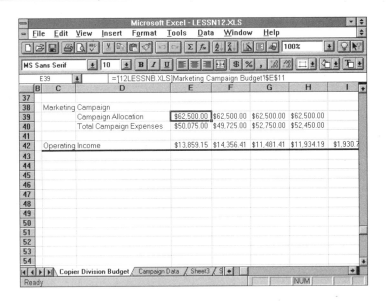

One Step Further

You've seen that you can link data easily by using a formula and pointing to the cell you want to link. When you link data with a formula, you can easily change the link or accidentally erase it if you are not careful. If you have a large range of data that you want to link to another worksheet and you do not want anyone to be able to change the data on the dependent sheet, even accidentally, you can link data by making use of an *array*, a formula that produces multiple results or operates on a range of cells.

You can also use arrays for writing multiple-value formulas and improving worksheet efficiency.

An array formula usually occupies only one cell, but it can calculate values in many cells in which you need to do similar calculations. You can greatly improve the efficiency of your worksheet by using array formulas instead of ordinary single-value formulas. In this case, you use a special application of an array, linking a range from a source worksheet to a range in the dependent worksheet. In the sheet, the linked array will occupy several cells on the dependent worksheet, but only use one linking formula. In other words, you only need to create the linking formula once, and the array takes care of the rest. You don't have to copy the formula or update the references.

For more information about arrays, refer to the Microsoft Excel User's Guide, *Chapter 10, "Creating Formulas and Links."*

You can use the Paste Special command to paste and link an array of cells to another sheet. When you use arrays, however, you cannot change anything in the cells of the dependent sheet after you've pasted the data. You cannot move or delete part of an array on a dependent sheet, or use part of an array and leave the rest. You can only use, update, or delete arrays as a whole. You should only use arrays if you need all of the data in exactly the same format on another sheet, and you will not need to change any individual cell.

Because you want to be able to view all of the marketing campaign budget information in the copier division budget worksheet, you can use an array to link the data to a range of cells in the copier budget worksheet. In the next exercise, you use an array to link data from the campaign budget worksheet (the source) to the copier budget worksheet.

Link all of the campaign information to the copier budget worksheet

1   Switch to LESSN12A.XLS.

2   Select cells D14:H19.

Copy

3   Click the Copy button on the toolbar.

4   Switch to LESSN12.XLS, and then click the Campaign Data sheet.

5   Select cell D14, and then from the Edit menu, choose Paste Special.

The Paste Special dialog box opens.

6   In the dialog box, click the Paste Link button.

The campaign information is pasted as an array into the Campaign Data sheet. Your workbook should look similar to the following.

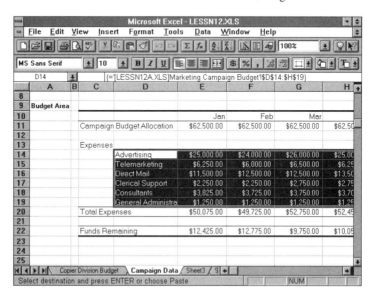

7 Click cell D14 and press DEL.

A dialog box appears, notifying you that you cannot change part of an array.

8 Choose OK.

The dialog box closes.

If You Want to Continue to the Next Lesson

1 From the File menu, choose Save.

2 Hold down SHIFT, and then from the File menu, choose Close All.

If you see the Save dialog box, click Yes.

If You Want to Quit Microsoft Excel for Now

▶ From the File menu, choose Exit.

If you see the Save dialog box, click Yes.

Lesson Summary

To	Do this
Create a link between two worksheets	Click the cell in the dependent sheet where you want the data to appear, and type = in the cell. Switch to the source sheet and click the cell that contains the data. Press ENTER.
Update a link	Open the dependent file. If you are prompted to update the links, click Yes.
Change a link	From the Edit menu in the dependent workbook, choose Links. Select the source filename of the link that you want to change and click the Change Source button. Select a new source file in the File Name list, and then choose OK.

For more information on	See in the *Microsoft Excel User's Guide*
Linking your data	Chapter 10, "Creating Formulas and Links"

Preview of the Next Lesson

In the next lesson, "Sharing Your Data with Other Applications," you'll learn how to import graphics, how to link information between applications, and how to embed information into a worksheet from another application. You'll also learn about the efficiency you can gain by using Microsoft Excel and Microsoft Word together.

Sharing Your Data with Other Applications

As you create reports, prepare presentations, or distribute information to other people, you will probably need to share your Microsoft Excel data with other applications. You might need to include a portion of a Microsoft Excel database in a letter to a potential contact, or you might need to use a Microsoft Excel table in a larger presentation. Sharing with other applications can go the other way, as well, when you use text or graphics from other applications in your Microsoft Excel sheets. With *Object Linking and Embedding* (OLE), you can link data from the sheet it resides on to another application, or vice versa. And, working with Microsoft Word and Microsoft Excel together has never been easier; you can copy and paste between Microsoft Word 6 for Windows and Microsoft Excel 5 without having to learn a new set of menus or buttons on the toolbar.

You will learn how to:

- Incorporate text and graphics from another application into a Microsoft Excel sheet.

- Take advantage of the similarities between Microsoft Word 6 for Windows and Microsoft Excel 5.

Estimated lesson time: 25 minutes

If your screen does not match the illustrations in this lesson, see the Appendix, "Matching the Exercises."

Start the lesson

1 Open 13LESSN.XLS.

2 Save the workbook as LESSN13.XLS.

3 Click the Maximize button on the document window, if it is not already maximized.

Sharing Data

You've already seen how linking data between sheets can make your work more efficient. You can apply this same principle to other applications, and make sharing data between applications efficient as well. You can copy and paste information between other applications and Microsoft Excel, or link the information so that you are able to update the information whenever it changes. You can also embed the information so that you can make changes to the copy of the information in your worksheet without altering the original file. For example, if you have a graphic that you created in Paintbrush, you can simply place the graphic in your Microsoft Excel worksheet. Or, you can create a link in your Microsoft Excel worksheet so that any time you change the graphic, it will be updated in the worksheet. You can also embed the graphic so that you can alter the graphic in your worksheet easily, without changing the original file.

Placing Graphics into Microsoft Excel

If you simply want to put a copy of a graphic into a Microsoft Excel sheet, you don't need to link or embed it. You can simply copy and paste, or use the Picture command on the Insert menu to place the picture in your sheet. The graphic will not retain any links to its original application; it will simply become an object like the text boxes and other graphic objects you've already used in your sheets.

In the next exercises, you'll place a new logo design created in Paintbrush into your Copier Marketing Budget sheet, and then delete it to make room for another version.

Place a graphic in your inventory

1 In the Copier Marketing Budget sheet, select cell F1.

The picture is not actually be inserted into a cell, you simply select a cell near where you want the graphic to appear. In this case, the graphic will cover from cell F1 to about cell G8.

2 From the Insert menu, choose Picture.

The Picture dialog box opens.

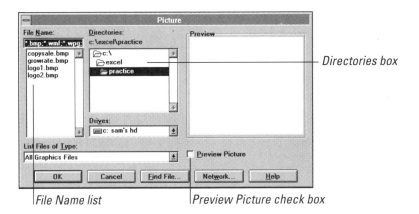

3 In the Directories box, be sure that your PRACTICE directory is the active directory.

4 In the File Name list, select LOGO1.BMP.

5 Click the Preview Picture check box.

The picture appears in the Preview box, similar to the following.

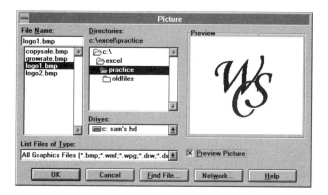

6   Choose OK.

The LOGO1.BMP picture is placed in your Copier Marketing Budget sheet. Your worksheet should look similar to the following.

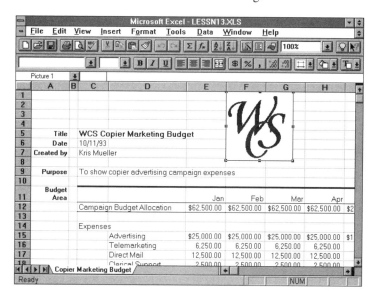

Delete a graphic

1   Click the LOGO1.BMP graphic in your Copier Marketing Budget sheet if it is not already selected.

2   Press DEL.

The graphic is removed from your Copier Marketing Budget sheet.

Linking Information Between Applications

Suppose that the Art department at West Coast Sales has created a library of graphic images for use in company correspondence, reports, and presentations. The Art department maintains this library and makes changes to the images occasionally. If you simply copy and paste or use the Insert Picture command to place one of these graphics in your sheet, you won't know if the original graphic changes, or if you have the most current copy. To be sure that the image in your sheet is the current image, you can *link* the graphic. When you link information, you retain an active connection to the source file, so that the information is updated automatically whenever the source file changes. Just as you linked data between sheets in Microsoft Excel, you can link graphics, text, or other types of information between a source file and your Microsoft Excel file. To link information between two applications, you use the Paste Special command.

Note   To link objects in Microsoft Excel 5, the application you want to use must support OLE version 1 or 2. Check the user's guide or online Help system for your application to determine this.

In the next exercises, you'll open Paintbrush, and then link the company logo graphic to your Copier Marketing Budget sheet.

Open Paintbrush

1   Minimize Microsoft Excel.

2   In Program Manager, open the Accessories group.

3   In the Accessories group, locate the Paintbrush icon.

4   Double-click the Paintbrush icon.

Your screen should look similar to the following illustration.

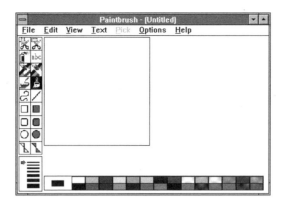

Link a graphic to your inventory sheet

1   In Paintbrush, open the file LOGO2.BMP in your PRACTICE directory.

The LOGO2.BMP picture should look like the following.

Pick tool

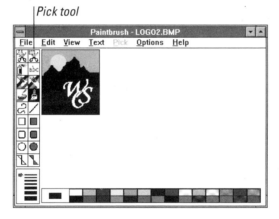

2   Click the Pick tool, and then with the cross hair pointer, drag from the upper-right corner to the lower-left corner of the picture.

The entire picture is selected.

3   From the Edit menu, choose Copy.

4   Switch to Microsoft Excel and select cell F1, if it is not already selected.

5   From the Edit menu, choose Paste Special.

The Paste Special dialog box opens.

You can easily switch between open Windows applications by pressing ALT+TAB until the name of the application appears.

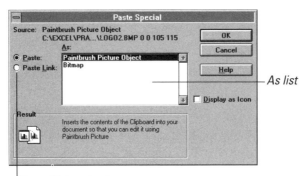

— As list

Paste Link option button

6 Click the Paste Link option button.

7 In the As list, select Paintbrush Picture object, and then choose OK.

The picture is pasted and linked to your Copier Marketing Budget sheet. Notice the linking formula in the formula bar, similar to the one you created to link data from one sheet to another in Lesson 12. Your worksheet should look similar to the following.

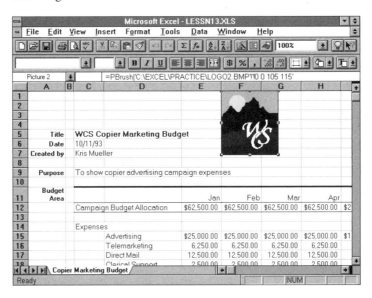

Change and then update a linked graphic

1 Double-click the logo in Excel.

Paintbrush appears, with the logo open.

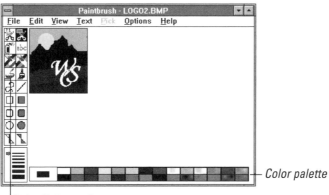

— *Color palette*

Paint Roller tool

2   In Paintbrush, select the Paint Roller tool.

3   Click the dark blue color on the Color Palette, and then click the purple area on the picture.

The purple area is changed to dark blue. Your Paintbrush picture should look similar to the following.

Area with changed color

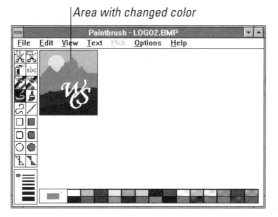

Note   If you reduce the size of the Paintbrush window and overlap it with Microsoft Excel, you can see the graphic change in Microsoft Excel at the same time as it does in Paintbrush.

4   Switch back to Microsoft Excel.

The picture is changed in the Copier Marketing Budget sheet, as well as in Paintbrush, as in the following illustration.

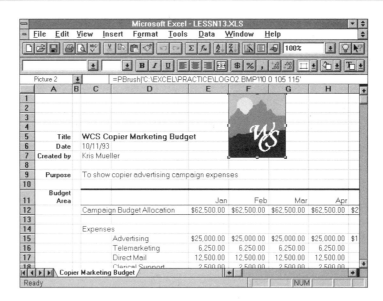

5   Switch back to Paintbrush, and then from the File menu, choose Exit.

A dialog box opens, asking whether you want to save the changes to the Paintbrush picture.

6   Click Yes.

Note   To complete the remainder of this lesson, you will need to use Microsoft Word version 6 for Windows. If you do not have Microsoft Word version 6 for Windows, go on to the Review & Practice for Part 4.

Working with Microsoft Word 6 for Windows

You probably don't spend your entire day working in Microsoft Excel. You might need to create memos or letters as well, and often you'll need to refer to your Microsoft Excel data in these documents. If you're creating a report or a memo in Microsoft Word, for example, you might want to insert data from a Microsoft Excel sheet, such as a budget or personnel report information. With Microsoft Word 6 and Microsoft Excel 5, you can create such combination documents easily. Microsoft Word and Microsoft Excel have similar menus, toolbars, and operations, so you don't need to learn a new interface when you switch between the programs.

The menu names in both applications are largely the same. The first few commands on each menu are also the same, so you can quickly find the commands you use frequently. Most of the keyboard shortcuts you rely on, such as CTRL+Z for Undo and F4 for Repeat, are identical between Microsoft Word and Microsoft Excel. Even the basic dialog boxes look the same, so you don't need to learn a new way to choose between a series of options.

With Microsoft Word and Microsoft Excel, you can either link or embed information from one to the other. When you embed information from Microsoft Excel, you place the information into Microsoft Word and retain a link to Microsoft Excel, but not to a specific document, as you would if you linked the information.

In the next exercises, you start Microsoft Word and open the file 13LESSON.DOC. Then you embed part of a Microsoft Excel sheet into your campaign budget report.

Start Microsoft Word for Windows

1   Switch to Program Manager.

2   Open the group that contains Microsoft Word 6 for Windows, and double-click the Microsoft Word icon.

3   In Microsoft Word, open the file 13LESSON.DOC in your PRACTICE directory, and then save it as LESSON13.DOC.

4   Click the Maximize button on the document window, if it is not already maximized.

Your document should look similar to the following.

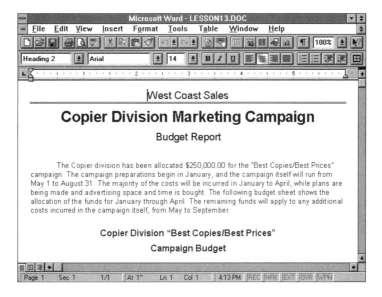

Embed information from Microsoft Excel into a Microsoft Word document

1 Switch to Microsoft Excel, and on the Copier Marketing Budget sheet, select cells C11:I23.

Copy

2 Click the Copy button on the toolbar.

3 Switch to Microsoft Word and place your insertion point at the end of the document.

4 From the Edit menu in Microsoft Word, choose Paste Special.

The Paste Special dialog box opens.

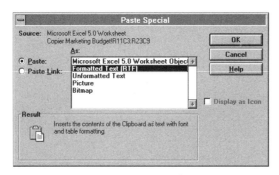

5 In the As list, select Microsoft Excel 5.0 Worksheet Object, select the Paste option, and then choose OK.

The Microsoft Excel data is embedded in your Microsoft Word document.

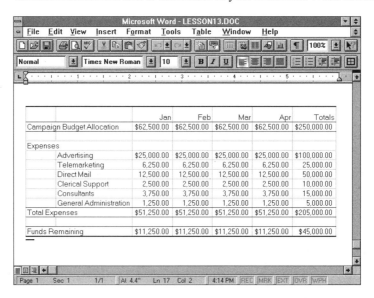

Editing Microsoft Excel Data in Microsoft Word for Windows

If the data that you embedded in your Microsoft Word for Windows document needs to be changed, you don't need to open Microsoft Excel before you can make the changes. You can make the changes right in your Microsoft Word document. When you select Microsoft Excel data that's linked to a Microsoft Word document, the menus change automatically to allow you to make any changes that you need. When you click in the text areas of the document outside of the linked object area, the menus change back to Microsoft Word menus so that you can continue with your text editing.

In the next exercise, you add formatting to your recently embedded Microsoft Excel data to polish the presentation in your report.

Note   The ability to edit Microsoft Excel data in a Microsoft Word document without leaving Microsoft Word is new with OLE 2. You can only perform this action with Microsoft Word version 6 or later, and Microsoft Excel version 5 or later.

Format Microsoft Excel data in your Microsoft Word document

1   In the Microsoft Word document, double-click the Microsoft Excel object.

The Microsoft Word menus are replaced by Microsoft Excel menus. Notice that the Table menu is gone, replaced by the Data menu.

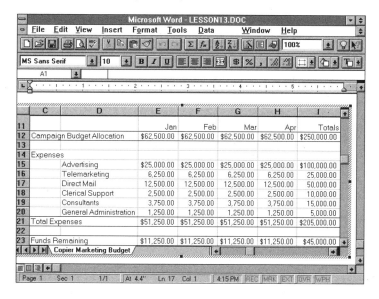

2   In the Microsoft Excel object, select cells C11:I23, and then from the Format menu, choose AutoFormat.

The AutoFormat dialog box opens.

3   In the list of formats, choose Classic 3, and then choose OK.

The AutoFormat dialog box closes, and the data is formatted.

4   Click in the text area of the document.

The Microsoft Word menus appear again. Your document should look similar to the following.

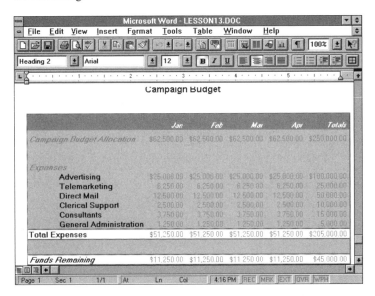

One Step Further

If you need to link to another electronic document, but you don't need to show the entire document in the sheet you're working with, you can link it with an icon. The icon acts as a placeholder that you can double-click to open the actual document. When you place only the icon on your sheet, you can save space (both visually and in your computer storage) while still calling the extra information to another user's attention. Use an icon whenever the information you need to link is not vital to the sheet but is more of a comment or an addition to it.

Try linking your Microsoft Word budget report to your budget sheet with only the icon, and then open the linked information by double-clicking the icon.

Link a Microsoft Word document with an icon

1   Switch back to Microsoft Excel.

2   On the Copier Marketing Budget sheet, select cell C32, type **Double-click this for more information:** and then press ENTER.

3   Select cell F32, and then switch to Microsoft Word.

4   In the LESSON13.DOC file, select all of the text.

Exclude the embedded Microsoft Excel data.

Copy

5   Click the Copy button on the toolbar.

6   Switch back to Microsoft Excel, and from the Edit menu, choose Paste Special.

The Paste Special dialog box opens.

7   In the dialog box, select the Paste Link option.

8   In the dialog box, click the Display As Icon check box to select it.

9   Choose OK.

The dialog box closes and a Microsoft Word icon appears in your sheet.

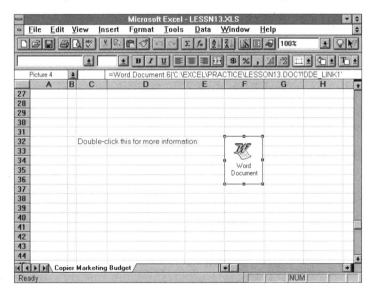

10   Double-click the Microsoft Word icon.

Microsoft Word opens with the document displayed.

If You Want to Continue to the Next Lesson

1   In Microsoft Word, from the File menu, choose Save.

2   From the File menu, choose Close.

3   Switch to Microsoft Excel, and from the File menu, choose Save.

4   From the File menu, choose Close.

If You Want to Quit Microsoft Excel and Word for Now

1   Switch to Microsoft Word, and from the File menu, choose Exit.

   If you see the Save dialog box, click Yes.

2   Switch to Microsoft Excel, and from the File menu, choose Exit.

   If you see the Save dialog box, click Yes.

Lesson Summary

To	Do this
Insert a graphic into a sheet	Open the sheet and click the cell near where you want to place the picture. From the Insert menu, choose Picture. Select the filename of the picture you want from the File Name list, and then choose OK.
Delete an inserted or linked object	Select the object, and then press DEL.
Link information from another application to a Microsoft Excel sheet	Open the file in the source application. Select the information you want, and then from the Edit menu, choose Copy. Switch to Microsoft Excel and select the cell where you want the information to appear. From the Edit menu, choose Paste Special. In the Paste Special dialog box, click the Paste Link option button. In the As list, select the type of object, and then choose OK.
Embed Microsoft Excel information into a Microsoft Word document	In Microsoft Excel, select the information that you want to embed. From the Edit menu, choose Copy. Switch to Microsoft Word, and place the insertion point where you want the information to appear. From the Edit menu in Word, choose Paste Special. In the As list, select Microsoft Excel 5.0 Worksheet Object, and then click the Paste option. Choose OK.
Edit Microsoft Excel data in Microsoft Word	Click the Microsoft Excel data in the Word document, make your changes, and then click outside of the Microsoft Excel data to return to Microsoft Word.

For more information on	See in the *Microsoft Excel User's Guide*
Placing graphics in Microsoft Excel	Chapter 41, "Sharing Data and Graphics with Other Applications"
Linking information between applications	Chapter 41, "Sharing Data and Graphics with Other Applications"
Working with Microsoft Word	Chapter 41, "Sharing Data and Graphics with Other Applications"

Preview of the Next Lessons

In Part 5, you'll learn how to customize the appearance of your worksheets and toolbars on your screen, and how to automate complex tasks that you might have to repeat often. In the next lesson, "Customizing Your Workspace," you'll learn how to customize Microsoft Excel to create the working environment that will best suit your needs. You'll learn about toolbars by moving and customizing the buttons where you need them. You'll also learn about options in Microsoft Excel that can make your work easier.

Review & Practice

In the lessons in Part 4, "Analyzing and Sharing Your Data," you learned skills to help you answer what-if questions and to share data between Microsoft Excel and other applications. If you want to practice these skills and test your understanding before you proceed with the lessons in Part 5, you can work through the Review & Practice section following this lesson.

Part 4   Review & Practice

Before you move on to Part 5, which covers customizing your workspace, you can practice the skills in Part 4 by working through the steps in this Review & Practice section. You will solve a what-if problem with goal seeking, link information between workbooks, link a graphic to your worksheet, and embed Microsoft Excel data into a Microsoft Word document.

Scenario

You've nearly completed the Sales Journal report. All you need to do is add a few finishing touches. You need to use goal seeking to find the sales growth figure that will allow the Copier division to reach its sales goal, and you need to create a data table and scenarios to show what happens to the sales figure at different growth rates. You also need to link the copier data to an all-division report in another workbook. Then you will insert an illustration to add emphasis to the sales figure in the Copier division part of the report, and link a graphic to your growth rate data. Finally, you'll open a Microsoft Word document that includes introductory text, and add the Microsoft Excel data and graphic to finish the report.

You will review and practice how to:

- Find a value using goal seeking.
- Use a data table to find a series of solutions to a what-if problem.
- Create scenarios to show several possibilities.
- Link data between workbooks so that the data will always be current.
- Insert a picture to illustrate and emphasize data.
- Link a picture to show the latest version of it at all times.
- Add Microsoft Excel data to a Microsoft Word 6 for Windows document to finish a report.

Estimated practice time: 30 minutes

Step 1: Seek a Value to Reach a Goal

From 1991 to 1993, the copier sales grew from $172,102.76 to $179,161.05, a constant annual growth rate of 2.03%. In 1995, you expect sales to reach at least $190,000.00. Find the percentage of sales growth that would be necessary to reach this sales goal.

1 Open the file P4REVIEW.XLS and save it as REVIEWP4.

2 Use the Goal Seek command to set cell G18 to 190,000 by changing the value in cell D8.

For more information on	See
Finding a specific value	Lesson 11

Step 2: Find a Series of Solutions to a What-If Problem

For your own information, you want to see what kind of sales income you could expect with growth rates between 3 percent and 10 percent. Build a data table to show the sales income that these rates could generate.

1 Copy the formula in cell G18 to cell D23.

2 Use the Table command on the Data menu to create a data table that replaces the column input value in cell D8 with the values in C24:C31.

For more information on	See
Using data tables to find a series of values	Lesson 11

Step 3: Create Scenarios for Different Growth Rates

You need to show how the changing growth rates could affect each product marketer's sales, as well as the total sales amounts. Create three scenarios for Low, Medium, and High Growth Rates, and use the 2 percent, 5 percent, and 10 percent rates to show the changes in each product marketer's sales for 1995.

1 Select cell D36 and use the Scenarios command to add scenarios for 2 percent, 5 percent, and 10 percent growth rates.

2 Use the Show button to see the results in each scenario.

For more information on	See
Creating and viewing scenarios	Lesson 11

Step 4: Create Links to an All-Division Workbook

Along with each division's sales records, the Administration department keeps track of the sales for all of the divisions. You need to put the Copier division's sales information into their all-division workbook. If you link the data, you won't have to update it every time the data changes.

1 Open the file P4REVWA.XLS and save it as REVWP4A.

2 In the Total Sales sheet, create a formula in cell D12 to link to cell C12 of the REVIEWP4.XLS workbook, on the Copier Sales sheet.

3 Copy the linking formula downward and across to cell H17.

You can either link the cells one by one, or copy the formulas to the rest of the total range and then update the references to the proper cells. Your sheet should look similar to the following.

You might need to reapply the autoformatting if your screen does not match this illustration.

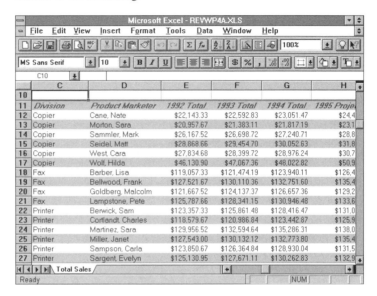

4 Save and close the REVWP4A.XLS file.

For more information on	See
Linking Your Data	Lesson 12

Step 5: Insert a Picture to Enhance the Information

The Marketing departments for each division have created division logos for different types of reports or correspondence. The logo for use with the Copier division's sales reports is the COPYSALE.BMP logo. Insert this logo into your sheet.

▶ Use the Picture command to insert the logo into cell G3 on your sheet.

For more information on	See
Inserting graphics into Microsoft Excel	Lesson 13

Step 6: Link a Picture to Show the Latest Version

The Art department has also created some logos that are more generalized and are available in the graphics library. The Art department is in the process of reviewing and revising the graphics, so it's hard to tell whether you have the latest version. Link the graphic in the GROWRATE.BMP file to your sheet, so that it will be updated automatically whenever it changes.

1   Open Paintbrush and open the GROWRATE.BMP file.

2   Use the Pick tool to select the entire graphic, and then copy the entire graphic.

3   In Microsoft Excel, use the Paste Special command to link the logo to cell F23 on your sheet.

4   In Paintbrush, change the background color to green and see the effect upon the linked object in the worksheet.

For more information on	See
Linking information	Lesson 13

Note   To complete the remainder of this Review & Practice, you will need to use Microsoft Word version 6 for Windows. If you do not have Microsoft Word version 6 for Windows, go on to the next lesson.

Step 7: Add Data to a Document in Microsoft Word 6 for Windows

Your Unit Manager likes all reports to have introductory information in Microsoft Word, with data from Microsoft Excel following the introduction. Rather than printing both documents, you will combine them in Microsoft Word to create a professional-looking document.

1   Open the Microsoft Word document P4REVIEW.DOC and save it as REVIEWP4.DOC.

2   In Microsoft Excel, use the Copy button to copy cells A1:G18.

3   In Microsoft Word, scroll downward to the end of the report, and then use the Paste Special command to link the Microsoft Excel data.

For more information on	See
Linking information	Lesson 13
Working with Microsoft Word 6	Lesson 13

If You Want to Continue to the Next Lesson

1   In Paintbrush, from the File menu, choose Save.

2   In Paintbrush, from the File menu, choose Exit.

3   In Microsoft Word, from the File menu, choose Save.

4   In Microsoft Word, from the File menu, choose Exit.

5   In Microsoft Excel, from the File menu, choose Save.

6   In Microsoft Excel, from the File menu, choose Close.

If You Want to Quit Microsoft Excel for Now

▶   From the File menu, choose Exit.

  If you see the Save dialog box, click Yes.

5

Customizing and Automating Microsoft Excel

Customizing Your Workspace

When you are working on a big project, with several workbooks full of information, you need some way to arrange your workspace so that the information you need is more accessible. You also need to access any tools you might want to use. In this lesson, you'll learn how to customize the Microsoft Excel screen display to meet your needs. You'll learn how to change your toolbars so that the tools you use most often are easy to find. In addition, you'll find out how to view and arrange worksheets so that you can see the information you need on all of your sheets. You'll view your sheets at different magnifications, and split your window into panes to show different parts of your sheet in each pane. Finally, you'll learn how to arrange your windows so that you can see as many files as you need at one time.

You will learn how to:

- Display and customize toolbars.

- Hide toolbars, menu bars, and the status bar to gain a full screen view of a worksheet.

- Zoom in or out to see as much of your sheet as you need.

- Split your worksheets so that you can see more than one section of data at a time.

- Arrange your sheets within windows so you can see more than one sheet at a time.

Estimated lesson time: 20 minutes

If your screen does not match the illustrations in this lesson, see the Appendix, "Matching the Exercises."

Start the lesson

1 Open 14LESSN.XLS.

2 Save the workbook as LESSN14.XLS.

3 Click the Maximize button on the document window, if it is not already maximized.

Customizing Your Workspace with Toolbars

Microsoft Excel comes with several preset toolbars with buttons that can save you time and effort. When you first start Microsoft Excel, you see two toolbars by default, the Standard and the Formatting toolbars. You've already used these toolbars, as well as the Chart and the Query And Pivot toolbars, in earlier lessons.

Toolbars are like SmartIcon palettes in 1-2-3.

In addition to these toolbars, there are several others that you can use as you work with Microsoft Excel. For example, in Lesson 15, you'll use the Stop Recording Toolbar. If you use Windows for Workgroups, you'll probably use the Workgroup toolbar. If you work with graphic elements, you'll become familiar with the Drawing toolbar. If you work with Microsoft Office, you'll probably want to use the Microsoft toolbar to switch to the other applications in the Office package. If you are a power user of Microsoft Excel, you might use the Auditing and Visual Basic toolbars as well.

Showing and Hiding Toolbars

You've seen how certain toolbars automatically appear when you perform a certain action or choose a particular command. For example, when you created a chart and then activated it to make changes, the Chart toolbar automatically appeared. When you created a pivot table in Lesson 10, the Query And Pivot toolbar appeared so you could make changes to the table. Other toolbars open automatically when you choose a certain command or activate an object. But what if you need to use a button on a toolbar that isn't open? You can easily open other toolbars by using the Toolbars command on the shortcut menu or the View menu. In the next exercise, you close the Formatting toolbar, and then open it again.

Close and then open the Formatting toolbar

1   Move the mouse pointer to an empty area on the toolbar, and then click the right mouse button.

The toolbar shortcut menu opens. Notice that Standard and Formatting have check marks beside their names indicating that the toolbars are currently open.

2   From the shortcut menu, choose Formatting.

The Formatting toolbar closes.

3   From the View menu, choose Toolbars.

The Toolbars dialog box opens. This is another way to display or hide a toolbar.

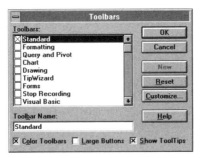

4   In the Toolbars list, select the check box next to Formatting, and then click OK.

The dialog box closes and the Formatting toolbar appears again.

Customizing and Moving Your Toolbars

The Customize command is like /Tools SmartIcons in 1-2-3.

If you find that you use a particular button often, or another button infrequently, you can customize your toolbars to make them work better for you. If, for example, you rarely use the sorting buttons on the Standard toolbar, or use only the Descending button, you can remove one or more of these buttons from the toolbar. Or, if you often need to add a new worksheet page to your workbooks, you can add the Insert Worksheet button to the Standard toolbar so it is within easy reach. You can create your own customized toolbars to contain only the buttons that you need to use. You can also move buttons around on your existing toolbar to make them easier to use, or move the entire toolbar to a new location.

Note   You can also create your own custom buttons for your toolbars. See Chapter 34, "Customizing Your Workspace," in the *Microsoft Excel User's Guide* for more information.

In the next exercises, you create a custom toolbar, add some buttons to it, and rearrange the buttons.

Create a new toolbar and add buttons to it

1   From the View menu, choose Toolbars.

The Toolbars dialog box opens.

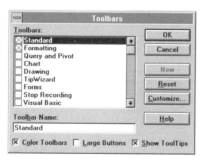

2   In the Toolbar Name box, type **My Tools** and click the New button.

The Customize dialog box opens. An empty toolbar appears in the upper-left corner of the screen.

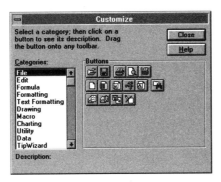

3 In the Categories list, select File, and then in the Buttons area, locate the Insert Worksheet button.

Insert Worksheet

The toolbar buttons are organized according to the action that they perform. You can click the buttons with your mouse to see their descriptions.

4 Drag the Insert Worksheet button to your new toolbar in the upper-left corner of the screen.

5 In the Categories list, select Edit, and then drag the Delete and Insert buttons to your new toolbar.

Delete   *Insert*

6 In the Edit category, drag the Clear Contents, Clear Formats, and Paste Values buttons to your new toolbar.

Clear   *Clear*   *Paste*
Contents   *Formats*   *Values*

7 In the Categories list, select Formatting, and then drag the AutoFormat button to your new toolbar.

AutoFormat

8 In the Categories list, select Drawing, and then drag the Arrow and the Create Button buttons to your new toolbar.

Arrow   *Create Button*

9 In the Categories list, select Utility, and then drag the Freeze Panes button to your new toolbar. You'll learn about freezing panes later in this lesson.

Freeze Panes

Arrange the buttons on your new toolbar

If your toolbar is vertical, rather than horizontal, drag the bottom-right corner of the toolbar border up and to the right. When you drag the border, it will change to a horizontal arrangement.

1 On your My Tools toolbar, click the Insert button and drag it to just before the Delete button.

The Insert button appears before the Delete button.

2 Drag the Insert button a little to the right, but not over the Delete button.

A space appears between the Insert Worksheet button and the Insert button.

3 Drag the Clear Contents button a little to the right to create another space between the Delete and the Clear Contents button.

4 Drag the Arrow and the Create Button buttons to the left, before the AutoFormat button.

5 Drag the Arrow button a little to the right to create a space between the Paste Values and the Arrow button.

6 Drag the AutoFormat button a little to the right to create a space between the Create Button button and the AutoFormat button.

7 Drag the Freeze Panes button a little to the right to create a space between it and the AutoFormat button.

Be careful not to drag it off of the toolbar. If you drag the Freeze Panes button off of the toolbar, you'll need to add it again. Your toolbar should look similar to the following.

8 In the Customize dialog box, choose Close.

You can move your toolbars to any position on your screen. If you move a toolbar to the top, bottom, or either side of your window, it will *dock* at that location. When your toolbar docks, it changes its shape to a single vertical row of buttons (at the side of your screen) or a single horizontal row of buttons (at the top or bottom of your screen). Toolbars that contain drop-down boxes, such as the Font box or the Size box, cannot dock on the sides of your window, since the boxes will not fit. If you move a toolbar to anywhere near the center of your window, it will *float* there.

In the next exercise, you move your new toolbar around on your screen to see how it docks at different positions and floats in others. Then you dock it at the top of your screen, below the other toolbars.

Move the toolbar around on your screen

1 Click the title bar on the My Tools toolbar, drag the toolbar to the left side of your screen, and then release the mouse button.

The toolbar moves to the left margin of your window and docks.

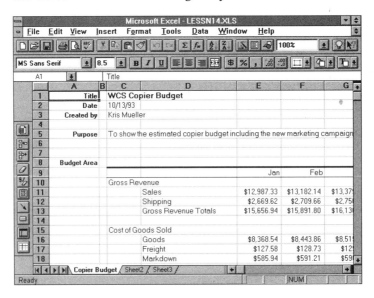

2 Position your cursor in the My Tools toolbar background, and drag downward to the bottom of your screen.

The toolbar moves to the bottom of the Microsoft Excel window and docks again.

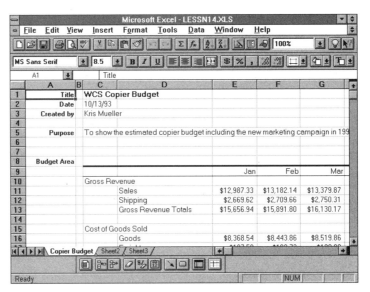

3 Using the toolbar background, drag the My Tools toolbar back to the center of the screen.

The toolbar appears near the center of the screen again.

4 Drag the My Tools toolbar to the top of the screen, immediately below the Formatting toolbar.

The toolbar docks at the top of the window, below your other toolbars.

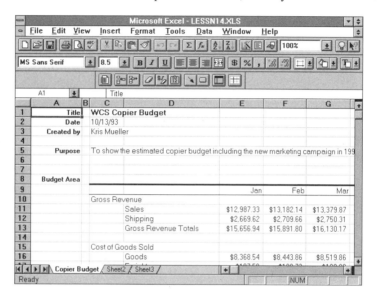

Hiding On-Screen Elements

If you find that you don't use the toolbars often, and you want to see more of your data at one time, you can hide the toolbars and other elements on the screen. The Full Screen command on the View menu hides the toolbars, the title bar, and the status bar, showing only your sheet, the scroll bars, and the menu bar. To restore the hidden elements to your view, you can choose the Full Screen command again, or you can use the Full Screen button on the Full Screen toolbar. In the next exercise, you arrange a full screen view of your sheet, and then restore the toolbars, status bar, and title bar to view.

Arrange a full screen view of a sheet

1 From the View menu, choose Full Screen.

The toolbars, title bar, and status bar are hidden from view and your sheet fills the entire screen. The Full Screen toolbar appears with the Full Screen button.

Full Screen button

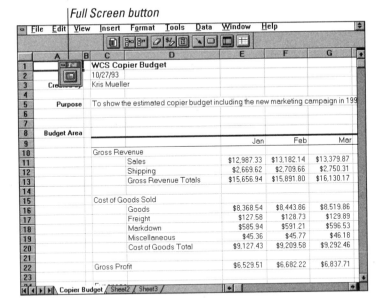

2   Click the Full Screen button.

You can also use the Full Screen command on the View menu again to restore the screen elements to view. The toolbars, title bar, and status bar appear again, and the Full Screen toolbar disappears.

Zooming In or Out to View a Worksheet

You've seen how to make more space to display your sheet by hiding the toolbars, status bar, and title bar, but what if you want to see even more data? To get a wider view of your data, you can zoom out to display more cells in the window. If you want to see fewer cells at a higher magnification, you can zoom in. As with zooming out, you can zoom in to show a certain percentage of the full screen, or to fit a particular selection to the size of the window. To zoom in or out, you can use either the Zoom box on the Standard toolbar or the Zoom command on the View menu. In the next exercise, you select part of your worksheet and then zoom out and in to see your data from different perspectives.

Zoom out and zoom in to view a selection

1   Select cells C9:G18.

2   Click the down arrow next to the Zoom box on the Standard toolbar.

The Zoom box opens, showing the standard zoom percentages.

`100%` ⬇

Zoom

3 In the list, choose 50%.

Your worksheet zooms out to show the data at 50% size.

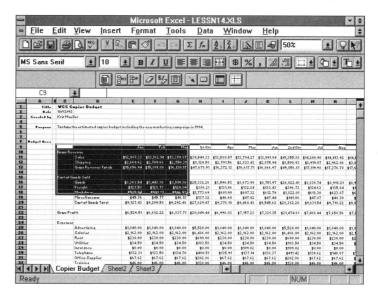

4 Click the down arrow next to the Zoom box.

5 In the list, choose Selection.

The worksheet zooms in to fit your selection to the window size. Notice that the percentage in the Zoom box adjusts precisely to the required magnification.

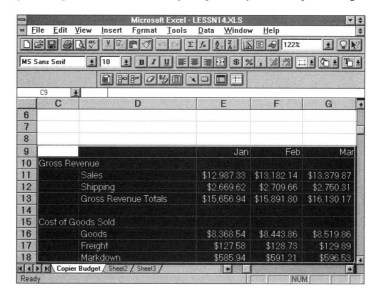

Note If your selection is larger than one screen, either horizontally or vertically, choosing Selection in the Zoom box will zoom out rather than in to display the entire selection.

---

6 Click the down arrow next to the Zoom box, and in the list choose 100%.

Your worksheet is returned to 100% size.

Splitting Your Worksheets into Panes

With large sheets, you'll often have headings at the top or the left of your sheet with data extending to the right and down. When you have scrolled past the point where the headings are visible, it can be difficult to remember what they were. If you want to see your headings all of the time while scrolling through your data, you can split your worksheet window into separate sections called *panes,* and then freeze the panes so that you can view both headings and data at the same time. For example, if you have headings in row 2, and you need to see data in row 55, it is difficult to see the heading and the data at the same time. But if you split your worksheet after row 2, and then freeze the pane with the headings, you can see the headings at all times, no matter where you have scrolled in the data.

To split a window into separate panes, you can use either the Split command on the Window menu or your mouse. You can freeze and unfreeze your window panes, or remove the split entirely, by choosing commands on the Window menu. In the next exercise, you split your worksheet into two panes with the mouse, scroll the top pane to show the headings, and then remove the split.

Split a window into panes

1 Scroll downward and over until cell C9 is in the upper-left corner of the screen.

 — *Split box*

2 Point to the small black area at the top of the vertical scroll bar and drag downward to the middle of the screen.

This small black box is called the *split box.* Your pointer changes to look like the following illustration, and the window is split into two panes.

3 From the <u>W</u>indow menu, choose Remove <u>S</u>plit.

The split panes are removed from the worksheet.

4 Be sure that cell C9 is the upper leftmost cell in your window.

You will split your window so that you see only the headings in one pane and all of the data in the other.

5 Select cell E10, and from the <u>W</u>indow menu, select <u>F</u>reeze Panes.

Your window is divided into panes, but without the extra scroll bars. The headings and the top and left of the screen are frozen into place, but you can scroll through the data in the lower-right section. Your worksheet should look similar to the following.

	Microsoft Excel - LESSN14.XLS					
File Edit View Insert Format Tools Data Window Help						

	C	D	E	F	G	H
9			Jan	Feb	Mar	1st Qtr
10	Gross Revenue					
11		Sales	$12,987.33	$13,182.14	$13,379.87	$39,549.33	$13
12		Shipping	$2,669.62	$2,709.66	$2,750.31	$8,129.58	$2
13		Gross Revenue Totals	$15,656.94	$15,891.80	$16,130.17	$47,678.91	$16
14						
15	Cost of Goods Sold					
16		Goods	$8,368.54	$8,443.86	$8,519.86	$25,332.26	$8
17		Freight	$127.58	$128.73	$129.89	$386.21	
18		Markdown	$585.94	$591.21	$596.53	$1,773.69	
19		Miscellaneous	$45.36	$45.77	$46.18	$137.32	
20		Cost of Goods Total	$9,127.43	$9,209.58	$9,292.46	$27,629.47	$9
21						
22	Gross Profit		$6,529.51	$6,682.22	$6,837.71	$20,049.44	$6
23						
24	Expenses					

Copier Budget / Sheet2 / Sheet3

Ready   NUM

Note You can also select a row or column and then freeze panes. The window will be split along that row or column, and the row or column will be frozen in place.

---

6 In the data area, scroll downward and to the right to cell U38.

Notice that even though you are scrolling through the cells in the data area, the headings remain in place. You can scroll anywhere to the right or to the bottom of your worksheet, but you cannot scroll past cell D9 to the left or top of your worksheet.

Freeze Panes

7 Click the Freeze Panes button on your My Tools toolbar.

You can also use the Unfreeze Panes command on the Window menu. The frozen panes are removed from the worksheet.

Arranging Windows

Splitting your windows and zooming in or out can help you see more information on a particular sheet. But what if you have several sheets in a workbook and you need to look at more than one at a time? Or what if you need to compare information that is stored in more than one workbook? You can arrange your windows so that you can see two, three, four, or more windows at a time. Of course, the more windows you have, the harder it will be to see very much information in them.

In Lesson 12, "Linking Your Data," you saw how you could arrange your windows horizontally to show smaller, horizontally aligned windows. You can also arrange windows in vertical, or *tiled*, panels. Alternatively, you can *cascade* your windows so that only the title bars of the inactive windows show behind the active window. To arrange your windows, you use the Arrange command on the Window menu. You can have several workbooks in separate windows, or one workbook displayed in several windows.

In the next exercises, you open a second and a third window for your workbook and then rearrange the three windows by cascading and tiling.

Open new windows to display different sheets in a workbook

1   From the Window menu, choose New Window twice.

Two new windows open showing your LESSN14.XLS workbook.

2   From the Window menu, choose LESSN14.XLS:2.

The LESSN14.XLS:2 window appears.

3   Click the Sheet2 tab.

Sheet2 appears in the LESSN14.XLS:2 window.

4   From the Window menu, choose LESSN14.XLS:3.

The LESSN14.XLS:3 window appears.

5   Click the Sheet3 tab.

Sheet3 appears in the LESSN14.XLS:3 window.

Cascade, tile, and then arrange windows horizontally

1   From the Window menu, choose Arrange.

The Arrange Windows dialog box opens.

2   In the Arrange area, select Cascade, and then choose OK.

Your windows are arranged so that LESSN14.XLS:3 is visible in front, and only the title bars of LESSN14.XLS:2 and LESSN14.XLS:1 are visible. You can click a title bar to make another window active and bring it to the front, as in the following illustration.

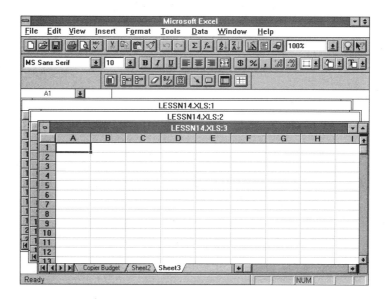

3   From the Window menu, choose Arrange.

The Arrange Windows dialog box opens.

4   In the Arrange area, select Tiled, and then choose OK.

Your windows are arranged so that LESSN14.XLS:3 is on the left, with
LESSN14.XLS:2 and LESSN14.XLS:1 tiled beside it.

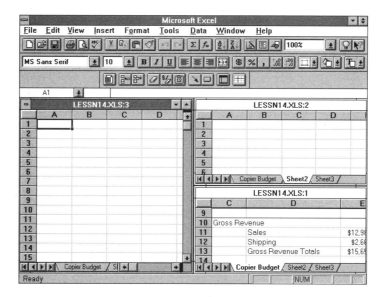

5 From the Window menu, choose Arrange.

The Arrange Windows dialog box opens.

The Horizontal option is like /Worksheet Window Horizontal in 1-2-3.

6 In the Arrange area, select Horizontal, and then choose OK.

Your windows are arranged horizontally, with all three windows visible and the LESSN14.XLS:1 window at the bottom.

To change all of the windows back to full size, you can simply maximize one of the windows. All of the others will be restored to full size automatically, with the inactive workbooks hidden behind the active workbook. In the next exercise, you restore your windows to full size and then close the duplicate windows.

Restore your windows and close the blank workbooks

1 Click the Maximize button on the LESSN14.XLS:3 window.

All three windows are maximized, but only LESSN14.XLS:3 is visible.

2 Double-click the Control-menu box on the LESSN14.XLS:3 and the LESSN14.XLS:2 windows.

The duplicate windows are closed. Your LESSN14.XLS file remains open and maximized.

One Step Further

In the budget sheet in the LESSN14.XLS file, you have columns for every month, as well as summary columns for every quarter and a totals column. In Lesson 9, you saw how you could outline your sheet and hide parts of the outline to show only a summary. If you have some data, however, that you do not need to view at the moment, but you don't want to outline your sheet, you can simply hide the rows or columns that you don't need. You can hide your rows or columns with the Row and Column commands on the Format menu. To restore your rows or columns, you select the rows or columns around the hidden rows or columns, and then use the Row and Column commands on the Format menu again.

Try hiding all of the months in your budget so that only the summary columns are visible, and then restore them so that you can see all of the data.

Hide columns of data and then restore them

1 Select columns E through G.

2 From the Format menu, choose Column, and then choose Hide.

The columns are hidden. A wider column border divides column D from column H, indicating that columns are hidden between them.

3 Select columns I through K, and then click the right mouse button to display the shortcut menu.

Be sure that your mouse pointer is still over the column header when you bring up the shortcut menu.

4 From the shortcut menu, choose Hide.

Columns I through K are hidden as well.

5 Click the column header button for column M, hold down CTRL, and select columns N, O, Q, R, and S.

Using the CTRL key, you can select individual, non-adjacent columns, rows, or cells.

6 From the shortcut menu, choose Hide.

All of your month columns are hidden. Only the quarterly summaries and the totals row remain.

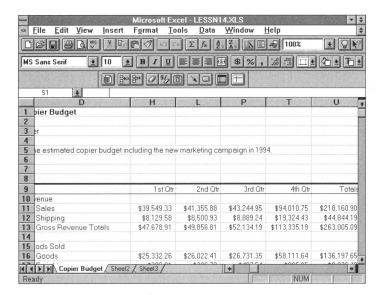

7 Select columns D through T.

You redisplay a column by selecting the columns on either side of it, or you can select the entire worksheet.

8 From the Format menu, choose Column, and then choose Unhide.

You can also use the Unhide command on the shortcut menu. All of the hidden columns are restored.

9 Close the My Tools toolbar.

If You Want to Continue to the Next Lesson

1 From the File menu, choose Save.

2 From the File menu, choose Close.

If You Want to Quit Microsoft Excel for Now

▶ From the File menu, choose Exit.

If you see the Save dialog box, click Yes.

Lesson Summary

To	Do this	Button
Display a toolbar	From the shortcut menu, select the toolbar that you want, or choose Toolbars from the View menu.	
Create a new toolbar	From the View menu, choose Toolbars. In the Toolbar Name box, type the name for your toolbar. Customize your toolbar using the summary that follows.	
Customize a toolbar	From the View menu, choose Toolbars. In the Toolbars dialog box, click the Customize button. Drag the buttons you want to remove from the toolbar to the Buttons area of the Customize dialog box. Drag the buttons you want to add from the Buttons area to the toolbar. Drag buttons you want to move within the toolbar to their new locations. In the Customize dialog box, choose Close.	
Gain a full screen view of a worksheet	From the View menu, choose Full Screen. *or* Click the Full Screen button on the toolbar.	
Display the toolbar, title bar, and status bar	From the View menu, choose Full Screen.	
Zoom in or out to view your sheet	Select the cells you want to view. From the View menu, choose Zoom, or click the down arrow next to the Zoom box on the Standard toolbar. In the Zoom box, select a percentage, type in a percentage, or select Selection, and then choose OK.	`100%`
Split a worksheet into panes	Drag the split box. *or* From the Window menu, choose Split.	

To	Do this	Button
Remove split panes	From the Window menu, choose Remove Split.	
Freeze or unfreeze panes	From the Window menu, choose Freeze Panes or Unfreeze Panes.	
Open a new window	From the Window menu, choose New Window.	
Arrange windows	From the Window menu, choose Arrange. In the Arrange Windows dialog box, choose Tiled, Horizontal, Vertical, or Cascade, and then choose OK.	

For more information on	See in the *Microsoft Excel User's Guide*
Customizing your workspace with toolbars	Chapter 34, "Customizing Your Workspace"
Viewing a sheet full screen	Chapter 32, "Changing How You View Your Worksheet"
Zooming in or out to view your sheet	Chapter 32, "Changing How You View Your Worksheet"
Splitting your worksheet into panes	Chapter 32, "Changing How You View Your Worksheet"
Arranging multiple windows	Chapter 32, "Changing How You View Your Worksheet"

Preview of the Next Lesson

In the next lesson, "Automating Repetitive Tasks," you are introduced to Microsoft Excel's macro language and you learn how to create simple macros to save yourself time and effort. You learn how to record keystrokes as a macro, how to add comments to make a macro more understandable, and how to add buttons to your sheets to automatically run the macros you create.

Automating Repetitive Tasks

Some of the data entry and formatting that you do in Microsoft Excel can be repetitive. For example, you might set up most of your worksheets with the same basic headings, or format all of your headings alike. Rather than performing the same sequence of tasks over and over again, you can create a *macro*. Then, instead of typing the same headings, or using the same formatting commands repeatedly, you can run the macro, which will enter and format the headings automatically.

A macro consists of a series of instructions written in a language called *Visual Basic* that Microsoft Excel can follow. To create a macro, you don't need to understand the language that is used—you only need to know what Microsoft Excel commands you want the macro to perform for you. You can *record* the commands in sequence, and they will be translated automatically into the language that Microsoft Excel uses. Recording a macro is similar to recording music on a tape—you don't need to understand how the music is recorded onto the tape—you only need to know what music you want to record.

In this lesson, you'll learn how to automate repetitive tasks by recording macros, how to add comments to your macros to make them easy to understand later, and how to create macro buttons so that you can access and run your macros quickly.

You will learn how to:

- Create macros to automate repetitive tasks.

- Add comments to your macro to make it easier to understand.

- Create a macro button to make the macro easier to run.

Estimated lesson time: 25 minutes

If your screen does not match the illustrations in this lesson, see the Appendix, "Matching the Exercises."

Start the lesson

1   Open 15LESSN.XLS.

2   Save the workbook as LESSN15.XLS.

3   Click the Maximize button on the document window, if it is not already maximized.

Creating Macros to Automate Tasks

If you find that you perform certain tasks frequently in Microsoft Excel, such as applying bold, italic, and a large type size to sheet titles, or typing the same categories into every budget sheet, you can save time by automating these tasks. You can record a macro for almost any series of actions that you perform with Microsoft Excel.

To create a macro, you simply turn on the *macro recorder*, perform the sequence of tasks that you want to record, and then turn off the macro recorder. As you record the macro, the commands are automatically translated into the Visual Basic language and stored in a separate *module* sheet in your workbook.

Note   You can also use any macros you created in Microsoft Excel versions 3 or 4, or record macros in the macro language used in Microsoft Excel version 4.

After your macro is recorded, you can run it by choosing the macro name in the Macros dialog box. As you will see later in this lesson, you can also run macros by clicking a macro button or by using a shortcut key combination.

Recording Macros

Before you record a macro, you need to plan out exactly what you want the macro to do, and in what order. After you choose Record New Macro, every cell you select, everything you type, and every command you choose is recorded, in a manner similar to a tape recorder. You also need to think of a name and a description for the macro to identify exactly what the macro does.

The Record New Macro command is like /Tools Macro Record in 1-2-3.

You should name your macro to reflect the actions it performs. In this exercise, the macro you will record adds area headings, a title, and the current date to a new budget sheet. The name of this macro will be "Budget_Info" because it adds the budget headings. Macro names, like range names, cannot include spaces or periods. If you include more than one word, you need to separate the words with an underscore.

It's a good idea to run through the steps in your plan before you actually record the macro. Since you will have exact instructions for creating macros in this lesson, however, you will not need to run through the steps before recording them. In the next exercises, you will record a new macro to enter budget area headings into a sheet.

Start recording a macro

1   Switch to Sheet1, and select cell A8.

You want to be able to use this macro anywhere in a sheet, so you need to select the cell you'll start with before you begin recording. If you start recording and then select a cell, that selection is part of the macro.

Note   Macros are automatically set to absolute references. If you record a macro to enter data or select a cell, you might need to switch to relative references. If the macro is recorded with absolute references, the data will appear in the same cells, no matter what cell you select before running the macro.

---

2   From the Tools menu, choose Record Macro, and then choose Record New Macro.

The Record New Macro dialog box opens.

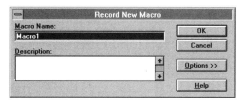

Note You can use the Record Macro button on the Visual Basic toolbar instead of the Record New Macro command, if you prefer. Either way, the Record New Macro dialog box appears, ready for you to name and describe your new macro.

3 In the Macro Name box, type **Budget_Info**

4 In the Description box, type **Sets up budget area headings.**

Note A macro is only available when the file it is stored in is open. If you want your macros to be available all the time, no matter which files are open, you can click the Options button in the Record New Macro dialog box, and then select the "Store In Personal Macro Workbook" option.

5 Choose OK.

The Stop Recording toolbar appears with one button. You might need to move this toolbar out of the way while you record the macro.

6 From the Tools menu, choose Record Macro, and then choose Use Relative References.

Switching to relative references allows you to use your macro wherever you need to, rather than in a particular cell or range.

Record the macro

1 In cell A8 type the following:

Budget Area ENTER ENTER TAB **Gross Revenue** ENTER **Sales** ENTER **Shipping** ENTER **Gross Revenue Totals** ENTER ENTER **Cost of Goods Sold** ENTER **Goods** ENTER **Freight** ENTER **Markdown** ENTER **Miscellaneous** ENTER **Cost of Goods Sold Total** ENTER

2 Click the Stop Macro button on the Stop Recording toolbar.

The macro stops recording and the Stop Recording toolbar disappears.

Stop Macro

Running Macros

After you've recorded a macro, it's a good idea to test it out before you store it permanently or pass it on to someone else. To run a macro, you use the Macro command and then select the macro's name from the list of available macros.

When you run a macro, it simply carries out all of the actions that you performed while you were recording. For some macros, you need to select the cell or cells that you want the macro to affect before you run it. Since the Budget_Info macro you created does not begin on any specific cell, you need to select a cell before you run it. In the next exercise, you'll run your Budget_Info macro to add another series of budget titles to your sheet.

Run the Budget_Info macro

1 Select cell E9, and then from the Tools menu, choose Macro.

The Macro dialog box opens.

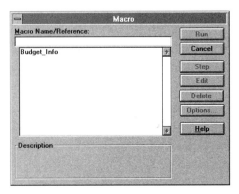

2 In the Macro Name/Reference list, select Budget_Info.

3 Click the Run button.

The macro runs and your budget titles are added to the sheet. Your worksheet should look similar to the following.

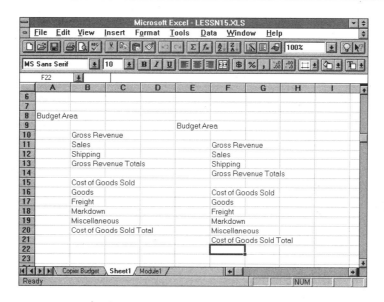

Documenting Macros

In Lesson 7, "Organizing Your Workbooks," you learned that it's a good idea to add comments, notes, or headings to your workbooks to describe them. In the same way, you should add comments to, or *document*, your macros so that you or other users can understand how they work. You have begun documenting the macros you created by adding both a title and a description. But what if you need to examine the macro steps at some point and find out what each part of the macro does? You can add comments to the macro steps to do this.

Macros are stored on special sheets in your workbooks called *modules*. These sheets can contain only macros and comments. When you record a macro, the codes are added automatically, along with your title and description. You can edit your macros on the module sheet to add additional comments to explain the particular steps. In the next exercise, you'll open the module that contains your macros and take a look at them.

If your module sheet displays dots instead of characters, you need to change the font used in your module sheets. From the Tools menu, choose Options. In the Options dialog box, select the Module Format tab, and change the font to Courier New. Choose OK.

Examine your macros

▶ Select the Module1 sheet in your workbook.

The Module1 sheet opens, with the Budget_Info macro displayed.

Notice that some text on the module sheet appears in green, some appears in blue, and some appears in black. The green text indicates a comment, the blue text indicates the beginning or end of a macro, and the black text indicates a macro step. In your macro, the title "Budget_Info Macro" and the description appear as comments in green. In addition, comments are preceded by an apostrophe to set them off from the steps.

The word "Sub" appears in blue text, followed by "Budget_Info". This line indicates the beginning of a macro called "Budget_Info". After this line, everything else is black, meaning that everything else is a step in the macro, until you reach the line that reads "End Sub" in blue. "End Sub" indicates that you have reached the end of the macro commands.

Note   Macros in Microsoft Excel version 5 are written in a language called Visual Basic. If you want to learn more about Visual Basic and the macros in Microsoft Excel 5, refer to the *Microsoft Excel Visual Basic User's Guide*.

To document your macro, you'll add comments to each section. Usually, you add a comment that describes a section immediately above the section, rather than following it. To add a comment, you simply type an apostrophe and then the comment; it will turn green automatically after you click away from the line. The apostrophe tells the program that the text is a comment rather than a step. Adding comments will not affect the macro when you run it, as long as you remember to add the apostrophe at the beginning of the line. If you don't, you will see an error message when you try to run the macro again.

In the next exercise, you'll add comments to explain each step of your Budget_Info macro.

Add comments to your Budget_Info macro

1 On the Module1 sheet, click at the end of the Sub Budget_Info line, after the closed parenthesis.

Remember that the first action you performed when you created the macro was to label the Budget Area. The "Budget Area" line performs that action.

2 Press ENTER twice, press TAB, and then type **' Adds heading to budget area.**

Be sure to type an apostrophe first.

3 Click at the end of the "Budget Area" line below.

Notice that the comment turns green.

4 Press ENTER twice, and then type **' Adds budget categories to budget area.**

Your macro code should look similar to the following.

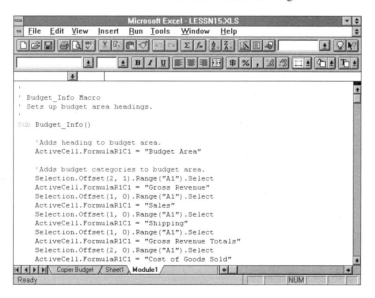

Making Macros Easier to Run with Macro Buttons

You can run any macro in your workbook from the Macro dialog box, but this is not always the quickest method. If you have a macro, such as the Budget_Info macro you created, which will often be used with a particular sheet, you can add a button to that sheet and assign the macro to the button. That way, you can click the button to run the macro, rather than using a menu command. You can still access the macro through the menu should you need to.

Creating Macro Buttons

When you want a macro button, you can simply draw a button and assign the macro to it. You draw buttons in the same way that you drew lines and text boxes earlier in this book, by selecting the Create Button button on the Drawing toolbar, and then dragging on your worksheet to create the button. You can make the button as large or as small as you like, depending on the amount of space available on your sheet. You can resize or move the button later. When you create the button, you also assign a macro to it from the list of macros in the workbook. After you've created the macro button and assigned a macro to it, it's a good idea to give it a descriptive name so that you can remember what will happen when you click the button.

In the next exercise, you add a macro button to run the Budget_Info macro and you name the button.

Add a macro button to run the Budget_Info macro

1 Switch to the Copier Budget sheet.

Drawing

2 Click the Drawing button on the Standard toolbar.

The Drawing toolbar appears, showing you the different buttons from which you can choose.

Create Button button

3 Click the Create Button button.

Your pointer changes to a small pair of cross hairs, ready for you to draw a button.

4 Drag to draw a button to cover cells E2:E3.

The button appears and the Assign Macro dialog box opens.

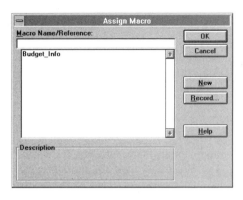

5 In the Macro Name/Reference list, select Budget_Info, and then choose OK.

The Assign Macro dialog box closes.

6 Be sure that the button is still selected, and then select the text "Button 1."

7 Type **Adds Budget Titles**, and then click outside the button.

The button is named Adds Budget Titles, although only part of the name might appear. Your worksheet should look similar to the following.

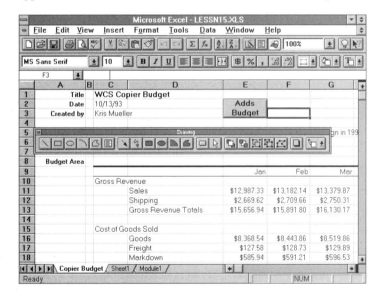

If your Drawing toolbar is docked above or to the side of your worksheet, you can close it by using the Toolbars command from the View menu.

8   Click the Control-menu box on the Drawing toolbar to close it.

When you first create a macro button, you might not place it exactly where you want it, or you might not size it correctly. If the button's name is too long, or if you decide that you need to move the button to a better location on your sheet, you can select it and resize or move it. Unlike most objects on a sheet, however, you cannot simply click the button to select it. (If you simply click the button, you will start the macro.) To select a macro button, you must hold down CTRL and then click the button.

Note   You can also copy a macro button by holding down CTRL and then dragging the button to a new location. When you copy a button, it retains its connection to the macro, so you can place a copy on several sheets in a workbook and then run the macro from any of them.

In the next exercise, you'll size your macro button to fit the size of the button name.

Select and resize a macro button

1   Hold down CTRL and then click the macro button.

The macro button is selected and a border appears around it with small square handles at each side and corner. Be careful not to drag the button. If you do this, you will create a copy instead.

2   Place your mouse pointer over the handle at the right side of the button, and then drag to enlarge the button until its entire name appears on the same line.

3   Release the CTRL key and click away from the button.

The button is resized to fit the text inside it.

Running Macros with a Macro Button

To run a macro from a macro button, you simply click the button once. If the macro is one that performs an action on a particular selection, like the Budget_Info macro, you need to select the cell or range that you want it to affect before you click the button. In the next exercise, you'll run the Budget_Info macro using the button you just created.

Run the Budget_Info macro

▶   Select cell C47, and then click the Adds Budget Titles button once.

The budget titles are added to cells C47:D59. Your worksheet should look similar to the following.

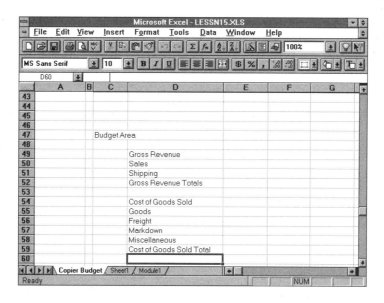

Note If you get an error message that you did not see when you ran the macro before, you might have forgotten an apostrophe when you were adding comments to the macro. Look over the macro on the Module1 sheet to add any apostrophes that you might have left out.

One Step Further

You can make your macros even easier to access by assigning a keyboard shortcut to them. You can assign any combination of CTRL + *key* or CTRL + SHIFT + *key*, as long as that particular key combination is not being used to access another command. For example, CTRL+C is already in use as the Copy shortcut, so you would not want to use that key combination. If you used CTRL+C for a macro, you would no longer be able to use it to copy data. To assign a shortcut to a macro, you use the Options button in the Macro dialog box. Try assigning the keyboard shortcut CTRL+SHIFT+I to your Budget_Info macro.

Important When you assign a shortcut key combination to a macro, Microsoft Excel does not notify you if that combination is already assigned. Exercise caution when you assign shortcut keys so that you don't reassign a combination that is already in use.

Assign a shortcut key to a macro

1 From the Tools menu, choose Macro.

The Macro dialog box opens.

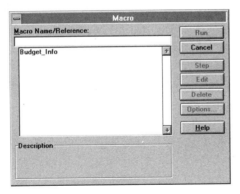

2 In the Macro Name/Reference box, select Budget_Info.

3 Click the Options button.

The Macro Options dialog box opens.

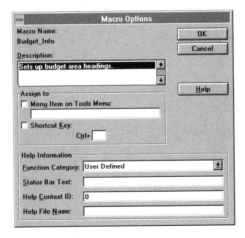

4 In the Assign To area, select the Shortcut Key check box, if it is not already selected.

5 Click in the Ctrl+ box. Select all the text in the box (if any), hold down SHIFT, and then type **I**

6 Choose OK.

7 In the Macro dialog box, choose Close.

8 Select cell E47, and then press CTRL+SHIFT+I.

The Budget_Info macro runs and adds budget titles.

If You Want to Continue to the Next Lesson

1 From the File menu, choose Save.

2 From the File menu, choose Close.

If You Want to Quit Microsoft Excel for Now

▶ From the File menu, choose Exit.

If you see the Save dialog box, click Yes.

Lesson Summary

To	Do this	Button
Create a macro	From the Tools menu, choose Record Macro, and then choose Record New Macro. In the Record New Macro dialog box, type a name and a description for the macro, and then choose OK. Perform the keystrokes that you want to include, and then click the Stop Macro button on the Stop Recording toolbar.	
Run a macro	From the Tools menu, choose Macro. In the Macro dialog box, select the macro, and then click the Run button.	
Document a macro	Select the module sheet that contains the macro you want to document. Click at the end of the line before the step you want to document. Press ENTER twice, press TAB, and then type an apostrophe followed by the comment.	
Assign a macro to a button	Click the Create Button button on the Drawing toolbar and draw a button on your sheet. In the Assign Macro dialog box, select a macro, and then choose OK. With the button selected, select the text on the button and type a button name. Click outside the button.	
Run a macro from a macro button	Click the macro button.	

For more information on	See in the *Microsoft Excel Visual Basic User's Guide*
Creating macros to automate tasks	Chapter 1, "Automating Repeated Tasks"
Documenting macros	Chapter 2, "Editing Recorded Macros"
Creating macro buttons	Chapter 1, "Automating Repeated Tasks"

Review & Practice

In the lessons in Part 5, "Customizing and Automating Microsoft Excel," you learned skills to help you customize your toolbars, modify your screen display, and create macros to automate repetitive tasks. If you want to practice these skills and test your understanding, you can work through the Review & Practice section following this lesson.

Part 5   Review & Practice

Before you complete this book, you can practice the skills in Part 5 by working through the steps in this Review & Practice section. You will create a new toolbar, zoom in to view part of your worksheet, arrange windows to show more than one sheet at a time, create a macro to save time and effort, document the macro, and then add a macro button to make it easier to run.

Scenario

You're preparing the final version of the ten-year sales history presentation, and you need to do a little more work to make the chart and worksheet even better. You need to get a close-up view of your chart to make sure everything is ready and in place, so you'll zoom in to see separate sections of the data. You also need to compare the values in the data and the chart to be sure that the chart type reflects your point. You'll add a macro to quickly show the chart at full screen and zoomed to 125% size. Finally, you'll document the macro and assign it to a macro button on the sheet. Sometimes, you'll find it's easier to use a button than a menu command. Since many of the buttons you use frequently are not on the default toolbars, first you'll create a new toolbar to make some of your tasks easier.

You will review and practice how to:

- Customize your workspace with toolbars.

- Zoom in to view part of a sheet.

- Arrange windows to show more than one sheet.

- Create a macro to automate a repetitive task.

- Document a macro.

- Add a macro button to make the macro easier to access.

Estimated practice time: 15 minutes

Step 1: Create a New Toolbar

Create a new toolbar and add the Record Macro and Stop Macro buttons to it, and then move it to the top of the window.

1 Open the file P5REVIEW.XLS and save it as REVIEWP5.

2 Use the toolbar shortcut menu and the Toolbars command to create a new toolbar called "My Macro."

3   From the View menu, select Toolbars. In the dialog box, click the Customize button to copy the Record Macro and the Stop Macro buttons from the Macro category to your new toolbar, and then close the Customize dialog box.

4   Drag your new toolbar to the top of the screen.

For more information on	See
Opening and customizing toolbars	Lesson 14

Step 2:   Arrange the Windows and Zoom in to See the Chart

You need to see both the data and the chart side by side to be sure that the chart shows the data clearly. Open a new window to show the chart and tile both windows. Zoom out to show all of the history data in one window and all of the chart in the other. Close the extra window after you have looked over the data and the chart.

1   Be sure the Sales History sheet is the active sheet, and then from the Window menu, choose New Window.

2   Tile the windows.

3   In the new window, switch to the Sales History Chart sheet, zoom the chart to 50%, and then scroll until all of the chart is visible in the window.

4   Zoom the Sales History sheet to 75%, and then scroll until all of the data is visible in the window.

5   Close the new window.

For more information on	See
Arranging windows	Lesson 14
Zooming in and out to see information	Lesson 14

Step 3:   Create a Macro to Show a Full-Screen View of the Chart

You find that you often need to switch to the chart sheet and zoom it to 75% size so that you can see a full-screen view of the chart. To save time later, make a macro that first switches to the chart sheet, then changes the view to full screen, then zooms to 75%.

1   Be sure that the Sales History sheet is the active sheet, and then use the Record Macro button on the My Macro toolbar to create a new macro.

2   Name the macro "Show_Chart" and add the description "Switches to chart sheet, changes view to full screen, and zooms to 75%."

3   To record the macro, click the Sales History Chart sheet tab, select the Full Screen command on the View menu, and then use the Zoom command to zoom the window to 75%.

4 Use the Macro and the Stop Recording commands on the Tools menu to stop recording and finish your macro.

For more information on	See
Recording a macro	Lesson 15

Step 4: Document the Macro

You need to document your macro so that others can understand exactly what each step does. Switch to the module sheet and add comments to the macro to explain each step.

1 After the line "Sub Show_Chart ( )," press ENTER twice and TAB once, and then type **' Switches to show chart.**

2 After the line "Sheets("Sales History Chart"). Select," press ENTER twice, and then type **' Changes the view to Full Screen.**

3 After the word "True," press ENTER twice, and then type **' Zooms out to 75%.**

For more information on	See
Documenting a macro	Lesson 15

Step 5: Add a Macro Button and Run the Macro

Your macro can save you repetitive keystrokes, but only if you can access it quickly. Create a macro button called "Show Chart" to run the macro.

1 Click the Full Screen button to display the toolbars, title bar, and status bar again, and then restore the chart sheet to 50% size.

2 Use the Create Button button on the Drawing toolbar to draw a macro button on the Sales History sheet.

3 Assign the Show_Chart macro to the button.

4 Name the button "Show Chart".

5 Use the Show Chart button to run the macro and check that it works.

For more information on	See
Viewing a sheet full screen	Lesson 14
Zooming in and out to view a sheet	Lesson 14
Creating macro buttons	Lesson 15
Running a macro from a macro button	Lesson 15

If You Want to Quit Microsoft Excel for Now

▶ From the File menu, choose Exit.

Appendix

Matching the Exercises

Microsoft Excel has many optional settings that can affect either the screen display or the operation of certain functions. Some exercise steps, therefore, might not produce exactly the same result on your screen as shown in this book. For example, if you cannot find the PRACTICE subdirectory or if your screen does not look like the illustration at a certain point in a lesson, you can turn to this appendix for guidance. Or, if you do not get the outcome described in the lesson, you can use this appendix to determine if the options you have in effect are the same as the ones used in this book.

Displaying the Practice Files

You begin most of the lessons by opening one of the sample workbooks that came on the Step by Step Practice Files disk. The practice files should be stored on your hard disk, in a subdirectory called PRACTICE. The PRACTICE subdirectory is located in Microsoft Excel's home directory, which might be named EXCEL, or something else depending on your installation. If you cannot locate the practice files you need to complete the lesson, follow these steps.

Open the PRACTICE directory

Open

1   On the Standard toolbar, click the Open button.

Clicking the Open button displays the Open dialog box, where you select the name of the practice file to open. You must tell Microsoft Excel on which drive and in which directory the practice file is stored.

2   If the Drive box does not display the drive where the practice files are stored, click the down arrow next to the Drive box, and then click the name of the correct drive.

Most users have the PRACTICE subdirectory stored on drive C.

3   In the Directories box, find the name of the directory where the PRACTICE subdirectory is stored. You might need to click the up or down arrow in the scroll bar to see all the directories in the list. When you find the name of the directory, double-click it to open the directory and display the PRACTICE subdirectory.

The Microsoft Excel home directory (typically EXCEL or EXCEL5) is the usual location for the PRACTICE subdirectory.

4   Double-click the PRACTICE subdirectory to open it.

When you open the PRACTICE subdirectory, the names of the Step by Step practice files (the sample documents) appear in the File Name box. Click the up or down arrow in the scroll bar to see all the names.

5   Return to the lesson to learn which file you need to open to complete the lesson. Double-click the filename to open the practice file.

Matching the Screen Display to the Illustrations

Microsoft Excel makes it easy for you to set up the application window to suit your working style and preferences. If you share your computer with others, previous users might have changed the screen setup. You can easily change it back, so that the screen matches the illustrations in the lessons. Use the following methods for controlling the screen display.

If you change the screen display as part of a lesson and leave Microsoft Excel, the next time you open Microsoft Excel, the screen looks the way you left it in the previous session.

Display toolbars

If toolbars are missing at the top of the screen, previous users might have hidden them to make more room for text. You can easily display the toolbars that contain the buttons you need in the lessons.

1 From the View menu, choose the Toolbars command.

2 In the Toolbars dialog box, click the check boxes for the toolbars you need.

Most of the lessons require that the Standard and Formatting toolbars appear.

Hide extra toolbars

To use specific features in some of the lessons, additional toolbars appear in the application window. If, after completing the lesson, you no longer want these toolbars to appear, use the Toolbars dialog box to hide toolbars you do not want to see. However, most of the lessons require that the Standard and Formatting toolbars appear.

1 From the View menu, choose the Toolbars command.

2 In the Toolbars dialog box, clear the check boxes for the toolbars you do not want to see.

If the vertical or horizontal scroll bars do not appear

If you do not see the vertical or horizontal scroll bars, a previous user might have hidden the scroll bars to make more room for data. You can easily display them again.

1 From the Tools menu, choose Options.

2 Click the View tab to display the view options in the dialog box.

3 In the Window Options area, click the Vertical Scroll Bar and Horizontal Scroll Bar check boxes so that an "X" appears in each, indicating it is selected.

If the Vertical Scroll Bar or the Horizontal Scroll Bar option was previously selected, complete step 4 and then see the following procedure, "If the Microsoft Excel application window does not fill the screen."

4 Click the OK button.

If the Microsoft Excel application window does not fill the screen

A previous user might have made the Microsoft Excel application window smaller to allow quick access to another application. You can enlarge the document window by doing the following.

Maximize

▶ Click the Maximize button to the far right of the Microsoft Excel title bar.

If the right edge of the Excel window is hidden so that you cannot see the Maximize button, point to "Microsoft Excel" in the title bar at the top of the screen, and then drag the title bar to the left until you see the Maximize button.

If the document does not fill the space that Microsoft Excel allows

A previous user might have displayed the workbook in a smaller size to get an overview of a worksheet. To see your workbook at the normal size, use the Zoom drop-down list on the Standard toolbar.

▶ Click the down arrow next to the Zoom box, and select 100%.

If the sheet tabs do not appear in your workbook

A previous user might have hidden the sheet tabs to see more of the worksheets. To view the sheet tabs, use the Options command on the Tools menu.

1   From the Tools menu, choose Options.

2   In the Options dialog box, click the View tab.

3   In the Window Options area, click the Sheet Tabs check box, and then choose OK.

If you see number signs rather than numbers in your practice files

If you see number signs (#) instead of numbers in your practice files, your column width might not be wide enough. To display the numbers, resize the columns.

▶ Select the affected columns and double-click the column header border between two of the selected columns.

If gridlines do not appear in your workbook

A previous user might have hidden the gridlines to see a cleaner view of the data. To view the gridlines again, use the Options command on the Tools menu.

1   From the Tools menu, choose Options.

2   In the Options dialog box, click the View tab.

3   In the Window Options area, click the Gridlines check box, and then choose OK.

If your columns are identified by numbers instead of letters

A previous user might have changed the reference style to R1C1. To change to the A1 reference style, use the Options command on the Tools menu.

1   From the Tools menu, choose Options, and then click the General tab.

2   In the Reference Style area, select the A1 option button, and then choose OK.

If the Summary Information dialog box does not open when you save a document

A previous user might have turned off the Prompt For Summary Info option. To turn the Prompt For Summary Info option on again, use the Options command on the Tools menu.

1   From the Tools menu, choose Options, and then click the General tab.

2   Click the Prompt For Summary Info check box, and then choose OK.

Changing Other Options

If you are not getting the results described in the lessons, follow the instructions in this section to verify that the options set in your application are the same as the ones used in this book.

Review each of the following dialog boxes to compare settings for those options that users change most often and are most likely to account for different results. You can view these dialog boxes by choosing the Options command from the Tools menu. Then you click the tab corresponding to the options you want to see. The following illustrations show the option settings used in this book.

View options

Click the View tab to change options that affect the appearance of the document window.

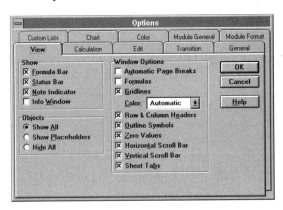

Calculation options

Click the Calculation tab to change options that affect the calculations of your formulas.

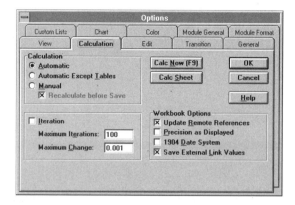

Edit options

Click the Edit tab to change options that affect how editing operations are performed.

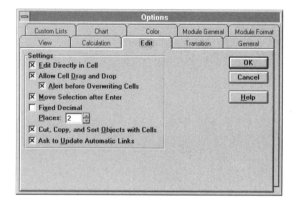

General options

Click the General tab to change options that affect the operation of Microsoft Excel in general.

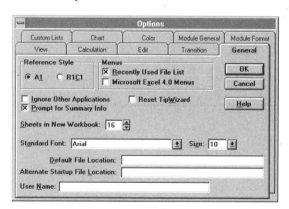

Chart options

Click the Chart tab to change options that affect how charts appear in Microsoft Excel.

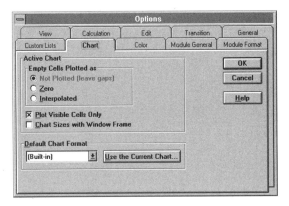

Module General options

Click the Module General tab to change options that affect how modules are set up.

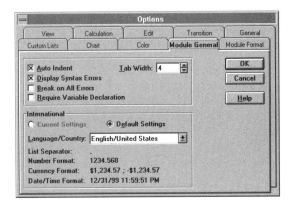

Module Format options

Click the Module Format tab to change options that affect how modules are formatted.

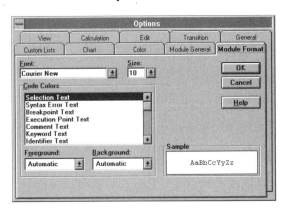

Glossary

absolute reference   A cell reference that refers to the absolute location of a specific cell, rather than a location relative to the current cell. If a formula containing an absolute reference is moved, the reference remains the same. In an absolute reference, the row and column are each preceded by a dollar sign ($). *See also* reference type.

active cell   The selected cell. When a cell is active, you can type new data or edit the data it contains.

argument   Information you supply to a Microsoft Excel function for calculation.

array   A set of data used to build formulas that produce multiple results or that operate on a group of arguments arranged in rows and columns. There are two types of arrays in Microsoft Excel: array ranges and array constants. An array range is a rectangular area of cells sharing one common formula. An array constant is a specially arranged group of constants used as an argument in a formula.

automatic updating   A form of data exchange in which changes in data are reflected immediately in all documents linked to the data. This form of linking allows you to see any changes to the dependent data immediately, but it gives you less control when shared data changes are incorporated into your document. *See also* link.

axes   Lines bordering the plot area that provide a frame of reference for measurement or comparison on a chart. A two-dimensional (2-D) chart has two axes. A three-dimensional (3-D) chart has two or three axes, depending on the data view selected.

cell   The intersection of a column and a row. Each cell can contain text, a number, or a formula, and is named by its position in the row and column.

cell note   A note that explains, identifies, or comments on the information in a specific cell or range of cells.

cell reference   The combination of the column letter and row number for a cell. For example, the intersection of the first column with the first row is a cell called A1. The cell one column to the right of A1 is called B1; the cell one row down from A1 is A2, and so on.

chart   A graphic presentation of data from a worksheet. You can create a chart in a separate chart sheet or embed it on the same worksheet as the data. An embedded chart can be linked to data on other worksheets.

Clipboard   The holding place for information you cut or copy with the Cut, Copy, or Copy Picture command. If you cut or copy worksheet cells, the Clipboard does not display the actual cells. Instead, it displays the action you are taking and the location of the cells you are cutting or copying. Example: "Copy 2R x 3C" or "Cut 2R x 3C."

column   A vertical set of cells. Each column is identified by a unique letter or letter combination (for example, B, F, AD).

comparison operators   There are six standard comparison (logical) operators you can use in Microsoft Excel formulas, as shown in the following table:

Operator	Meaning
=	Equal to
>	Greater than
<	Less than
>=	Greater than or equal to
<=	Less than or equal to
<>	Not equal to

consolidation by category   Consolidates worksheet cells based on their category name. The worksheet cells you want to consolidate must have identical category labels, but the position of the categories within each worksheet can vary.

consolidation by position   Consolidates worksheet cells based on their position. The worksheets that contain the cells you want to consolidate must have identical layouts so that similar categories of data occupy exactly the same location in each source area.

data series   A group of related data points to be plotted on a chart. Each data point consists of a category and a value. You can plot one or more data series on a chart.

data sheet   A worksheet in which you save input values that you want to substitute in your worksheet cells.

data table   A range of cells summarizing the results of substituting different values in one or more formulas on your worksheet. In Microsoft Excel, there are one-input data tables and two-input data tables.

database   A range of cells on a worksheet. The first row of the database contains the field names. Each additional row of the database is one record; each column in the record is one field.

dependent worksheet   A worksheet that contains an external reference formula or a remote reference formula. When you link two Microsoft Excel worksheets, the dependent worksheet relies on another worksheet for the value in the external reference formula. When you link a Microsoft Excel worksheet to a document in a different application, the worksheet is dependent on that document for the value in the remote reference formula.

embedding   The process by which an object is copied into another document. Embedding can take place between documents within the same application or between documents in different applications, as long as both applications support the embedding process. Because an embedded object maintains "ties" with its original application, you can open that application and edit the embedded object by double-clicking the object.

external reference   A reference to another Microsoft Excel worksheet. An external reference can designate a single cell, a cell range, or a named cell or range.

field   A column or cell in a database. Each column in a database contains a different category of data, and each cell in a database shares a common characteristic with other cells in the same column.

file format   The way information in a document is stored in a file. Different programs use different file formats. You can save documents in a variety of file formats using the Save As command on the File menu.

fill handle   A handle that appears when you select a cell or range. By dragging the fill handle to the adjoining cell or range, you can automatically copy or extend a data series into the cells or range.

filtering   A method by which you can extract data that meets certain criteria from a database. You use the field names in your worksheet to filter the data.

floating toolbar   A toolbar that appears in a window with a title bar, stays on top of the other windows, and is not fixed in position.

formula   A sequence of values, cell references, names, functions, or operators that is contained in a cell and produces a new value from existing values. A formula always begins with an equal sign (=).

formula bar   A bar at the top of your Microsoft Excel window that is used to enter or edit values and formulas in cells or charts. It displays the constant value or formula contained in the active cell.

function   A built-in formula that takes a series of values, uses them to perform an operation, and returns the result of the operation. You can use the Function Wizard to select a function and enter it into a cell as part of a formula.

goal seeking   A process in which you enter your goal value, select the variable that you want to change, and then let the program find the value that will allow you to reach your goal. With goal seeking, you can test values and then enter them into your worksheet when you find the ones you need.

graphic object   A line or shape (button, text box, oval, rectangle, arc, picture) you draw using the tools on the toolbar, or a picture you paste into Microsoft Excel.

handles   Small black squares located in the lower-right corner of selected cells or around selected graphic objects, chart items, or text. By dragging the handles, you can perform actions such as moving, copying, filling, sizing, or formatting on the selected cells, objects, chart items, or text.

input cell   A cell into which values from a data table are substituted.

insertion point   A blinking vertical line that shows where text is entered; for example, in the formula bar.

legend   Lists each pattern or symbol that is used as a marker in a chart, followed by the corresponding data series or category name.

link   To create a data connection between a dependent worksheet, the worksheet that will use the data, and a source worksheet, the worksheet in which the original data resides. Your dependent worksheet is updated whenever the data changes in the source worksheet. You can link graphics, text, or other types of information between a source file and your Microsoft Excel file.

linking formula   A formula in a worksheet that contains a reference to a single cell, a cell range, or a named cell or range in another worksheet. A linking formula creates the actual link between Microsoft Excel worksheets.

macro   A sequence of commands you record on a module. Later, you can run the recorded macro to automate your work. A macro can be assigned to a shortcut key, a button, an object, or a tool, for easy use.

module   A document that is similar to a worksheet and that contains sets of instructions (macros) for accomplishing specific tasks.

moving border   A moving dotted line that surrounds a cell or range of cells. A moving border appears around a cell or range that has been cut or copied, or around a cell or range you are inserting into a formula.

name   An identifier you create to refer to a cell, a group of cells, a constant value, an array of values, or a formula. When you use names in a formula, the formula is easier to read and remember than a formula containing cell references.

nested subtotals   Multiple levels of subtotals that provide additional levels of detail in a complex report.

nonadjacent selection   A selection of noncontiguous cells and/or objects.

one-input data table   A table you produce using the Table command on the Data menu. Using a formula containing one variable and a series of values to be substituted for that variable, you can generate a one-row or one-column series of results based on the series of values you entered.

operator   *See* comparison operators.

pane   A separate section of your worksheet window resulting from splitting your window. By splitting your window into panes and then freezing the panes, you can view both headings and data at the same time, no matter where you have scrolled in the data.

paste area   The destination for data you cut with the Cut command or copy with the Copy command.

personal macro workbook   A separate workbook that contains macros that are available every time you start the program. When you record a macro, you can choose to include it in your personal macro workbook.

pivot table   A table, similar to a crosstab, that can display two-dimensional summaries of selected data from a database in different combinations. You create a pivot table with the PivotTable Wizard.

plot area   The area of a chart in which Microsoft Excel plots data. On a 2-D chart, the plot area is bounded by the axes and includes all markers that represent data points. On a 3-D chart, it is defined by the walls and floor of the chart. The walls and floor can be formatted independently.

print title   A heading that you repeat on successive printed pages of a worksheet to identify the data.

range   On a worksheet, a rectangular section containing two or more cells.

record   One row in a database. The first row of the database contains the field name. Each additional row of the database is one record. Each record contains the same categories of data as every other record in the database.

reference   The location of a cell or group of cells on a worksheet, indicated by column letter and row number. Examples: C5, A1:D3, R1C1, and R[1]C[3].

reference style   A method of identifying cells in a worksheet. In the A1 reference style, columns are labeled with letters and rows are labeled with numbers. In the R1C1 reference style, R indicates row and C indicates column; both columns and rows are labeled with numbers.

reference type A relative reference (A1) in a formula indicates the location of another cell in relation to the cell containing the formula. An absolute reference ($A$1) always refers to the exact location of a specific cell. A mixed reference ($A2; A$2) is half relative and half absolute.

refresh The action of updating the data in a pivot table to reflect changes to the data in your worksheet.

relative reference A cell reference that refers to the location of a specific cell relative to the current cell, rather than its absolute location. *See also* reference type.

result cell A cell on your worksheet that is recalculated when you apply a new scenario.

rows Cells that run horizontally and are identified by numbers.

scenario A set of input values you can apply to a worksheet model. You create scenarios with Scenario Manager.

scroll bars Bars along the right and bottom sides of a worksheet or module that allow you to scroll through the document vertically and horizontally, using a mouse. Clicking an arrow moves one column or row at a time. Clicking a shaded area moves one window at a time. The length of the scroll bar represents the entire document. Dragging the scroll box to a different position on the scroll bar and releasing the mouse button displays the part of the document that is in that relative location.

sheet tab A tab at the bottom of the screen that represents a sheet in a workbook. You select sheets by clicking their tabs. By selecting several sheets, you can enter the same information on all sheets at the same time.

shortcut menu A menu that appears when you click the right mouse button while pointing to any of several areas on screen. You can display shortcut menus from cells, columns, rows, text boxes, objects, buttons, charts, chart items, toolbars, tools, or workbooks.

sort key The field name or criteria that you use to sort by. To sort a range, you can select any cell within the range, and then use the Sort command. When you choose the Sort command, the range around the active cell is automatically selected for sorting.

source worksheet A Microsoft Excel worksheet referred to by an external reference formula or a remote reference formula. The source worksheet is the source of the value contained in the external reference formula or the remote reference formula; it provides source data to the dependent worksheet.

startup directory   An optional directory named XLSTART, which is located in the same directory as EXCEL.EXE. Any documents you place in the startup directory are automatically opened when you start Microsoft Excel. Templates placed in the startup directory or folder are not automatically opened, but they are listed as options in the New dialog box.

status bar   The bar at the bottom of the screen that displays information about the currently selected command, the active dialog box, the standard keys on the keyboard, or the current state of the program and the keyboard.

text box   A graphic element that you can place on a worksheet or chart. You can use text boxes to explain or label any part of a worksheet or chart.

toolbar dock   The region above the formula bar and below the menu bar, or the regions on the left, right, and bottom sides of the application window, where toolbars can reside.

trendline   A line plotted in a chart that points out the progress of one data series in a chart of several data series. You can add a trendline to one data series that will clearly show the changes in that series relative to the others in the chart. You can add trendlines to bar, column, area, line, and xy (scatter) charts.

two-input data table   A table you produce using the Table command on the Data menu. Using a formula containing two variables and two series of values to be substituted for those variables, you can generate a two-dimensional matrix of results based on the series of values you entered.

workbook   A Microsoft Excel document in which you can store other documents. A workbook can include multiple worksheets, modules, and charts.

worksheet   A set of rows, columns, and cells in which you store and manipulate data in Microsoft Excel. Several worksheets can appear in one workbook, and you can switch among them easily by clicking their tabs with the mouse.

XY (scatter) chart   A 2-D chart that has numeric values plotted along both axes rather than having values along the vertical axis and categories along the horizontal axis. This kind of chart type is typically used to analyze scientific data to see whether one set of values is dependent on or affects another set of values.

Index

Build Your Spreadsheet Expertise

Train Yourself
With *Step by Step* books from Microsoft Press

The *Step by Step* books are the perfect self-paced training solution for the busy businessperson. Whether you are a new user or you're upgrading from a previous version of the software, the *Step by Step* books can teach you exactly what you need to know to get the most from your new software. Each lesson is modular, example-rich, and fully integrated with a timesaving practice file on the disk. If you're too busy to attend a class or if classroom training doesn't make sense for you or your office, you can build the computer skills you need with the *Step by Step* books from Microsoft Press.

**Microsoft® Excel Visual Basic®
for Applications Step by Step**
Reed Jacobson
Covers version 5 for Windows.
350 pages, softcover with one 3.5-inch disk
$29.95 ($39.95 Canada)   ISBN 1-55615-589-1

**Microsoft® Windows™ 3.1
Step by Step**
Catapult, Inc.
296 pages, softcover with one 3.5-inch disk
$29.95 ($39.95 Canada)   ISBN 1-55615-501-8

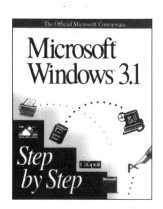

**Microsoft Access® for Windows™
Step by Step**
Microsoft Corporation
Covers version 1.0.
384 pages, softcover with one 3.5-inch disk
$29.95 ($39.95 Canada)   ISBN 1-55615-482-8

**Microsoft® Word 6 for Windows™
Step by Step**
Catapult, Inc.
336 pages, softcover with one 3.5-inch disk
$29.95 ($39.95 Canada)   ISBN 1-55615-576-X

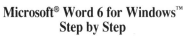

MicrosoftPress

Microsoft Press® books are available wherever quality books are sold and through CompuServe's Electronic Mall—GO MSP.
*Call 1-800-MSPRESS for direct ordering information or for placing credit card orders.**
Please refer to BBK when placing your order. Prices subject to change.

*In Canada, contact Macmillan Canada, Attn: Microsoft Press Dept., 164 Commander Blvd., Agincourt, Ontario, Canada M1S 3C7, or call (416) 293-8464, ext. 340. Outside the U.S. and Canada, write to International Sales, Microsoft Press, One Microsoft Way, Redmond, WA 98052-6399.

The Step by Step Companion Disk

The enclosed 3.5-inch disk contains timesaving, ready-to-use practice files that complement the lessons in this book. To use the practice files, you'll need the Microsoft® Windows™ operating system version 3.1 or later and Microsoft Excel version 5 for Windows.

Each *Step by Step* lesson is closely integrated with the practice files on the disk. Before you begin the *Step by Step* lessons, we highly recommend that you read the "Getting Ready" section of the book and install the practice files on your hard disk. Remember, as you work through each lesson, be sure to follow the instructions for renaming the practice files so that you can go through a lesson more than once if you need to.

Please take a few moments to browse the License Agreement on the previous page. If your computer uses only 5.25-inch disks, we will gladly send you a replacement disk, free of charge. For ordering information, please see the bottom of the License Agreement page.